The Novels of Fernando del Paso

Florida A&M University, Tallahassee
Florida Atlantic University, Boca Raton
Florida Gulf Coast University, Ft. Myers
Florida International University, Miami
Florida State University, Tallahassee
University of Central Florida, Orlando
University of Florida, Gainesville
University of North Florida, Jacksonville
University of South Florida, Tampa
University of West Florida, Pensacola

The Novels of Fernando del Paso

Robin W. Fiddian

University Press of Florida

Gainesville · Tallahassee · Tampa · Boca Raton

Pensacola · Orlando · Miami · Jacksonville · Ft. Myers

05 04 03 02 01 00 6 5 4 3 2 1

Library of Congress Cataloging-in-Publication Data
Fiddian, Robin W.
The novels of Fernando del Paso / Robin W. Fiddian.
p. cm.
Includes bibliographical references and index.
ISBN 0-8130-1806-4 (cloth: alk. paper)
1. Paso, Fernando del, 1935—Fictional works. I. Title.
PQ7298.26.A76 Z65 2000
863'.64—dc21   00-032586

The University Press of Florida is the scholarly publishing agency
for the State University System of Florida, comprising Florida
A&M University, Florida Atlantic University, Florida Gulf Coast
University, Florida International University, Florida State
University, University of Central Florida, University of Florida,
University of North Florida, University of South Florida,
and University of West Florida.

University Press of Florida
15 Northwest 15th Street
Gainesville, FL 32611–2079
http://www.upf.com

Contents

Acknowledgments   iv

Introduction   1

1. Paradigms, Contexts, and Affiliations: Reading the Novels
   of Fernando del Paso Intertextually   9

2. *José Trigo:* A Novel of Hybridity and Regeneration   29

3. *Palinuro de México:* The Body, the Nation,
   and the Book of the World   72

4. *Noticias del Imperio* and the New Historical Novel   105

5. *Linda 67:* The Homeland Strikes Back   141

Conclusion   155

Notes   157

Bibliography   163

Index   179

Acknowledgments

I am grateful to Fernando del Paso and the staff of the Agencia Literaria Carmen Balcells (Barcelona) for their kindness in allowing me to reproduce a range of material from his novels. I also wish to thank Susan Fernandez and her colleagues at the University Press of Florida for the speedy and professional handling of my manuscript.

Several other institutions and individuals have assisted with the present project. I wish to acknowledge the Faculty of Medieval and Modern Languages, the Hayter Committee, and the Interfaculty Committee for Latin American Studies—all at Oxford University—for awarding me a series of travel and research grants that enabled me to produce a final text between 1994 and 1999; some years earlier, the University of Newcastle upon Tyne supported the project at an initial stage and is entitled to a proportional share of the credit.

John Wainwright of the Hispanic section of the Taylor Library at Oxford University gave me unfailing support throughout the time of writing; Ian Michael, aka David Serafín, shared with me his encyclopedic knowledge of *la novela negra;* Robert Young and Christina Howells, both of Wadham College, Oxford, were a constant source of encouragement and intellectual stimulus, as were Donald Shaw of University of Virginia, Clive Griffin of Trinity College, Oxford, and Sir Peter Russell of Belsyre Court, Oxford. I am especially grateful to Enrico Mario Santí for his continuing friendship and endless supply of materials and information; to Rebecca Biron of University of Miami for alerting me to the presentation of the Empress Carlota in *El eterno femenino* by Rosario Castellanos; and to Blanca Merino Juti, Jane Garnett, Alfonso González, John King, and Ilan Stavans for providing me with various types of material, including bibliographical references.

In other latitudes, René Avilés Fabila, Juan José Barrientos, Alberto Blanco, Elizabeth Corral Peña, Hugo Iriarte, Hector Manjarrez, Carlos Monsiváis, Miguel Rodríguez Lozano, Alberto Ruy Sánchez, and Ignacio Solares all showed interest in the project and gave it their unfailing support. Special thanks go to Fernando del Paso and his wife, Socorro, in recognition of the unlimited friendship and hospitality that they have heaped on me since we first met in 1980; to Prof. Enrique Pupo Walker, for several years of encouragement with this project; and to Dr. Leopoldo Zea, who generously interrupted a busy schedule to grant me a lengthy interview in his offices in the Universidad Nacional Autónoma de México on 9 March 1998. Finally, María Donapetry contributed massively to the completion of this book through her patience and companionship in locations in and around Los Angeles, Oxford, Gijón, and Vivero.

Note on Translation

All translations from Spanish into English are by the author.

Introduction

Fernando del Paso (Mexico City 1935) is the author of four highly acclaimed novels that exemplify many of the major trends in Mexican and Spanish American fiction of the last four decades of the twentieth century. His first literary endeavor was a volume of poetry, *Sonetos de lo diario*, published in 1958. In April 1959 he began work on *José Trigo*, an ambitious novel that took seven years to complete. Upon its publication in 1966, *José Trigo* won the prestigious Xavier Villaurutia Prize, awarded annually to the work deemed to have made the most significant contribution to Mexican literature of the year.

The success of *José Trigo* was surpassed in 1977 by the reception given to *Palinuro de México*, an extravagant novel that won numerous national and international prizes and consolidated del Paso's reputation in literary circles throughout Spanish America and elsewhere. A decade later, *Noticias del Imperio* (1987) met with a level of commercial and critical acclaim that astonished even the author's most fervent admirers: treating a historical subject—the tragic failure of the Habsburgs, Maximilian and Carlota, to establish a viable empire in Mexico in the mid-1860s—*Noticias del Imperio* received the plaudits of critics and popular audiences alike. Del Paso's fourth novel, *Linda 67: Historia de un crimen*, appeared in 1995. Regarded by its author as a divertissement, it represented a departure from his normal style of writing, as he ventured into the territory of crime fiction.

The immediate frame of reference of del Paso's fictional output is the Mexican narrative tradition since 1940. Through a series of connections that will be documented fully in the chapters that follow, the four novels of Fernando del Paso reflect different moods and literary imperatives as they draw on, and modify, the literary models successively available to Mexican fiction writers over the past sixty years. It is customary, in histories of Mexican literature, to account for the period 1940 to the present by decades and to signal watersheds around the end of the 1950s and in 1968 before charting further developments in the 1980s and 1990s. Making all due allowances for possible mismatches between the historical and literary processes, the scheme of description by decade can provide some practical assistance in mapping the place of the novels of Fernando del Paso within the broad context of contemporary Mexican narrative.

In rough outline, Mexican narrative of the 1940s comprised a number of types and trends that were first defined and then invariably broken by one or more texts that have come to be seen as landmarks. Principal among the dominant types were (i) the novel of the Mexican Revolution, now nearing the end of its productive life; (ii) the subcategory of the *novela cristera,* promoted by such writers as José Guadalupe de Anda; (iii) novels about the Mexican railroad, written in a *costumbrista* idiom; and (iv) a proletarian literature concerned with social and political issues. The single most important exponent of this latter category of writing was José Revueltas (1914–1976), whose influence on Mexican literature and politics would continue to the end of the twentieth century. A prolific and polemical figure, Revueltas produced one book in particular that broke the ideological and aesthetic mold of Mexican fiction of the 1940s. *El luto humano* (1943) paints an uncompromising, highly textured picture of human suffering in postrevolutionary Mexico, borrowing narrative devices from the works of William Faulkner and adapting them to a Mexican setting in an exemplary way.

Another milestone in Mexican fiction of the 1940s was *Al filo del agua* (1947) by Agustín Yáñez (1904–80). Set in an imaginary location in the province of Jalisco on the eve of the Mexican Revolution, the novel explores the troubled responses of members of a rural community to an imminent political schism. The representation of characters' inner lives is achieved through the use of interior monologue; narrative fragmentation in the style of Joyce, Faulkner, and Dos Passos provides further evidence of the abandonment of the conventions of Balzacian realism, which had prevailed in Mexican fiction before the iconoclasm of *El luto humano* and *Al filo del agua.*

The next significant staging posts in the nation's narrative evolution were *El llano en llamas* (1953) and *Pedro Páramo* (1955), both by Juan Rulfo (1918–1986), and *La región más transparente* (1958), which was the debut novel of Carlos Fuentes (1928). Rulfo's two books delved into the collective imagination of the Mexican people, offering glimpses of the complex motivations of a national character driven by atavistic instincts and anxieties. Oedipal conflict and impotence in the face of authority are constituent features of a mind-set haunted as much by the types of pre-Columbian culture as by those of the Catholic Church; the inward turn of Rulfo's narratives exemplifies again the all-pervasive influence of Faulkner, first absorbed, as we have seen, by Revueltas in the early 1940s.

La región más transparente brought about a major sea change in the style and subject matter of Mexican fiction. Conceived by its precocious author as a vast frieze of the social conditions obtaining in Mexico City in the mid-1950s, *La región más transparente* renders the dynamic conflict between different forces—social, political, psychological, and cultural—in the life of the capital and inaugurates a type of novel that will mushroom over the following decade. In the process, the modernist paradigm of *Ulysses* is incorporated definitively into Mexican fiction, bringing with it all of the linguistic and technical innovations of Joyce's seminal text.

After the publication of *La región más transparente*, there was a veritable explosion of creativity in Mexican fiction. Revueltas wrote *Los errores* (1964) and Yáñez produced *La tierra pródiga* (1960) and *Las tierras flacas* (1962). They were accompanied fitfully in their efforts by Juan José Arreola (1918), who in 1961 brought out *Confabulario total* (a revised collection of short stories first published in 1952) and the only novel in a distinctive and varied output, *La feria* (1963). The hallmarks of Arreola's work include humor, fantasy, and a strong intertextual impulse that manifests itself in forms of parody, transposition, and carnivalesque writing.

Arreola offered tremendous support to younger writers in literary workshops in Mexico City. Salvador Elizondo (1932), José Agustín (1944), and Fernando del Paso were three such writers who benefited from Arreola's teachings and who made their narrative debuts in the 1960s. In the case of del Paso, Arreola exercised a literary influence that is plain to see in the pages of *José Trigo*, interwoven with those of Revueltas, Yáñez, Rulfo, the precocious example of Carlos Fuentes, and the various styles and currents of writing exemplified in their work. All told, *José Trigo* impressed most literary commentators as a comprehensive summa of Mexican fiction, replete with echoes of the novel on proletarian subjects, the *novela cristera*, the stylistic idiosyncrasies of Rulfo and Arreola, the iconoclasm of *La región más transparente*, and numerous other literary models and precursors.

A significant phenomenon in Mexican fiction of the mid to late 1960s was la Onda (The Wave), epitomized in the works of Gustavo Sainz (1940), José Agustín, and Parménides García Saldaña (1944–1982). *Gazapo* (1965), *De perfil* (1966), and *Pasto verde* (1968) are typical narratives about urban adolescents who rebel against the social, moral, and linguistic norms of their middle-class milieu. Inspired by the waves of youthful protest and counterculture that were breaking on the international scene, these Mexican novels of the 1960s express their repudiation of decorum in a language that incorporates blasphemy, obscenity, the *albur* (offensive sexist wordplay), and other forms of linguistic barbarism.

The liberation of language from the constraints of good taste and literary decorum, along with an attitude of total frankness toward the body and adolescent sexuality, are aspects of Onda writing that are found elsewhere in Mexican fiction of the time—in the work of Héctor Manjarrez (1945), for instance. As far as the work of del Paso is concerned, linguistic play and the reevaluation of the body and sexuality are more prominent in *Palinuro de México* than in *José Trigo,* where, as we shall see, they are grounded in an outlook different from that of la Onda. All things considered, the first two novels of Fernando del Paso have slightly more in common with an alternative current of Mexican writing of the 1960s known as Escritura (writing), which is represented habitually as Other to la Onda and perceived as being focused not on social and moral issues but on aesthetic questions concerning language, narrative, and representation. Exemplified in *Farabeuf* (1965) by Salvador Elizondo, Escritura accords with a view of the novel as an antirepresentational form and self-conscious verbal artifact—properties that can be detected in *José Trigo* and *Palinuro de México* but that constitute only a partial definition of those two novels.

At the same time as it represents a continuation of certain aspects of Mexican fiction of the 1960s, *Palinuro de México* also typifies a set of social and literary concerns that are very much of the 1970s. With respect to literary paradigms, what was known as the "total novel" would reach its apex in *Terra nostra* (1975) by Carlos Fuentes and *Palinuro de México.* Derived from sources including *Ulysses* and *Finnegans Wake* and, in the Hispanic field, *Adán Buenosayres* (1948) by Leopoldo Marechal and *Rayuela* (1963) by Julio Cortázar, the total novel had flourished in Mexico in the 1960s and would maintain its relative strength well into the following decade. The moral and philosophical example of Cortázar also prospered in Mexican fiction of the 1970s, in the works of writers such as Héctor Manjarrez and Jorge Aguilar Mora (1946), as well as that of Fernando del Paso.

The bloody repression of a peaceful pro-democracy rally in Mexico City in October 1968 shocked the nation and had a decisive impact on the political and cultural life of Mexico. Although the political legacy of 1968 is still a matter of debate, the cultural legacy began to crystallize in various forms immediately and throughout the 1970s. In the field of prose narrative, the literary chronicle proved to be a most effective form for dealing with the traumatic events of the time. Carlos Monsiváis (1938) and Elena Poniatowska (1933) produced the first testimonial accounts, *Días de guardar* (1970) and *La noche de Tlatelolco* (1971), in step with Luis

González del Alba (1947), author of *Los días y los años* (also of 1971). A testimonial tendency continues to be evident eight years later in *Manifestación de silencios* (1979), the third novel by Arturo Azuela (1938). The events of 1968 received a more elaborate and imaginative treatment in *Compadre Lobo* (1977) by Gustavo Sainz and *Si muero lejos de ti* (1979) by Jorge Aguilar Mora—texts that can be considered companion volumes to *Palinuro de México* in their use of a nonrealist idiom to represent elements of tragedy and the absurd in the experience of the Mexican people at a watershed in the nation's history.

On the twin basis of its continuing adherence to the conventions of the total novel and its engagement with the tragedy of 1968, *Palinuro de México* stands out as representative of the main lines of Mexican fiction during the 1970s. The relationship of del Paso's next novel to the dominant narrative paradigm of the 1980s is equally close, inasmuch as *Noticias del Imperio* (1987) exemplifies a type of fiction that is cultivated not only in Mexico but throughout Spanish America over that time. Alongside crime fiction, *testimonio* narrative, and women's writing, all of which thrive in Spanish American literature of the 1980s, the "new historical novel" of Spanish America is arguably the most substantial cultural achievement of the decade. While *Los perros del paraíso* (1983) by Abel Posse (Argentina, 1936) and *El general en su laberinto* (1989) by Gabriel García Márquez (Colombia, 1928) are outstanding examples of the type in the field of continental writing, Mexican literature of the period boasts a plethora of impressive titles including *La campaña* (1990) by Carlos Fuentes, *Madero, el otro* (1989) by Ignacio Solares (1945), and *Noticias del Imperio*. In point of fact, Fuentes, Solares, and del Paso were tapping a rich national vein of historical writing that had produced *Los relámpagos de agosto* (1965) and *Los pasos de López* (1982) by the humorous writer Jorge Ibargüengoitia (1928–1983) and that would continue into the 1990s when Angeles Mastretta (1949) published *Mal de amores* (1996) and was awarded the prestigious Premio Rómulo Gallegos of 1997. The humorous, often irreverent treatment of historical sources, combined with a revisionist attitude toward relations between the European powers and their former colonial possessions, are two features of *Noticias del Imperio* that represent a challenge to traditional historical discourse; polyphony, parody, and pastiche further distinguish del Paso's novel from a traditional type of historical fiction, contributing to the profile of a brilliant piece of creative writing that is now universally acknowledged as the leading example of the Spanish American new historical novel of the 1980s.

Mexican literature of the 1990s does not lend itself yet to the kind of discriminating analysis that literary historians have been able to conduct in connection with the production of earlier decades. Given a lack of critical perspective and appropriate analytical tools, those who would attempt to survey a field of such vast proportions and shifting outlines must for the time being fall back on standard strategies, of which differentiation by generation is as useful as any other. With the aid of this well-worn tool, it is possible to distinguish as many as four generations of writers of fiction in Mexican literature of the 1990s, beginning with those authors who are long-standing members of the literary academy—authors such as Carlos Fuentes, Elena Poniatowska, Gustavo Sainz, and Fernando del Paso. A second generation includes Ignacio Solares, Héctor Manjarrez, and María Luisa Puga (1944); their literary debuts occurred later than those of the previous generation, and their reputations also took longer to establish. A third generation includes Carmen Boullosa (1954) and Juan Villoro (1956). Finally, a younger generation is made up of writers born after 1960.

In an attempt to categorize the dominant types of writing that constitute Mexican fiction of the 1990s, a prolific number of labels could be used, including the urban novel, rural and regional novels, women's fiction of several hues, gay fiction, fiction in a humorous idiom, and fiction in the fantastic mode. Particularly relevant to a study of the novels of Fernando del Paso is the type of the *novela negra,* which enjoyed great popularity in Mexico during the 1980s and 1990s. In writing *Linda 67: Historia de un crimen* (1995), del Paso was trying his hand at a genre that was already an integral part of the national literary tradition and that an author some fifteen years his junior had been cultivating and promoting with considerable success throughout the 1970s and 1980s. By the time del Paso began work on *Linda 67,* Paco Ignacio Taibo II (1949) had produced a number of detective novels that had secured him both a popular and a critical following in many parts of the Spanish- and English-speaking worlds. Taibo's readers were enthralled by the effortless style of a series of narratives featuring a highly individual Mexican detective, Héctor Belascoarán Shayne, and by the humorous and often satirical perspectives that Taibo brought to bear on contemporary Mexican institutions and mores. On a superficial reading, del Paso's experiment with the conventions of the *novela negra* in *Linda 67* cannot compare with Taibo's mastery of the genre. However, it is important to note differences in conception between *Linda 67* and Taibo's well-wrought novels: crucially, *Linda 67* is set, for the most part, outside Mexico, with a resulting redirection of the focus of the narrative away from crime and corruption in Mexico and onto an alternative canvas. Set principally in and around San Francisco, with a brief excursion to Switzerland and another to Cuernavaca over an idyllic but ephemeral weekend, the plot of *Linda 67* serves largely as a vehicle for exploring the deeply ingrained sickness that the novel detects in the body politic of the United States. A Mexican dimension to the fiction is embodied in the character of Olivia, who is the beautiful and morally irreproachable girlfriend of the main protagonist, Dave Sorensen. Modeled on Rosario in *Los pasos perdidos* (1953) by Alejo Carpentier (1904–1980), Olivia helps to transform *Linda 67* from an imitation *novela negra* into a skillful late twentieth-century allegory of civilization and barbarism in which the former is identified with Mexico and the latter with the United States.

This summary description of *Linda 67* and its divergent relation to one of the dominant trends in Mexican fiction of the 1990s serves to highlight the dialectic of sameness and difference that links the novels of Fernando del Paso to the Mexican narrative tradition of the past sixty years. The references made earlier to José Revueltas, Carlos Fuentes, and Ignacio Solares prefigure an essential part of the agenda of the present study, which will explore connections between the novels of Fernando del Paso and a variety of Mexican texts. Other references, to authors such as Alejo Carpentier and Gabriel García Márquez, indicate a wider range of interest that encompasses the narrative traditions of continental Latin America and will at times extend even further to take in landmarks of the literary traditions of countries as varied as the United States, England, Ireland, France, and Spain. In view of the multiple contexts and perspectives that can legitimately be applied to the novels of Fernando del Paso, it is perhaps helpful to provide some words of clarification concerning the protocols governing the comparative method adopted in this study and its grounding in theories of intertextuality.

Intertextual approaches to the novels of Fernando del Paso have become a standard feature of the critical tradition, from the early essays of Ramón Xirau (1967) and Jesús Flores Sevilla (1970) to a recent article by José T. Espinosa-Jácome (1997). In this book I elaborate on those approaches, which I have sought to promote since 1981 when I published the first of a number of essays devoted to del Paso's novels. In the chapters that follow, I analyze relations between each of his four novels and a set of cultural contexts and narrative traditions that I consider relevant to the construction and categorization of *José Trigo, Palinuro de México, Noticias del Imperio,* and *Linda 67*. Those contexts and traditions are identified and distinguished by the labels "national," "regional," "continental," and "universal"—terms which are utilized here in wholly conventional senses as exemplified in the discursive writings of Jorge Luis Borges, Leopoldo Zea, and others including Fernando del Paso himself, and sanctioned, in the realm of the academy, in a substantial body of scholarship ranging from the essays of Angel Rama on transculturation to others by Lois Parkinson Zamora, Gustavo Pérez Firmat, Amaryll Chanady, Arnold Peñuel, and Maarten van Delden. As a general procedure, I invoke the contexts and traditions just mentioned when they promise to heighten appreciation of a text under consideration, when I believe that a reading of a text by del Paso will benefit from the stratagem of relating it to other texts and cultural contexts, through a comparative method that seeks either to highlight properties shared by a number of narratives, or actively to differentiate one text or set of texts from another on the basis of a discernible pattern of distinctive features.

Angel Rama's seminal theory of narrative transculturation lends an important cultural dimension to my investigation of the novels of Fernando del Paso and their relation to the European and North American literary avant-garde. Following Rama and others including Manuel Pedro González and Morton Levitt, I identify James Joyce, William Faulkner, and Aldous Huxley with the international currents of modernism, and posit an aesthetic and, specifically, a paradigm of novel writing that exercise a determining influence on Mexican fiction from Revueltas to del Paso. Throughout this study I consider the manifestations of a modernist paradigm in del Paso's narratives from *José Trigo* on and plot their evolution from the late 1950s to the mid-1980s and beyond, when the modernist project in the cultures of Mexico and other parts of Spanish America is forced to confront the challenges and ruptures of the postmodern. The history of assimilation and adaptation of the literary forms of modernism, of which del Paso's work is a signal example, has salutary implications for the integrity and creativity of Latin American culture, which I address below. In the final analysis, a concern with narrative form, intertextuality, and the cultural parameters of writing is what defines my study, the ultimate goal of which is to provide a readership based in Latin American studies, comparative literature, and postcolonial studies, with a newly drawn profile of the novels of Fernando del Paso and their place in the narrative traditions of Mexico, Spanish America, and a broader international field of writing.

Paradigms, Contexts, and Affiliations

Reading the Novels of Fernando del Paso Intertextually

> Any text is constructed as a mosaic of quotations; any text is the
> absorption and transformation of another. The notion of *inter-*
> *textuality* replaces that of intersubjectivity, and poetic language is
> read as at least *double.*
> **Julia Kristeva, "Word, Dialogue, and Novel"**

> Cultural and literary traditions (including the most ancient ones)
> are preserved and continue to live, not in the subjective memory
> of the individual, nor in some collective "psyche," but in the ob-
> jective forms of culture itself (including linguistic and discursive
> forms); in this sense, they are intersubjective and interindividual,
> and therefore social; that is their mode of intervention in literary
> works—the individual memory of creative individuals almost
> does not come into play.
> **Mikhail Bakhtin, "Concluding Remarks"**

The contradictions and variations in the definitions cited above are both
an indication of the quite legitimate and fundamental differences of opinion that can exist between two equally authoritative and influential exponents of theories of intertextuality, and a reminder of the continuing fluid-
ity of the concept and its applications, about which Graham Pechey
remarked: "The urgent task of Bakhtin's readers is [. . .] to push his concepts still further on in their journey, putting them to still more demanding
tests" (57). In Latin American literary studies, Bakhtinian and Kristevan
models of intertextuality have been in circulation for some time, alternating with those of Borges, Harold Bloom, and Michael Riffaterre—to name
only the most prominent figures in a long established and still expanding
field of intellectual inquiry. Work carried out by Lois Parkinson Zamora
on Cortázar and Vargas Llosa (1982; revised in 1997), by Gustavo Pérez
Firmat on Cuban literature (1989), by Arnold Peñuel on García Márquez
(1994), and by Bernard McGuirk on a selection of topics in Latin Ameri-

can literature (1997) illustrates the successful application of theories of intertextual relations to a variety of literary materials and casts Pechey's clarion call into a perspective of near-obsolescence as far as the study of Latin American literature is concerned.

Given the history of colonial and neocolonial relations between the countries of Latin America and the metropolitan powers that have sought to influence their development, it is perhaps inevitable that intertextual studies of Latin American literature should choose to privilege cultural considerations over more narrowly defined aesthetic concerns. For the author of one such study, "It is evident [. . .] that intertextuality brings a broad cultural approach to the study of a text, postulating that any text is a reflection of one or more cultural traditions" (Peñuel x). In an early instance of this mode of criticism, Lois Parkinson Zamora, writing on European intertextuality in *Conversación en la catedral* by Mario Vargas Llosa and *62 Modelo para armar* by Julio Cortázar, addresses the issue of the relation between Latin American writers and a hegemonic European literary culture that provides imitable models at the same time that it sets a gold standard against which non-European achievements have tended to be measured. Allowing for the possibility of a reciprocal "infusion of energy" by Vargas Llosa and Cortázar into a canonical tradition exemplified by Cervantes, Fielding, Flaubert, Unamuno, James Joyce, and others, Parkinson Zamora still characterizes that narrative tradition as "venerable," in a concluding sentence that seems curiously devoid of irony and whose wider political implications are subjected to some eye-catching strategies of formal containment: They are bracketed, first, inside a textual parenthesis that nevertheless advocates "the central importance of the comparative consideration of contemporary Latin American texts" (34) and then displaced onto an endnote reproducing a statement by Julio Ortega, who more than a decade earlier had ascribed Cortázar and Fuentes to the category of "Latin American narrators of the highest universal standing" and identified a certain "impulse toward integration" in Latin American writing, which in Ortega's view represented "the Latin American response to a dialogue whose aesthetic and philosophical terms [. . .] had been formulated in multiple instances of division [en múltiples escisiones]" (*La contemplación y la fiesta* 8). Echoing Borges in his classic essay "El escritor argentino y la tradición," Alfonso Reyes ("Notas sobre la inteligencia americana"), and Octavio Paz (*Posdata*), and anticipating Angel Rama (*Transculturación narrativa* 39), Ortega championed Latin America's active involvement in the give-and-take of global cultural exchange and spoke tellingly from the margins of Parkinson Zamora's text to defend the sovereign value of Latin American cultural discourse and to assert its equal status vis-à-vis the cultural production of other areas of the world.

A study in which the politics of cultural interaction occupies center stage is Gustavo Pérez Firmat's major essay, *The Cuban Condition: Translation and Identity in Modern Cuban Literature*. Published seven years after Parkinson Zamora's pioneering article, Pérez Firmat's study combines an intertextual focus with an explicit political agenda valid for Cuba and Latin America as a whole. According to Pérez Firmat, the "fundamental interest [of *The Cuban Condition*] lies in the complicated intercourse between New World and Old World Culture, and, more particularly, in how Cuban texts rewrite some of the masterworks of the Spanish and European literary tradition" (14). Postulating a mismatch, at the moment of encounter, between a local "American" sensibility and exogenous forms of expression, Pérez Firmat traces the emergence in Cuba of a literary vernacular which, at the levels of idiom, rhetoric, and structural aspects of narrative, effects a continuous "antiauthoritarian, anticolonial gesture" whose business is the promotion of cultural autonomy and the assertion of difference (26–27). Redolent, once more, of Borges's valorization of the periphery as the site of subversion, this reading of cultural interaction in Cuba reiterates the connection between the textual and the political in terms that hold for the cultures and peoples of Latin America in general.

With regard to Mexico, the issues under discussion here figure prominently in the work of intellectuals such as José Vasconcelos, Alfonso Caso, Alfonso Reyes, and especially Leopoldo Zea. Through his various activities as editor (most famously of *Cuadernos americanos,* which he founded in 1942), scholar, and teacher, Zea strove to account for the history of Mexican and Latin American philosophical ideas and to elucidate the conditions of their specificity vis-à-vis the dominant traditions of Europe and the United States. For more than half a century, Zea persistently reworked a number of essential themes while evolving in directions that kept him in touch with the major political and intellectual developments of his times.

The main lines of Zea's thinking are laid down in two early essays, "North America in the Spanish American Consciousness" (1947) and "Philosophy as Commitment" (1948). The first of these essays commemorates the centenary of the war between Mexico and the United States and surveys the attitudes to their northern neighbor of several generations of Spanish American intellectuals of the modern period. Concentrating, first, on the nineteenth century, the essay registers the widespread call for a "mental emancipation" to match the political freedoms gained in the initial phase of independence from Spain. With thinkers such as Esteban Echeverría, Juan Bautista Alberdi, and José María Luis Mora in mind, Zea comments: "In spite of having secured political emancipation from [Spain], they know that this does not go far enough, and that they must tear Spain out from their entrails. Political emancipation must be followed by another kind of emancipation, which they will term 'emancipation of the mind'" (reproduced in Zea, *La filosofía como compromiso y otros ensayos* 57). Moving ahead to the twentieth century, Zea then praises Enrique Rodó and Antonio Caso for their "stance of promoting Spanish American interests," and identifies two strands in their attitude toward the United States. On the one hand, they and other intellectuals like them found much to admire in the democratic traditions of the United States; on the other, they were united in their abhorrence of "the North America of territorial ambitions [and] 'Manifest Destiny,' of acts of racial discrimination and imperialist practices" (82). Compared with the former, the political and cultural institutions of Spanish America left much to be desired; with the latter, they gave cause for satisfaction, even pride.

Some of the implications of Zea's historical analysis for the Spanish American intelligentsia of the day are spelled out in "Philosophy as Commitment." Taking for granted a connection (reminiscent of Sartre) between philosophy and ethics, this pithy and combative essay asks, "What obligations are incumbent on us Spanish Americans? What situation must we answer to? What commitments must we undertake in our philosophy?" It calls for "a mode of philosophizing that is aware of our situation," that is, a way of thinking appropriate to the circumstances of Spanish American societies and the intelligentsias that serve them (31). In fundamental terms, this urgent, "circumstantialist" approach is at odds with the discourse of universalism: "We might be told: philosophy is universal and philosophers can only address universal and eternal issues." To which Zea retorts, "To answer in those terms is not to answer at all. [. . .] It is, quite simply, a subterfuge, an easy way of avoiding one's responsibilities" (32). Rejecting such strategies of evasion, Zea envisages a future close to hand involving the construction of new types of community founded on solidarity between colonial peoples and their united opposition to imperialist nations—a global scenario in which the peoples of Spanish America will, he anticipates, occupy "a very prominent place" (36).

Together and in their essential respects, these two early essays spell out a program promoting the political and cultural integrity of Spanish America. Consistent with the anti-imperialist ideology of a Pablo Neruda or a Gabriel García Márquez of the time, the ideas expressed in them will surface again and again in later writings by Zea—through the 1970s, when he publishes a collection of essays under the title "Dependence and Liberation in Latin American Culture," into the 1980s, when he publishes *Discourse from the Site of Marginalization and Barbarism* (1988), and thereafter to the century's end. Reviewing the content of the first of these volumes, we find an anti-imperialist message and defense of the specificity of the Latin American experience in "From the History of Ideas to the Philosophy of Latin American History" (originally of 1973); a statement of the continuing need for a "fight for the psychological or cultural liberation" of the peoples of Latin America, in "Latin American Philosophy as Philosophy of Liberation" (*Dependencia y liberación* 32); a renewed call for solidarity with other "dependent, colonized peoples" in "From the History of Ideas to the Philosophy of Latin American History" (26); and a high-minded invitation to "participate in the making of a broader, more humane world, beyond the limits of the one we inherited and which is considered by its architects to be in crisis. A world designed for another kind of human being," in "Colonization and Decolonization of Latin American Culture" (originally of 1970) (*Dependencia y liberación* 56).

In addition to these obvious continuities with Zea's earlier writings, the essays in *Dependence and Liberation in Latin American Culture* also contain elements that are novel and indicative of major developments in the author's political thinking. Signaled most readily at the level of terminology, the changes in question can all be subsumed under the concepts of decolonization and postcolonial awareness. In no particular order of importance or hierarchy, aspects of this revised outlook include the idea of the Third World—Zea mentions parts of Africa and Asia—with which Latin America is encouraged to adopt a common perspective; the sense of being poised at a crossroads in world history, and of the benefits of participating in large-scale processes of decolonization; a rejection of dependence theory and its replacement by the philosophy of liberation expounded by the likes of Enrique Dussel and Augusto Salazar Bondy; and identification with other thinkers of the moment, of whom the most significant, by any criteria, are Frantz Fanon, Aimé Césaire, and Léopold Sedar Senghor. Looking beyond the—by no means narrow—frame of reference of Latin American affairs, of which he was as cogent an interpreter as any other Latin American intellectual of the second half of the twentieth century, Zea chose to relate the subcontinent's current situation and trajectory to contemporary trends in world history, within which, he implied, the ultimate significance of contemporary Latin American experience could best be gauged.

One of the most noteworthy features of the essays of *Dependence and Liberation in Latin American Culture* is the intermingling of references to local thinkers such as Salazar Bondy and the three intellectuals named above. Of the triad, Frantz Fanon is the most widely mentioned, appearing in three of the six essays that make up the volume. More tellingly: at the midpoint of "Latin American Philosophy as Philosophy of Liberation," Zea pointedly invokes "Frantz Fanon, a fellow Latin American" in a review of contemporary continental thinking on the subjects of liberation and decolonization of the mind. Paying tribute to Salazar Bondy's contribution to liberation philosophy, Zea glosses his thoughts with a two-part quotation from Fanon: "Decolonization is quite simply the replacing of a certain 'species' of men by another 'species' of men [. . .]; for Europe, for ourselves and for humanity, we must turn over a new leaf, we must work out new concepts, and try to set afoot a new man" (Fanon, *The Wretched of the Earth* 27, 255), going on to cite and summarize Fanon profusely yet again in the penultimate and closing paragraphs of the essay (*Dependencia y liberación* 41). There, Zea praises the integrity of Fanon's position and his commitment to mankind, noting, "For that reason, Fanon, writing not as a black man, a Latin American or a person of African origins but as a concrete human being endowed with the concreteness that is a feature of all human beings, remarks, 'If we want humanity to advance a step farther, if we want to raise it to a higher level than that which Europe has imposed on it, then we must invent, and we must make discoveries'" (47). Throughout the essay, what is significant is the repeated gesture of identification with an individual whom Zea clearly regards as a front-line representative of a current of thinking that is of unquestionable relevance to the situation of postcolonial societies everywhere, whether in Africa, Asia, Latin America, or other parts of the world.

"Negritude and Indigenism" is the title of a lecture that Zea delivered to the *Négritude et Amérique Latine* colloquium held at the University of Dakar, Seneghal, in January 1974. Indebted to the work of Aimé Césaire and Léopold Sedar Senghor, it provides further evidence of the expanded parameters of Zea's view of the world while it illustrates his use of material drawn from diverse sources to illuminate the situation of the peoples of Latin America—specifically, the indigenous populations of Mexico and the Andean region. Zea's acquaintance with the work of Césaire stems in part from the interviews that he had read in a number of *Casa de las*

Américas published in the summer of 1968, where the Haitian intellectual had discussed issues of race, colonialism, culture, and revolution. By the time he composed "Negritude and Indigenism," Zea had absorbed the ideology of Césaire and his fellow intellectual, the Senegalese Sedar Senghor, and was able to apply their analysis of racialist oppression in French and British colonial territories to areas of Latin America.

As his starting point, Zea states, "Negritude and indigenism are ideological concepts which originate in a situation that is common to the peoples of black Africa and Afro-America on the one hand, and Latin America or Indo-America on the other: the situation of dependency. In both cases, [the concepts] express recognition of a situation of marginality and subordination that has to change" (*Dependencia y liberación* 57). Acknowledging the very different circumstances in which the two concepts arose and developed, Zea nevertheless sees them as addressing similar questions to do with ethnicity, culture, and subalternity, and he reassesses Latin American *indigenismo* in the light of postcolonialism's unmasking of white mythologies and other categories of western thought and power. In the course of his argument, Zea cites Aimé Césaire and his recuperation of oppressed colonial subjects epitomized by "the black man [who] was a man like any other and who had accomplished things worthy of consideration within the frame of universal creation, to which we wished to continue to give recognition" (Césaire, in Aratán and Depestre 135). Next mentioned is the resoundingly titled *Liberté I: Négritude et Humanisme* by Sedar Senghor, in the context of a discussion envisaging new forms of "cultural mixing" in which the goal of each community or tradition would be "to assimilate, without being assimilated" (*Dependencia y liberación* 73). Finally, Zea rounds off his argument with one more quote from Fanon, anchoring his study ever more firmly in the discourse of postcolonialism which, without being named as such, is the matrix surrounding "Negritude and Indigenism" along with the other essays dating from the early 1970s under consideration here.

Moving ahead in time, *Discourse from the Site of Marginalization and Barbarism* (1988) and *Philosophizing at the Level of Mankind* (1993) demonstrate the principal continuities and developments in Zea's thinking near the century's end. In some of its ten chapters, *Discourse* reformulates concerns already documented in earlier work by Zea; in others, it engages with issues that are the focus of intense contemporary debate (see, e.g., Mignolo). Thus, at the same time as it repeats the analysis of the history of Latin American thought worked out in "North America in the Spanish American Consciousness" (1947), it gives an even higher profile than before to issues of colonialism and decolonization, discussing relations between Latin America and Europe from a perspective of reversal that privileges the discourse of the barbarous Other who occupies the margins, over the claims to represent civilization made by those who inhabit the center. Upsetting traditional assumptions about relations between the local and the universal, Zea articulates a range of positions representing national, continental, and global interests and provides a sharpened perspective on political and cultural issues of Latin America. Indeed, the multiple facets of Zea's intellectual profile constitute a paradigm, or type, against which other intellectuals might be measured, including the literary author who is the primary focus of this study, Fernando del Paso.

Americanismo and Postcolonialism, Humanism, and Universalism: The Discursive Affiliations of Fernando del Paso

> No one today is purely *one* thing. Labels like Indian, or woman, or Muslim, or American are not more than starting points, which if followed into actual experience for only a moment are quickly left behind. Imperialism consolidated the mixture of cultures and identities on a global scale.
>
> Edward Said, *Culture and Imperialism*

Known as one of his country's most prestigious novelists and retired diplomats, del Paso is also a painter, poet, dramatist, and essayist who has inserted himself into the discursive framework outlined above through numerous polemical and artistic means. Whether as a journalist, polemicist, or obliging subject of press interviews that became ever more frequent as his creative star ascended, del Paso has made a regular stream of public declarations that over the years have built up a clearly defined artistic and political profile. In general outline, the statements concerned reveal a pattern of evolution away from an initially apolitical stance toward increasing involvement in political issues of the day and a more vigorous expression of political views, which have invariably been bound up with questions of cultural identity.

The earliest recorded interview with del Paso dates from the summer of 1966 and captures the excitement surrounding the publication of *José Trigo*. Offering a highly informative summary of features of the novel, the text of the interview is remarkable for the absence of any mention of social or political matters. Indeed, concerning the storyline of *José Trigo* and its re-creation of incidents from the Mexican railway workers' strike of 1959, del Paso insists, "It was not my intention that it should have any specific social content." Instead, he emphasizes the linguistic and mythological dimensions of *José Trigo* and offers a formulation of his aesthetic creed: "My position on art is a mystical one." More specifically, del Paso acknowledges the example of Poe, expresses a belief in the permanence of "beautiful objects," and aligns himself with a Symbolist aesthetic that stretches as far as T. S. Eliot and James George Frazer and is not generally noted for the closeness of its attention to the accidents of history (Carvajal iii).

A decade later, all of this has changed. Speaking in 1978 in the wake of the publication and tumultuous reception of his second novel, *Palinuro de México,* del Paso radiates political conviction: "I don't believe that anybody, at the present time, can be apolitical. [. . .] Politics is related to concrete circumstances which impinge on us in the street, on television, in the newspapers." He continues, "To be apolitical is tantamount to closing your eyes to reality. And to do that is to take up a political position: it means you become an accomplice of dictatorships, oligarchies, and the multinationals, [an accomplice] of the people who assassinated Ché Guevara, dropped the bomb on Hiroshima and sprayed napalm on Vietnam. And of those who wounded a student in the Plaza Mayor of Mexico City" (Parra 69). Remarkable in part for its rhetoric of restraint, the statement lists many of the classic bogeymen of the political Left of the 1960s and 1970s and identifies the major determinants of del Paso's political outlook after 1968.

An important aspect of the author's evolved self-image at this time is the view of himself as a continental writer who shares many of the aims and concerns of other Latin American intellectuals. Answering a question fed him by two journalists from Madrid about his relationship to the writers of the *boom,* del Paso replied: "I am connected to them by something more than geographical and historical coincidence, and my books, [. . .] whether I like it or not, form part of the intellectual consciousness of Latin America" (Sánchez Bardón and Javier Goñi 49). As he subsequently explained elsewhere, this sense of a common identity grew out of a collective response to historical conditions in Latin America and the world beyond: "I believe that we all belong to a current of sorts that is of considerable importance and in which most of us have become keenly aware of our history—the history of Latin America, including our present-day position in the world. [I also believe that] in one way or another we express that awareness in our respective work" (Ruffinelli, "Fernando del Paso: la novela como exorcismo" 199). Inseparable, no doubt, from the overall climate of responsibility and enthusiasm generated by the successes of

Latin American writing from the mid-1960s on, the outlook described by del Paso responds at the deepest level to events in the political sphere, from the Cuban Revolution and its aftermath, through U.S. military intervention in Southeast Asia and the international student protests of 1968 (whose impact on del Paso is attested to in several interviews),[1] to numerous other conflicts and flashpoints in Latin America and the world at large.

It is at this moment in del Paso's career that his ideological profile begins to overlap quite clearly with that of Leopoldo Zea as outlined above. Two statements, recorded in 1980 and 1983, respectively, reveal the extent of the alignment. The first appears in the context of a discussion about del Paso's experience of life in London, where he resided from 1971 to 1985. In a lengthy conversation, the author of *Palinuro de México* lays claim to an anti-imperialist position that, he says, "would have reaffirmed itself in a different way if I had not lived in London for all these years." Commenting on the attitudes that he had observed among the British and continental Europeans, del Paso remarked: "The imperialist history of the European powers, their contempt for what we today call the Third World, is still reflected in the behavior and attitudes that persist at both the national and the continental levels; it is found among those who believe themselves to be free of the old prejudices, and even in those who fight for our causes" (Trejo Fuentes 10).

The second statement sketches a portrait of del Paso in the following unequivocal terms: "Without question I am a Mexican and a Latin American, one who has been caught in the cross fire and has the mind-set of a colonized country. That is the way I am and that is the role that I have assumed" (Echegoyen, "Nuevas conversaciones con Fernando del Paso" 32). As a declaration of identity and ethical purpose, this forthright statement could serve equally well to describe Leopoldo Zea, whose views are further reflected in incidental details of del Paso's experience such as his acceptance of nomination to the jury of the Casa de Las Américas literary prize for 1983 in Havana, and his authorship of a polemical article in 1980 on the continuing colonial plight of the New Hebrides—two ideologically significant gestures that place him in the same camp, if not in the same generation, as Zea (who was born twenty-three years before del Paso, in 1912).

In the overall trajectory of del Paso's career, the single most significant event is unquestionably the award in 1982 of the prestigious Rómulo Gallegos Prize, for *Palinuro de México*. At the award ceremony in Caracas in August of that year, del Paso delivered a formal address combining evocative autobiographical reflections with a resounding declaration of fundamental principles and beliefs. Reproduced subsequently in the pages of *Casa de las Américas,* "Mi patria chica, mi patria grande" furnishes a definitive statement of the author's political views, refashioned in the crucible of recent political events that had taken place in the United Kingdom and the south Atlantic in the spring of 1982. From his vantage point in London where he was working for the World Service of the British Broadcasting Corporation, del Paso was witness to the reactions of the British people and their government to the Argentine occupation of the Falkland Islands/Islas Malvinas. At that critical moment in world history, he also shared in the collective unease and indignation of a large community of Latin Americans based in London, who saw in the British military response an unwelcome replay of scenarios of nineteenth-century imperialist aggression. Admitting to a lifelong feeling that Latin Americans "belong to a kind of extensive, common homeland," del Paso told his audience in Caracas, "This kind of supranationality was strengthened more than ever at the point when the arrogance, the overreaching pride of some of those foreigners who do not belong to that common homeland, exacerbated, in me and in my friends, all that is Latin American about us" ("Mi patria chica" 159–60).

A fierce denunciation of imperialism and an accompanying proclamation of "a Latin American continental vocation" are, perhaps, not wholly unexpected ingredients of a public address written in the wake of the Falklands War and intended for a Latin American audience. Yet such views and proclamations echo precisely the fundamentals of del Paso's political philosophy expressed elsewhere, and chime in perfectly with his thoughts on the other subjects treated in "Mi patria chica, mi patria grande" — subjects ranging from geopolitics, patriotic sentiment, and nationalism to linguistic exile and cultural themes. The bearing of historical and political questions on the construction of del Paso's novels is something that I explore in greater detail in later chapters; at this point, I turn my attention to themes of culture — identity, heritage, affiliation — in order to fill out the literary-cum-political profile of Fernando del Paso being drawn here.

A strong affiliation with the cultural traditions of Latin America is evident in the foregoing analysis and is reiterated by del Paso in several interviews from the mid-1970s on. In a typical account of his literary apprenticeship, del Paso cites Latin American authors (Carpentier, Cortázar, Uslar Pietri, Roa Bastos, Lezama Lima, Neruda) who influenced his development and comments, "It was with them, with the authors of Latin

America, that I learned to write" ("Mi patria chica" 158). On the face of it, such statements are unexceptional—a logical consequence of the author's life and education in Mexico City in the 1940s and early 1950s. Yet they often carry within them the implication of a binary relationship between self and other, between Latin American and non-Latin American points of reference, which is crucial to the present inquiry. The interplay between the local and the universal is seen in the continuation of del Paso's account of his literary apprenticeship, quoted from above. Arbitrarily cutting short the roll call of famous Latin American authors to whom he acknowledges a debt, del Paso remarks, "Suffice it to say that they all taught me, not only to write, but also what to write about and for what purpose." He adds "And this is not to say that I do not recognize the instructive examples and the influence of the grand masters of world literature: because it was through those Latin Americans that, to a large extent, I acquired them" (158). In this two-part declaration, the second, qualifying sentence is noteworthy, above all, for its problematization of the categories of "Latin American" and "non-Latin American." Couched in the terms of a rhetorical denial, the sentence simultaneously asserts and negates difference between those two categories; what is more, it effectively enacts the proposition that it is in the process of advancing, by exemplifying from the author's own life the mechanisms of mediation through which material originating in non-Latin American sources enters the mainstream of Latin American cultural discourse, where it circulates freely thereafter. According to del Paso, the canonical authors of world literature became known to him largely through the mediation of other Latin American writers—writers such as Borges, Asturias, and Marechal, who, as I shall attempt to show below, served as vehicles for the transmission, to del Paso and other writers of his generation, of the influence of James Joyce (in particular) and, through him, of the examples of Homer, Dante, Shakespeare, Rabelais, Swift, and a voluminous *et caetera*.

Del Paso's relationship to what he terms "universal culture" and his view of the relation between it and Latin American culture are subjects that merit close attention. He has acknowledged the roots of his work most immediately in Symbolism (Poe), surrealism (Breton, Magritte), and modernism (Joyce) and, from a longer perspective, in a millenial tradition of (largely western) art and science, narrative, and philosophy. On the other hand, he has acknowledged a strong affiliation to a broad Latin American tradition including Bolívar, Borges, Reyes, Neruda, Rulfo, Paz, and others, whose work has debated the question of American identity vis-à-vis European culture vigorously and insistently.

Fernando del Paso's most important statements in this regard have revolved around the crucial event of his move to England in 1971. At a certain moment in the biographical narrative of "Mi patria chica, mi patria grande," del Paso recalls, "I went to live in London in order to confirm and reaffirm the western, European, and Judeo-Christian components of my culture, my way of life, my traditions, both past and present" (156). In an earlier account of his motives for moving to Europe, he had remarked: "I wanted to see the old cities, walk through their streets to the point of exhaustion, visit museums and monuments, and to try to recover that part of the history of Europe which also belongs to us" (Trejo Fuentes 10). Speaking in terms of reaffirmation and recovery, about a project intended and willed, del Paso lays claim here to the entire cultural heritage of the Old World, as well as to a selective identification with the history of Europe. A rhetorical question communicates vividly the right of access to the storehouse of western culture: "Surely Homer and Thomas Aquinas, Haydn and Botticelli belong to us to the same extent that they belong to Europe?" ("Mi patria chica" 156).

This attitude was given its most controversial formulation in a public address at the Sorbonne in Paris in the spring of 1991. The occasion was a celebration, sponsored by the French Ministry of Culture, of the achievements of contemporary Mexican literature. At the time, del Paso was Mexico's consul general in France, recently promoted from the position of cultural attaché there, and it fell to him to reply to the speech of welcome delivered by the rector of the Sorbonne. Beginning in a conventional vein, del Paso thanked the French authorities for their hospitality and acknowledged the existence of historic ties between France and Mexico. He then turned to the topic of cultural identity and introduced a mildly discordant note, querying some widely held perceptions of the literature of Latin America: "Our literature is not that far removed from European literature and thought. But neither is it as exotic as some might imagine, or as the inventors of the myth of the so-called *boom* of Latin American literature would have wished." With the part-French, part-Mexican audience now hanging on his every word, del Paso delivered the main thrust of his argument as follows:

Through religion and language, which were the two most powerful weapons in the conquest of the Latin American continent, the Spaniards made us a party to western culture. Put another way, the processes of *mestizaje* and transculturation, which began five hundred years ago and continue today, have resulted in the peoples of Latin

America acquiring co-ownership of all the values of western history and the Judeo-Christian cultural tradition. This means that Shakespeare, Ucello, Bergson, and Mahler, to mention just a few names, belong to us just as much as they belong to the peoples of Europe. (Excerpts 46)

On behalf of the peoples of Mexico and Latin America, del Paso restates the proposition of equal ownership of cultural goods, shrewdly citing the name of Bergson as a token of the French intellectual tradition alongside famous representatives of English, Italian, and German culture.

The reference to Bergson adds a certain edge to the critique of Eurocentrism that is implied in the Sorbonne speech and ushers in the most controversial section of the address. Centering on a text by the doyen of Mexican letters, Octavio Paz (who did not attend the proceedings), the material concerned shows del Paso taking issue, first and to a modest extent, with the organizers of the Paris event and, for the most part, with a paragraph from the prologue to Paz's essay of 1970, *Posdata,* reprinted, without the author's permission, as a preface to the program of the weeklong event:

> I disagree with the text that has been chosen [for this occasion], and especially with a paragraph that says: "Inhabitants of the periphery, living on the outskirts of history, we Latin Americans are the uninvited guests who came into the West via the tradesmen's entrance, the intruders who arrive at the spectacle of modernity at the moment when the lights are about to go out." (Paz, *Posdata* 13)

Without a break, del Paso continued:

> I, who as a child was nurtured on Jules Verne, Alexandre Dumas, Walter Scott, and who subsequently fed my sentimental education with Flaubert, Marcel Proust, André Gide, and William Faulkner, do not feel at all like a "man of the periphery," "an inhabitant of the outskirts of history," or an "uninvited guest." I have not gained access to the culture of the West by the tradesmen's entrance, nor do I feel at all that I am an intruder there. (Excerpts 46)

Predictably, these remarks drew a sharp reply from Paz, to which del Paso responded, the whole exchange being published in the pages of the weekly journal *Proceso* in April 1991. From my position on the sidelines, and at a temporal remove of several years, I am not going to attempt to adjudicate between the two parties involved in the dispute. For the purposes of this study I simply note the robust spirit of del Paso's remarks and the firmness of his conviction concerning his personal relation to western culture.

It is significant that the categories of the West and Judeo-Christian civilization overlap, in del Paso's thinking, with that of the universal. The conception of the universal that informs del Paso's work is both a personal one and the offshoot of a Latin American branch of political thought stemming from Bello and Bolívar and flowering much later in the work of Reyes, Zea, and others. Del Paso's personal conception is encapsulated in the following: "We are members of a single race of equals whose homeland is the world and whose common language is hope" ("Mi patria chica" 154) and "[We are] beings who have the capacity to think and who are universal" (155). A further statement, "All men are brothers of ours, and all their noble causes, too" (154–55), shows the humanist and idealist cast of del Paso's worldview, converging, once again, in key respects with the outlook of Leopoldo Zea, who near the close of "Colonization and Decolonization of Latin American Culture" had looked forward to the emergence of "a more fully developed human subject": "one who will express himself through all the forms of culture at his disposal," and who will be capable of representing "all men, of the past and of the present, along with those who have yet to be" (*Dependencia y liberación* 55).

From a continental perspective, the towering figure of Alfonso Reyes stands as a synecdoche of a long-running inquiry into relations between the national and the universal in Latin America. In a lecture entitled "Notas sobre la inteligencia americana," which he delivered to an international audience in Buenos Aires in 1936, Reyes spoke for all the peoples of Latin America when he demanded international recognition of "the right to citizenship of the world, which we have already acquired" [el derecho a la ciudadanía universal que ya hemos conquistado] (15). Through his calculated choice of words, Reyes asserted the right of all Latin Americans to enjoy the political fruits of a modern-day *conquest,* which they had at long last undertaken as subjects and not experienced merely as spectators and objects. Declaring their "citizenship of the world" a fait accompli, he blazed a trail for later thinkers who would press the same claim and, in del Paso's case, take absolutely for granted a personal place in the universal order of culture.

In light of the above, it is clear that del Paso does not share the suspicion of universalist concepts harbored by some postcolonial intellectuals (for example, Ngugi wa Thiong'o) who have regarded the rhetoric of universalism as nothing more than an instrument for the propagation and perpetuation of western hegemony (Ngugi 1986). Del Paso views the universal as part of a continuum beginning with the local and the regional and opening out onto wider horizons that either connect with, or actually constitute, the universal. Maintaining that "We proceed thus, from the lesser order to the greater" ("Mi patria chica" 155), he envisages staged access to the universal through the local, the regional, and the continental, and thereby plays out the scenario outlined by Leopoldo Zea in his conception of the evolution of Latin American ideas. Writing in the early 1970s, Zea bore witness to the following:

> A realization of the manner in which our peoples, the peoples of Latin America, have received and assimilated the expressions of other cultures. The way in which these peoples, in spite of everything, have appropriated values which were once used to justify acts of domination and relations of dependency, and have adapted them to their innermost personality. A realization which has gradually permitted us to make those values the expression of our own personality and indispensable complements of it. This history has also made us conscious of the universal dimension of our personality without this affecting our material specificity as human beings, which is equal to that of the architects, past and present, of the multiple creations of what is called universal culture. (*Dependencia y liberación* 31)

Rendering vividly the situation of colonial and postcolonial societies the world over, these words illuminate the study of the works of Fernando del Paso, which give sustained literary form to the political and ideological convictions rehearsed in this section.

Text, Intertext, and Narrative Transculturation in the Work of Fernando del Paso

Literary texts and literary culture were probably not foremost in Leopoldo Zea's mind when he made the declaration reproduced above, but they are, without question, sites of some of the most compelling operations of the phenomenon to which he was referring in all but name, which is the phenomenon of transculturation. Observations on the "assimilation of the expressions of other cultures," "adapting the values of others to one's own personality," and the relationship between local and universal categories are essential to Latin American theories of transculturation as analyzed by Silvia Spitta in an authoritative and invaluable study. *Between Two Wa-*

ters: Narratives of Transculturation in Latin America (1995) deals with the subject of transculturation from two complementary angles. The first of these traces the historical parameters of colonialism and neocolonialism, which have framed the societies and cultures of Latin America since the Conquest, while the second examines some specific narrative instances of transculturation that have taken place in the fields of painting and fiction over the past five hundred years. Each of these angles offers something of value to the present study of the work of Fernando del Paso.

In the opening pages of her book, Spitta acknowledges Cuban anthropologist Fernando Ortiz as the originator of a general theory of transculturation to which significant refinements were added in the work of the Peruvian José María Arguedas. Privileging "the Arguedian understanding of the intercultural dynamics that have arisen because of the Conquest," Spitta recalls the distinction drawn by Arguedas between *acculturation* and *transculturation* and offers the following summary: "On one side is acculturation, the sheer and irredeemable loss of one's culture, language, history, tradition—even the body and its rhythms; on the other side is transculturation, the overcoming of loss by giving new shape to one's life and culture after the catastrophes of Conquest, colonization, and modernization" (1–2). She concludes, "Transculturation can thus be understood as the complex process of adjustment and re-creation—cultural, literary, linguistic, and personal—that allow for new, vital, and viable configurations to arise out of the clash of cultures and the violence of colonial and neo-colonial appropriations" (2).

Spitta's account and definition of the concept of transculturation resembles Fernando del Paso's 1991 address at the Sorbonne. There, the Mexican novelist likewise traced the phenomena of *mestizaje* and transculturation in Latin America back to the moment of Conquest and depicted them as the prime determinants of Latin American cultural experience right up to the present day. In conjunction with other material that will be cited in due course, del Paso's familiarity with the basic principles of the subject of transculturation authorizes an approach to his novels as instances of "the two-way, multi-leveled cultural interchanges, borrowings, displacements, and re-creations characteristic of both Latin American and European literatures, languages, and cultures" (Spitta 14–15). In the specific case of *José Trigo*, European symbols interact with others from a Mesoamerican tradition and result in a subversive resemanticization of metropolitan values, similar to the operations Spitta observes in a range of early colonial texts (Spitta chapters 2–4). In *Palinuro de México*, a minor fictional character is recuperated from the margins of the western canon

(Virgil's *Aeneid*) and assimilated to a novelistic project that redefines him as a contemporary Mexican hero. *Noticias del Imperio,* through the narrative of the emperor Maximilian and the native Indian president Benito Juárez, thematizes military and ideological conflict between Europe and the Americas, and explores the political and moral consequences of a misguided imperial adventure on Mexican soil. And *Linda 67* exposes flaws in contemporary North American society through a polarized contrast with Mexican values that builds on Alejo Carpentier's earlier critical meditations on relations between Spanish America, the United States, and Europe. In the detailed design of their plots, therefore, del Paso's novels dramatize scenarios of conflict that are invested with varying degrees of political significance and intent.

Besides articulating a general historical explanation of intercultural encounter, the theory of transculturation offers a model for the study of processes of narrative transculturation in particular. This element of transculturation theory is also applicable to the novels of Fernando del Paso, which provide fascinating examples of the phenomenon. Spitta's recuperation of the seminal work of Angel Rama is especially helpful in this connection, inasmuch as it sets out the agenda for any serious inquiry into narrative transculturation. Such an inquiry must concern itself with (1) the relationship between foreign models and local narrative traditions, (2) the negotiation of the modernizing impulses of the European novel, and (3) processes of cultural mediation and assimilation which Rama, using a spatial metaphor and focusing exclusively on mid-twentieth-century examples, located at one of two poles of Spanish American writing: the transculturating pole represented, in his scheme, by authors such as Arguedas, Asturias, García Márquez, Rulfo, and Roa Bastos, and the cosmopolitan pole represented by authors such as Borges, Cortázar, and (quite problematically) Fuentes.

The polarized conception underpinning Rama's theory of narrative transculturation in Latin America is arguably both a strength and a weakness, as my bracketed comment on the identification of Fuentes with the cosmopolitan pole is meant to indicate. For, if there is a persuasive coherence to Rama's canon of "transculturadores" who, in Spitta's words, "take on the task of *mediating* between the different fields of tension created by the diverse cultures, languages, and worlds that coexist in different relations of power in their countries" (9), the attribution of the author of "Chac Mool," *La región más transparente, Terra nostra,* and other fictions to a completely opposite pole is, at least to my mind, counterintuitive. This objection is, in fact, anticipated by Rama, who concedes the possibility of certain authors' occupying a point of intersection between the two arcs that divide the field of Latin American culture according to his scheme ("La tecnificación narrativa" 70–71). This capacity for self-adjustment in Rama's theory opens the way to accommodating writers like Fuentes and del Paso at just that point of intersection.

In broad outline, Rama's theory of narrative transculturation concentrates on the impact, on Latin American fiction of the mid-twentieth century, of modernizing impulses deriving from the European avant-garde and its North American offshoots. In that context, the greatest influence was exerted by the modernist novels of such writers as Kafka, Joyce, Woolf, and Musil and, from North America, Faulkner and Dos Passos. Notwithstanding the prominence given to named authors in his survey, *Transculturación narrativa en América Latina,* Rama's account of the field of Latin American literature rests at bottom on culturalist foundations that privilege the cultural system, heritage, and community over the creative capacities of individuals: hence the dynamic role assigned in his discourse to literary "tendencies," "models," "structures," and "systems" — terms which appear under the nomenclature of "literary paradigms" in my study and reinforce the intertextual approach that I take to the novels of Fernando del Paso. The incorporation of a modernist paradigm of narrative fiction, exemplified quintessentially in *Ulysses* and *Finnegans Wake,* is crucial to the design of *José Trigo.* Elaborating on a process that was already well advanced in Mexican fiction, the most significant aspect of del Paso's novel was its interweaving of "foreign" modernist strands with native Indian cultural material, giving rise to a hybrid text whose transculturated nature, passed over by virtually all of the novel's commentators,[2] is one of the main focuses of my study. After *José Trigo, Palinuro de México* repeats the Joycean formula to produce what may be considered the most accomplished Mexican rewriting of *Ulysses* of all time. In del Paso's prize-winning novel of 1977, a template derived from the universal narrative tradition is made to conform to local conditions as part of a project that openly interpellates universal culture and inscribes itself within global parameters. Through a two-way process that involves the Mexicanizing of Mediterranean source material and the bold assumption of membership of universal culture, *Palinuro de México* places itself firmly at the cosmopolitan pole of Latin American writing according to Rama's scheme. A decade or so later, *Noticias del Imperio* models itself on the type of historical novel cultivated, in its classic nineteenth-century form, by European writers such as Scott and Stendhal. However, *Noticias del Imperio* sets out very self-consciously to subject the inherited paradigm to radical modification. Mixing the dogma of Lukács with the metaphysics of Borges, and generally contesting interpretations of Mexican history that have been written from external, imperialistic perspectives, *Noticias del Imperio* promotes and exemplifies a new Latin American historical novel pulsating with political assertiveness and conviction. In terms of narrative style, *Noticias del Imperio* exploits the modernist paradigm once more but subverts its totalizing pretensions in a postmodernist spirit that infuses several other Spanish American texts of the time. Finally, *Linda 67* experiments with the borrowed form of the crime novel as practiced by European and North American writers from Georges Simenon to Patricia Highsmith. Largely ignoring the national and continental Latin American branches of that tradition, del Paso uses the *novela negra* to paint a deprecating picture of life in the United States and to refute conventional views of Mexico as a site of backwardness and barbarism.

In the light of this summary, del Paso's work evidences a constant negotiation between different narrative paradigms and traditions, each with their own ideological inflections and baggage. His work further mediates between cultural fields ranging from the national through the regional and continental to the universal. Overall, these fields operate as arenas for the staging and, in some cases, for the symbolic resolution of conflicts that have both their origins and, arguably, their final explanation in the colonial, neocolonial, and postcolonial histories of Latin America. The highly elaborate novels of Fernando del Paso offer a singular opportunity for the study of multiple connections between texts, intertexts, and the broader historical and political contexts of writing in Latin America throughout the final third of the twentieth century.

2

José Trigo

A Novel of Hybridity and Regeneration

> Christianity, in its warm, blood-thirsty sense of sacrifice and
> ritual, becomes a natural and novel prolongation of native
> religion. The aspects of charity, love, and turning the other
> cheek are rejected, however. And everything in Mexico boils
> down to this: It is necessary to kill a human being so that oth-
> ers may believe in him.
>
> Carlos Fuentes, *Los días enmascarados*

Del Paso's debut novel has its immediate origins in a specific combination
of personal, social, and literary circumstances. Written between April
1959 and July 1966, it was the tangible result of seven years of creative
activity that del Paso carried out with the aid of a fellowship awarded by
the Centro Mexicano de Escritores in his native Mexico City.[1] For those
living in Mexico at the time, the late 1950s were characterized by rapid
social change and a considerable degree of labor unrest.[2] The epitome of
the latter was the railway workers' strike of 1959, which pitted a band of
workers, with labor leader Demetrio Vallejo at their head, against the
government of President Adolfo López Mateos aided and abetted by the
charros—pro-government union officials—who orchestrated a "dirty
tricks" campaign to discredit the strike movement.[3] "The turbulent conflict of the railways" (54) lies behind the narrative of *José Trigo,* where
it is transposed to a time frame beginning on 13 January and ending on 20
December 1960. Basing his plot "partly on what happened around Demetrio Vallejo, and partly on events from the 1940s, when the *charro*
movement was born" (Carvajal iii), del Paso uses the figure of Vallejo as a
model for Luciano, the main protagonist of *José Trigo.* Luciano is an
elected representative of the railway workers of Nonoalco-Tlatelolco who
campaigns vigorously for strike action and rejects government-sponsored
moves to impose on the workers a settlement that would be to their disad-
vantage. He is opposed by a local *charrista* sympathizer, Manuel Angel,
who contrives to undermine the strike through acts of bullying, sabotage,
and dishonesty. Manuel Angel attempts to bribe Luciano but is rebuffed;

in a later encounter he stabs his rival to death, thus depriving the movement of direction and leadership.

Luciano and Manuel Angel stand at the center of a network of narrative relationships that include their families and the local community of Nonoalco-Tlatelolco and stretch beyond the boundaries of Mexico City to encompass the nation as a whole. Among a plethora of secondary characters, the most important are *madrecita* Buenaventura and her husband, Todolosantos, of whom Luciano was "coincidentally both son and grandson" (137), and José Trigo—a fantasmal being whose story is tied up with that of Luciano and Manuel Angel and who represents an enigma to be elucidated in the course of the narrative. Within the temporal frame of *José Trigo,* a crucial point of reference is the historic Cristero rebellion of 1926–29 in which Luciano's family fought on the side of the defeated Catholic rebels. Further back in time, the narrative recalls the inauguration of the first section of the Mexican railway system in 1850 and evokes aspects of life in the capital city in the colonial era; it also mentions in a chronological note the founding of Tlatelolco by the Aztecs in 1337.

This summary of a large amount of the narrative content of *José Trigo* bears witness to a powerful centrifugal impulse at work in del Paso's novel; at the same time, it affords an insight into the almost limitless ambition that fires del Paso's artistic enterprise. Taking his immediate inspiration from sociopolitical events of the time, del Paso creates a novel of immense and far-reaching proportions, whose principal characteristics include (i) a highly elaborate formal design, which many critics have likened to a pyramid; (ii) a chorus of narrative voices, led by a first-person narrator who comes in search of information about José Trigo and is met by a group of interlocutors peddling unreliable memories, gossip, and half-truths; (iii) a showcase of styles, modes, and discourses, including the ode and the elegy, drama and the epic, historical discourse, scatology, parody of the official discourses of church and state, and pastiche of various literary styles; (iv) an exuberant display of verbal mastery and inventiveness that is grounded in encyclopedic knowledge of several lexical fields and enlivened by a playful attitude to the physical properties of words and their arrangement on the page; (v) a repertoire of cultural and psychoanalytical themes, of which family relations and Oedipal conflict are the most extensively deployed; and (vi) a mythical framework that matches each of the characters and main events in the plot of *José Trigo* with antecedents in pre-Columbian mythology.

As a system of formal and linguistic procedures, del Paso's novel corresponds to a modernist paradigm derived from authors such as James

Joyce, John Dos Passos, and William Faulkner, who together exerted a crucial, modernizing influence on Mexican fiction from the 1940s on. *El luto humano* (1943), *Al filo del agua* (1947), and *Pedro Páramo* (1955) are the most significant staging posts in a process of technical experimentation, which was well established in Mexican fiction midway through the century and which peaked with the historic publication of *La región más transparente* in 1958. The impact of Fuentes's debut novel on the contemporary literary scene cannot be overestimated: Reviled by a handful of detractors and enthused over by many more admirers, *La región más transparente* polarized literary debate in Mexico in the late 1950s and early 1960s and affected all those who were involved in writing fiction.

Testimony to the force of that novel's impact can be found in essays by José Donoso (1972), Gustavo Sainz, and, most pertinent to the present study, by Fernando del Paso in a retrospective declaration made in the mid-1990s. In a 1996 interview with Ilán Stavans, del Paso recollected:

> *Where the Air Is Clear* was a revelation to me. It was a novel that revolutionized Mexican fiction in that it stationed itself in a decisively urban atmosphere—its protagonist [. . .] is Mexico City. It influenced me in its attitude and openness to other styles. [Fuentes and I] were at the time reading the same set of authors: Flaubert, whose approach to the novel we admired, as well as Joyce; and in more technical terms, John Dos Passos, Hemingway, Virginia Woolf, and Faulkner. Without them we wouldn't be who we are today. (129–30)

Two main points emerge from this passage: first, the author's acknowledgment of the decisive influence on him of *La región más transparente,* and second, the mention of a wider community of literary authors and procedures that del Paso claims enabled him, as they did Fuentes, to evolve as a writer of fiction.

Evidence of the influence of *La región más transparente* on *José Trigo* resides most conclusively in the texts themselves. Under comparative scrutiny, the pair reveal a set of likenesses that identify *La región más transparente* quite clearly as a template for *José Trigo.* To start with, both books are novels of the city that double as novels of the nation. Through a narrative perspective that pretends to be all-embracing, *La región más transparente* constructs a vast frieze of life in Mexico City, reproducing "the unstable pastiche" of different milieux and social classes (52) and focusing in particular on "the fact, so obvious yet so rarely reflected in Mexican fiction, of the emergence for the first time ever in the history of the nation, of a middle class and an upper bourgeoisie" (García Gutiérrez, *La región más transparente* 21). Resolutely contemporary in its orientation, *La región más transparente* considers the minutiae of life in the Mexican capital in precise historical terms, locating the action in the period 1946 to 1952 when major social and economic changes were wrought by the administration of President Miguel Alemán. At the same time, the temporal perspective of Fuentes's novel fans out to include the period of the Mexican Revolution and, at a further remove, the pre-Hispanic era of Mexican history; through the medium of a narrative consciousness that spans several centuries, the novel offers a "compendium and review of the history [of the nation]" (García Gutiérrez 19).

More restricted in its sociological focus, *José Trigo* concentrates narrative attention on a small proletarian community living in a disused railway yard in Nonoalco-Tlatelolco. Differences of scale notwithstanding, this setting stems directly from the final scene of *La región más transparente* where the roving eye of Fuentes's narrative comes to rest on the figure of the prostitute, Gladys García, as she stands on the Nonoalco Bridge, looking down on the city below: "Gladys García stops on the Nonoalco bridge. [. . .] She lights up the last cigarette of the night and allows the ash to fall onto the laminated roofs, and takes in the panorama of the city at daybreak" (459–60). In a very literal sense, Fernando del Paso's novel starts up, in 1959, from the very point where Carlos Fuentes had left off, one year earlier, at the end of *La región más transparente*.

A key feature of the Fuentes novel is its incorporation of a mythical perspective on reality, which is provided by the indigenous character, Ixca Cienfuegos. A ubiquitous presence in the social world of the mimesis, Ixca effectively determines the shape of the narrative of *La región más transparente* inasmuch as it is his voice which opens and closes the novel and his vision and values which acquire prominence at strategic points in the narrative. At the thematic level, he and his mother, Teódula Moctezuma, embody certain "elements—cruel and vital—of that stony, eternal Mexico" which Carlos Fuentes suggests lie submerged beneath the surface of everyday social reality in postrevolutionary Mexico (García Gutierrez 21). At the same time, Ixca represents the racial and cultural diversity of a nation whose identity derives in large part from the historical fact of *mestizaje:* in Fuentes's hands, he exemplifies the amalgam of two worldviews—the Christian and the native Indian—which have contributed to the definition of Mexican cultural identity.

José Trigo reproduces the mythical perspective of its forerunner in the overall scope and some of the details of its design. Thus, Luciano evokes the ancient god Quetzalcóatl, while his opponent, Manuel Angel, is portrayed throughout as a modern-day Tezcatlipoca. The eponymous José Trigo, while lacking a concrete referent, seems to embody, like Ixca Cienfuegos before him, the transcendental spirit of the race, and *madrecita* Buenaventura, described as a centenarian "expert in enchantments and sorcery" (535), shares some features with Teódula Moctezuma, excepting her benevolent and charitable nature, which constitutes a major contrast with the bloodthirsty and destructive character of Teódula. In addition to their structural function in the narrative of *José Trigo,* the mythological framework and perspective of the novel permit a more systematic exploration of the phenomenon of cultural *mestizaje* dealt with in the earlier novel by Carlos Fuentes.

In the context of the modern renovation of Mexican narrative, *La región más transparente* attempted a radical experiment with forms and procedures of composition which, while not completely new to Mexican fiction, had not previously been foregrounded to the extent demonstrated in *La región más transparente.* The book's conspicuous technical virtuosity provoked great controversy and met with the disapproval of some commentators. Manuel Pedro González, for one, accused Carlos Fuentes of pursuing gratuitous technical aims and dismissed *La región más transparente* and *La muerte de Artemio Cruz,* along with *Rayuela* by Julio Cortázar and *La ciudad y los perros* by Mario Vargas Llosa, as "the four most scandalously applauded novels" in Spanish American writing of the early 1960s (38). However, it is clear in retrospect that what Georgina García Gutiérrez calls "the avant-garde impulse of Fuentes" was an essential part of a bold, iconoclastic project that resisted containment within the conventional bounds of prose fiction (16). Fuentes's disregard for accepted norms of narrative economy and proportion carries over into the verbal texture of *La región más transparente,* which offers a copybook example of the Bakhtinian categories of carnivalesque and multivocal writing.[4] The dynamics of Fuentes's prose are typified in passages where the author cultivates an encyclopedic style built around extravagance and excess.

José Trigo shares the extravagant technical ambitions of *La región más transparente.* The multiplicity and complexity of its narrative structures, the contrivance of its form, and the seemingly boundless variety of its rhetorical and stylistic repertoire are a mirror image of the operations of Fuentes's text, and they bear out the contemporary evaluation of *José Trigo* as "the most ambitious novel to have been written in Mexico since Carlos Fuentes published *La región más transparente*" (Xirau 24). Xirau's opinion can legitimately be read as a comment on the formal similarities between the two texts in question. Yet a bedazzlement by form should not obscure the fundamental point at issue, which is the affiliation of both texts to a common paradigm deriving from European and North American modernism, a paradigm whose full incorporation into the Mexican narrative tradition is linked unquestionably to the social dynamics of the age. Urban expansion, industrial growth, and further differentiation between the social classes were visible indices of a modernity in the making in Mexico in the 1950s and 1960s. In other latitudes, those conditions had developed some decades earlier and had been reflected in a modernist aesthetic that produced works such as *Ulysses* and *Manhattan Transfer*. In Mexico, the modernizing idiom of *La región más transparente* was a timely response to the conditions and imperatives of social change, shortly to be echoed in the multifarious accents of *José Trigo*.

Evaluating the temporal and causal relation between the two texts, it is possible to view *La región más transparente* as a trailblazing precursor of del Paso's debut novel; alternatively, we may look on the two works as complementary symptoms of a widespread desire to find adequate forms of fictional expression for the evolved realities of Mexican life around the midpoint of the twentieth century. This consideration highlights the fundamental question of the intertextual nature of literary production. To credit Carlos Fuentes with authorship of a text that answered the needs of the moment, as far as certain strata of urban Mexican society were concerned, with singular timeliness is fair. To privilege him as the sovereign creator of a text that single-handedly revolutionized Mexican fiction is to overlook his debts to previous writing and to overstate his importance in the evolution of a literary tradition. Fuentes's debts are legion, not only to James Joyce, about whom he would write at length in *Cervantes o la crítica de la lectura* (1976), but also to a number of traditions of which a single example would be the long line of Mexican writing about the nation's capital, which stretches from the chronicles and tableaux of life in Tenochtitlan in the sixteenth and seventeenth centuries as portrayed by Hernán Cortés, Bernal Díaz del Castillo, and Bernardo Balbuena, to essays, written in Fuentes's lifetime, by Alfonso Reyes and Salvador Novo, and an experimental novel, *La luciérnaga,* by Mariano Azuela.[5] Seen from this angle, Fuentes and his debut novel are not so much individual landmarks on a map of literary achievement as part of a densely populated nucleus—links in a genealogical chain that transmits formal and other features of the literary tradition to later writers and texts, including, of course, Fernando del Paso. Del Paso's frank acknowledgment of writers such as Poe, Flaubert, Joyce, and Borges, and his openness to influence by these and countless other figures belonging to the Mexican and non-Mexican literary traditions, invites an approach to his work through comparative literature. Furthermore, if we grant precedence to texts over authors and envisage the literary process as, to some degree, a history of forms and paradigms which coalesce in individual texts, then his work offers an extraordinary opportunity for systematic analysis in the light of current theories of intertextuality.

As remarked in the Introduction, a primitive notion of intertextuality informed the initial critical response to del Paso's novel, with commentators such as Ramón Xirau and Dagoberto Orrantia pointing out connections between *José Trigo* and *Ulysses* and emphasizing links between del Paso's novel and the Mexican narrative tradition, of which it represented an impressive *summa* in their eyes. What was missing in the early assessments and would remain underdeveloped in later studies by Lilvia Soto, Inés Sáenz, and others, was both a systematic theorization of the phenomenon of literary intertextuality and any awareness of the problematical implications of that phenomenon for the cultural and political profile of a body of work marked so distinctly with the badge of heterogeneity. For, as suggested in my account of the thinking of Gustavo Pérez Firmat, Leopoldo Zea, Silvia Spitta, and other theorists of postcolonial culture of Latin America, the integration, within the textual fabric of a novel like *José Trigo,* of material drawn from multiple sources has decisive consequences for the identity and symbolic value of that text, which requires a corresponding plurality of frames of interpretation to account for its semantic and cultural density.

My reading of *José Trigo* focuses on the construction of a cultural identity that has its most immediate relevance in the Mexican context but also reaches beyond the boundaries of that nation into the cultural landscapes of Mesoamerica and Latin America as a whole. The connections between *José Trigo* and a number of narrative traditions are essential to the profile of del Paso's text, and they will be discussed at length in a later section of this chapter. First, it is necessary to examine the anatomy of *José Trigo* more closely, concentrating on three of its features which historically have been the object of repeated analysis and often heated debate. Since the mid-1960s, critical attention has centered on the triad of myth, structure, and language in *José Trigo,* perpetuating a broadly structuralist approach to the analysis of narrative that dominated the academy throughout the

1960s and lasted into the 1970s.[6] Such a triad remains particularly well suited to a novel that is structured around pairs of characters, doubles, oppositions, symmetries, and the like; a timely reformulation of its basic terms demonstrates its continuing usefulness as a methodological tool for elucidating the formal and conceptual design of *José Trigo*.

Hybridity, the Metropolitan Standard, and the Myth of Resurrection

The presence of a clearly outlined mythical discourse in *José Trigo* has been a leitmotif of the criticism of the novel for the last three decades (e.g., Flores Sevilla and Soto). Miguel G. Rodríguez Lozano has tried to play down the importance of this element in the novel's design. Yet the system of mythical correspondences and allusions remains a dominant feature of *José Trigo*, which must be addressed in any examination of the text.

Historically, the critical tradition has documented the pervasive presence of pre-Columbian mythology in del Paso's novel where it underpins the entire narrative and provides a comprehensive exegetical key. What has not been sufficiently acknowledged is the presence of a set of Christian references, alongside the code of Aztec mythology, resulting in a text of cultural hybridity. A review of the mythological referents of the two main characters in the story illustrates the workings of hybridity in del Paso's novel and reveals some of the implications of a strategy of double-coding for the projection of a cultural identity. Some specific observations on the myth of resurrection provide an additional signpost for interpreting the humanist message of *José Trigo*.

Starting with Luciano, his character is made up of many archetypal features. As he washes in the garden outside his boxcar in the second chapter of the novel, we are reminded of the ritual behavior of classical heroes; the liquid reflection of Luciano's face "as big as the world" (29) suggests a figure who is larger than life. A retrospective section of the narrative then recalls how the adolescent Luciano had lived "with compassion and truth tied around his neck, written in his heart and attached to his fingers" (143), before he matured into a self-effacing and circumspect adult who shows courage in the defense of lofty principles. When he disappears in mysterious circumstances, "Luciano the agreeable, the archetypal, Luciano the only-begotten" (384) is acknowledged as "a symbol and corner-stone of the workers' movement" (404), and he is sorely missed. In death, the figurative dismemberment of his corpse ("Everybody received a piece of Luciano. They all shared Luciano amongst themselves," 509) completes the process of his ennoblement: conforming to mythical accounts of the fate of religious and culture heroes like the Egyptian god Osiris, it effectively sanctifies him.[7]

Consistent with this pattern of characterization, Luciano is assimilated to the type of Quetzalcóatl, the ancient Mexican "god of self-sacrifice and penance, of books, the calendar and the arts, the symbol of abnegation and culture" (Soustelle 171). That relation emerges unambiguously in the central section of the narrative, the "Parte Intermedia," which recounts a fantastic flight "through the thirteen heavens of the celestial world [and] the nine infernal regions of the underworld" (253) of Aztec cosmology.[8] Led by Nance Buenaventura, who assumes the form of a mockingbird (sinsonte/cenzontle), the narrator beholds a vision of Nonoalco-Tlatelolco *sub specie aeternitatis,* during which the fictional protagonists of *José Trigo* appear to him in mythical guises. In this vivid tableau, Luciano is distinguished by insignia associated with Quetzalcóatl: he wears "a belt of stars" and holds "a reed scepter" (254); a "small jewel [emblematic] of the wind" is emblazoned on his chest (255), and a quincunx adorns his forehead (260), as in Diego Rivera's famous representation of the god in his painting *The Legend of Quetzalcóatl,* housed in the National Palace in Mexico City.

Numerous analogies with the experience of Quetzalcóatl are incorporated into the narrative of *José Trigo.* In one incident, Luciano gets up from a stone on which he had been sitting and leaves behind "the impression of his buttocks" (327). The detail would appear to be trivial, but in fact it can be traced back to a poetic tradition of Nahuatl literature devoted to Quetzalcóatl. An anthology prepared by Angel María Garibay records the following story:

> And finally he came to another place and sat down on a stone and rested his hands on it. And there where he placed his hand was left an impression as though in soft clay. And likewise the outline of his buttocks remained in the stone on which he was seated. (32)

When Luciano subsequently pays a visit to the fairground, his itinerary is pictured as "a symbolic trajectory from the highest level to the lowest of the underworld" (350) in the unwelcome company of an albino half brother who drowns in a cauldron and acts as a replica of Xolotl, who accompanied Quetzalcóatl to the underworld. Finally, the mystery surrounding Luciano's ultimate fate recalls that of the god after his expulsion from the religious city of Tula: some people believe that Luciano "headed northwards, in the direction of the Mar Amarillo, which is where he disappeared," while "There are those who are of the opinion that he went east" (367). The myth of Quetzalcóatl thus determines much of the overall shape of Luciano's life story in *José Trigo,* as it had that of Lorenzo in *La muerte de Artemio Cruz* (1962) by Carlos Fuentes.

Manuel Angel's character and conduct also have their roots in Aztec mythology. Devious and hypocritical, hateful and prone to violence, Manuel Angel appears in the guise of Tezcatlipoca, "the protean god of the night, of war and of youth" (Soustelle 20). Tezcatlipoca, whose name signifies "smoking mirror,"[9] was typically shown carrying four arrows and a shield in one hand and a mirror in the other; the narrator of *José Trigo* sees "Manuel Angel little huntsman, smoking mirror" in the vision inspired by Nance Buenaventura, and thereby confirms his identity as an avatar of the Aztec god. The image of Manuel Angel playing a "flute made from a deer's horn," which he then breaks on the steps of a temple (258), has equally precise connotations. As George Vaillant observes, Tezcatlipoca was honored in a holy ceremony involving that very sequence of actions:

> The ceremony in honor of the god Tezcatlipoca was strikingly dramatic. [. . .] The handsomest and bravest prisoner of war was selected a year before his execution. Priests taught him the manners of a ruler, and, as he walked about, playing divine melodies upon his flute, he received the homage due to Tezcatlipoca himself. A month before the day of sacrifice four lovely girls [. . .] became his companions and attended to his every want. On the day of his death he took leave of his weeping consorts to lead a procession in his honor, marked by jubilation and feasting. Then he bade farewell to the glittering cortege and left for a small temple, accompanied by the eight priests who had attended him up the steps of the temple, and he followed, breaking at each step a flute which he had played in the happy hours of his incarnation. At the top of the platform the priests turned him over the sacrificial block and wrenched out his heart. (197)

In *José Trigo* an element of this ritual appears in debased form in a narrative episode set in a brothel that is frequented "religiously" by Manuel Angel and his cronies:

> Now, framed by a hyaline brilliance, [Manuel Angel] was surrounded by four women. Concerted resplendence of damsels: he [had] picked up four red hearts. Fulana, Mengana, Zutana y Putana. [. . .] One of them was putting a carnation in his buttonhole. Another

was sociable enough to offer him a cigarette. [. . .] Yet another, with a certain indifference, was removing cuticle with "Cutex" acetone. What a popular copulator [popular copulachero] was Manuel Angel. (210)

A final detail in the mythical depiction of Manuel Angel is the "assassin's dagger" (327) with which he stabs Luciano. In the context of Aztec mythology, this weapon identifies Manuel Angel with Itzalcoliuhqui, a surrogate of Tezcatlipoca, whose name signifies "curved obsidian knife" (Vaillant 181).

Luciano and Manuel Angel, Quetzalcóatl and Tezcatlipoca—these characters form antagonistic pairs who are locked in a conflict made all the more dramatic in the case of Quetzalcóatl and Tezcatlipoca by the fact that the two gods were brothers and sibling rivals. In *José Trigo,* Manuel Angel and Luciano are not related by blood, but when, after years of friendship, they clash over the right to occupy a boxcar and "become irreconcilable enemies" (370), their enmity matches that of the god-twins. An extract from the "Intermediate Part" illustrates their antagonism, drawing on a crucial episode of the Quetzalcóatl myth—the hero's deception by Tezcatlipoca—and featuring the distinctive motif of a mirror which is fabled to have induced shame in Quetzalcóatl:

> The man with the mirror [. . .] was telling the one with the starry eye in the crown of his head: look at yourself in this mirror. And he was inviting him to drink, and was intoxicating him. These two were none other than Manuel Angel and Luciano. (257–58)[10]

Luciano's death at the hands of his rival is also represented in mythical terms. The narrator rebukes Manuel Angel, "Ah, night wind, shaveling, enemy: [. . .] What did you do to your precious twin?" (258), and Nance Buenaventura predicts, "The youthful god, the little huntsman, will murder his precious twin" (263–64).

The symbolic depiction of Luciano and Manuel Angel's "age-old antagonism" (489) is not limited to the terms of Aztec mythology. It is also rendered through the Christian code. In general outline, Luciano corresponds to the type of Jesus Christ and Manuel Angel to that of Satan. Luciano's experience recalls that of Christ in a number of respects. On a personal level, his love for María Patrocinio and the decision to rescue her from a career in prostitution evoke Christ's rehabilitation of Mary Magdalen. In his public life, Luciano enjoys the exalted status of "Messiah of the tracks" (348), but he is nevertheless betrayed, as was Christ by Judas

Iscariot: Nance Buenaventura foresees his end, "taking for granted that the young man would be tempted by the owner of the precious stone of bribery and betrayed by the false witness who was destined to die with his mouth full of gravel" (141). The sequence recounting Luciano's walk in the yard—"a freshly fertilized garden, with a sort of pond covered in slime" where he "pushed a crucified shirt to one side" (175)—adumbrates his death and mysterious resurrection "to the astonishment and delight of the railway workers who were attached to his branch" (404). Narrated in the mode of magical realism, the resurrection episode carries strong cannibalistic overtones reminiscent both of an Aztec rite in honor of Xipe Totec, in which "the god's flesh was eaten by the faithful" (Soustelle 98), and of the Christian Eucharist.

Manuel Angel's principal Christian referent is Satan, an equivalence conveyed by conventional Christian symbolism of the snake and darkness. Eduviges had seen "the shadow of the man slithering [culebreando] through the grass" (75) when Manuel Angel first seduced her; in the narrative present "the ignoble one, violator of women, who was always delighted to dishonor" (489) is compared to the Prince of Darkness: "It was Manuel Angel, arrogant, princely [. . .] and eaten away by envy" (327).

The casting of Luciano and Manuel Angel in these archetypal molds is generally consistent with the polarized value system of western Christianity. Acting out the roles of a virtuous Messiah figure and a satanic force of evil, the two men perpetuate an antagonism of recognizable biblical origins that gives expression to a wholly conventional view of morality. Fernando del Paso nevertheless takes great care to avoid an excessively crude, unnuanced antithesis that would reduce his characters to one-dimensionality and he endows them instead with a moral and psychological complexity that confounds the "stupid, dried up dichotomies [of] the Christian dialectic"—that philosophical and ethical system repudiated by Julio Cortázar in *Rayuela* (27, 616) and analyzed by Ixca Cienfuegos and Rodrigo Pola in a central section of *La región más transparente* (249–58). As a result, the symbolic portraits of Luciano and Manuel Angel become complicated and enriched to a point where they can no longer be accommodated within established schemes of Christian thought and morality.

Elaborating on the descriptions of Luciano and Manuel Angel just given, we have to acknowledge that Luciano is essentially a flawed hero. In chapter 7 of part 1, he succumbs to sexual temptation, defying the dictates of his conscience as he commits adultery with Rosita, a waitress employed at the pointedly named Eden Oyster Bar. In the corresponding chapter of part 2, he is shown to be avaricious as he muses, in a moment's distraction from the main business of a political meeting that he is attending, "The only thing worthwhile is to swim in wool [*lana,* meaning "money" in Mexican slang], without being fleeced. Good business deals to provide a rich source of income, and you can forget everything else" (343). He also entertains feelings of hatred and jealousy, admitting on a visit to the fairground where his rival had consummated an idyllic love affair with Genoveva, "Oh, how much he would have liked to have been in Manuel Angel's skin" (353).

For his part, Manuel Angel, though reviled as "a mean son of a bitch [and] a traitor," is nevertheless partially redeemed by his love for Genoveva. Described as "a really genuine love," his devotion compensates for the earlier abuse of Eduviges, "who was never anything more than a lover whom he did not particularly love." "It has to be faced," the narrator admits, "the same Manuel Angel who up to that point had worshipped only himself really fell for Genoveva" (363).

For the critic Nora Dottori, such complexities in the two men's makeup are evidence of the author's intention to achieve a verisimile character portrayal through the allocation of a balanced set of positive and negative traits (291–93). The text, however, provides an alternative explanation more in keeping with the thematics of our inquiry. That explanation centers on the religious and philosophical doctrine of Manichaeanism, which posits that co-eternal principles of good and evil embodied in God and Satan dispute control of the world. At the fairground Luciano wonders, "Does the Devil really exist?" and formulates the response, "Yes, by aseity, just as God does. And we are all made in his likeness and image" (363). This proposition, which is consistent with Eduviges's view of José Trigo as one who "could be two people at the same time, of whom one could drag the other along or simply kill off the goodness and prudence in him" (26), has surprising consequences for the symbolic projections of both Luciano and Manuel Angel.

Contrary to normal expectations, Luciano, who, as we have just seen, displays some traits of Jesus Christ, is also cast in the mold of Lucifer, the Bringer of Light. This duality may surprise some orthodox readers, yet it is entirely congruous with the principles of Manichaeanism rehearsed above, according to which even a virtuous and godlike individual may be host to diabolical qualities and tendencies. Luciano's name is an important indicator in this respect, bringing together concepts of light and anality—*luz y ano*—which the western mind has traditionally associated with the Devil. "The star of Luciano" is identified variously with "the evening star" (263) and "the morning star" (366) and thus connotes Venus, the celestial star which the pre-Columbian mind equated with Quetzalcóatl. In a figurative sense, Luciano demonstrates a remarkable facility for "enlightening" his audience when he addresses a political rally of disaffected railway workers. Yet, for all its rhetorical magnificence, his address consists of "a torrent of words [and] hot air" (346) which he releases at the end of a day spent combatting the afflictions of diarrhea and flatulence. In *José Trigo* the scenes of Luciano on the lavatory, redolent of the "Calypso" episode of James Joyce's *Ulysses,* point humorously to the anal and diabolical basis of his character. We read how that morning, "[He had] had another bowel movement: the fourth in under twelve hours. That damned diarrhea. [. . .] Off to the bathroom again" (304–5).

At certain moments of the narrative Luciano displays attitudes and behavior that verge unquestionably on the satanic. A thirst for absolute power inspires the thought, "Ah, when I become leader of the entire Union organization, and not just a local branch," and prompts the narrator to conclude that Luciano is guilty of "Megalomania" (327). Also, in his sexual desire for Genoveva, he aspires to "dethrone" Manuel Angel (364), just as Satan had sought to dislodge God from His heavenly throne.

Looked at from these various angles, Fernando del Paso's symbolic portrait of Luciano fuses images of Christ and Satan/Lucifer in an intriguing *coincidentia oppositorum* that is sustained throughout the bulk of the narrative. Ultimately, the conflict between positive and negative values resolves itself in favor of the former: we sense the narrator's unconditional authority behind the description of Luciano as "the devil's own skin, but as we've said often enough: a model of integrity and the art of public speaking" (489). However, that resolution cannot detract from the originality of a characterization that involves two conflicting archetypal referents.

Nuances of character also produce a more complex symbolic portrayal of Manuel Angel. His first Christian name echoes that of Emmanuel, which was the name of Jesus Christ, and is combined with an assertion of angelic status in his second name. While the latter is consistent with Manuel Angel's primary role as Fallen Angel, the former asserts a likeness with Christ, in a further instance of *coincidentia oppositorum,* which contradicts monologic assumptions to do with character and morality.

In the light of this analysis, the symbolic identities of Luciano and Manuel Angel are both more varied and more complex in their interactions than has been acknowledged heretofore. Our findings can be summarized in the form of two paradigms:

Luciano	Manuel Angel
Jesus Christ	Satan
Lucifer	Emmanuel
Quetzalcóatl	Tezcatlipoca
-Venus	

According to this diagram, Fernando del Paso superimposes on an Aztec base Christian types representing antagonistic values. Christ vs. Satan, Lucifer vs. Emmanuel, and Quetzalcóatl vs. Tezcatlipoca add up to a set of horizontal oppositions that reflect the values of the two dominant cultural traditions of Mexico since the Conquest. In addition, each paradigm also houses vertical oppositions, which we have explained up until now in the terms of Manichaeanism. Having established this much, it is important to note a congruity between Manichean philosophy and the Aztec conception of god-heroes. As the researches of Eva Hunt and others have shown, the gods of Mesoamerica, unlike the figureheads of monotheistic Christianity, were enigmatic and ambivalent: "None of the deities were without ambivalent images, none of them were pure metaphors for good or bad, wholly beneficial or destructive" (Hunt 170). The oppositions that are contained in the vertical paradigms listed above thus find a rationale from within the domestic American cultural tradition, and bear witness to the thoroughgoing transculturation of Christianity on American soil.

The intertwined Aztec and Christian registers of del Paso's novel identify *José Trigo* as a hybrid text of considerable sophistication. In part, the narrative of Luciano, Manuel Angel, Nance Buenaventura, and the remaining characters mirrors an extratextual syncretism that is a fact of Mexican life. At the same time, it speaks to and promotes an ideology of syncretism that has a long pedigree in the Mexican intellectual tradition and has often been brandished as an affirmation of Mexican difference vis-à-vis other nations and cultures—in the work of Vasconcelos, Reyes, and others. In this respect, the treatment in *José Trigo* of Roman Catholicism, its themes and images, and, above all, its ethical schemes implies a devastating critique of the metropolitan standard. An entire history of spiritual colonization is repudiated in del Paso's description of his characters "struggling under the weight of four centuries of Catholicism" (Carvajal iii). Read politically, the unorthodox contexts and combinations of Catholic motifs in the narrative of *José Trigo* are motivated, at least in part, by a rejection of the values of Rome, depicted in the character of Todolosantos as patriarchal, authoritarian, intolerant, and unforgiving.

In the final analysis, the Christian references in *José Trigo* merge into a structure of religious beliefs representing a strategic accommodation with the types of pre-Columbian mythology that have resisted obliteration by the paradigms of Catholic culture.

Within the hybrid world of *José Trigo* there is one element that possesses particular importance: the myth of resurrection. Integral to the belief systems of both the Old and the New Worlds, the myth of resurrection pervades the narrative of *José Trigo* at the levels of theme, structure, and language, and it all but determines the reader's response. An arresting image of death and resurrection appears in the narrator's vision as he flies through the heavens: "Mockingbird said to me: This is the resurrection, this is the god of fire: old Todolosantos bursting into flame, the killing of the birds" (254). The scene refers to the Aztec god Xiuhtecuhtli, and at the same time it conjures up the image of Quetzalcóatl, who with his colorful plumage is a further instance of the type. According to mythical narratives, Quetzalcóatl destroyed himself by fire and descended to the underworld, from which he returned some days later in the form of Venus, the morning star. The story is recorded in the *Códice de Cuauhtitlan* and reproduced in Angel Garibay's anthology of Aztec poetry:

> And it is recounted that in the year 1 Reed [Quetzalcóatl] reached the sea shore, on the edge of the great ocean. He got to his feet there and burst into tears. He took hold of his personal objects and put them on in turn: his costume of quetzal feathers and mask of turquoise stones. As soon as he was properly attired, he set fire to himself. And he was consumed in the flames. And legend has it that when he started to burn and his ashes rose into the air, all the birds of beautiful plumage that fly across the sky came to see him and watched him intently. And when the ashes ceased to burn, Quetzalcóatl's heart rose up on high. Whence he has taken the name "Lord of the Dawn." And it is recounted further that he was not seen for four days, because he had descended to the realm of the dead, and in that region he acquired a set of small spears and after the eighth day he began to shine as a grand star. And it is said that he began to reign from that precise moment. (34)

To the native populations of Central America, these mythical events were evidence of Quetzalcóatl's resurrection and accession to immortality: Having entered the realm of the dead, the god suffers a miraculous transformation and becomes part of the natural order, which is governed by cyclical processes of life, death, and renewal. As Jacques Soustelle explains in her reconstruction of the Indian worldview, Venus, who is Quetzal-cóatl's astral equivalent, "is born in the east; then she disappears, and she is seen again as the evening star in the west. She has therefore traversed the world as a shuttle traverses the cloth: she is the symbol of death and re-birth" (105).

In del Paso's novel the promise of resurrection and renewal of vital potential is embodied, primarily, not in Luciano—the character modeled most closely on Quetzalcóatl—but in José Trigo, who in some respects is his double. As we have seen, Luciano fights for a noble cause but dies without having fully achieved his goals; it is therefore important that his positive lead be taken up by another character in whom the reader may be able to recognize similar traits and experiences. Notwithstanding some fundamental differences in their characters—José Trigo is cowardly, Luciano initially courageous—there are a number of coincidences be-tween the two men's experiences. Both are hounded by Manuel Angel, both disappear mysteriously from the railway camp, and both are associ-ated with the light of stars.

José Trigo's association with the stars invests him with other, related meanings. At the beginning of the novel, in the "madcap month" of Feb-ruary, the narrator seeks him out on an "interlunar night with stars clus-tering in the sky" and remarks, "As they revolved in their vaults, I imag-ined I saw José Trigo's eyes" (18). Near the end of the book, the narrator envisages a repetition of the search for his elusive quarry and conjures up the nocturnal scene of "the blessed whereabouts of José Trigo," using the optative mood:

> May it be a dusty night. [. . .] May the night breathe in the dust through the stigmas of its skin and sprinkle stars across the entire firmament. May the seafarers' stars sail across an ocean as dark and shiny as a black beetle's elytron. May Castor and Pollux, Sirius and Aldebarán form clusters in the sky above the encampments, scintil-late, and remain silent. (524)

The twin stars Castor and Pollux are particularly important here, for they may be considered symbolic counterparts of Luciano and José Trigo and images of a shared immortality. In Greek mythology Castor and Pollux were twin sons of Zeus who were inseparable companions until Castor was killed by a wild boar in a hunting accident. Pollux lamented his brother's death so poignantly that Zeus allowed him to share with Castor the privilege of immortality. Thus, in one version of the myth, the Dios-curi—as they were known—continued to live on alternate days, while in another they assumed a place among the stars in the constellation Gemini, where they became tutelary divinities of sailors.[11] In the penultimate chapter of del Paso's novel, it is the second tradition that underpins the reference to Castor and Pollux, prompting us to consider José Trigo an avatar of Pollux and a symbol of immortality.

As Luciano's double, or figurative twin, José Trigo may reasonably be expected to conform in some respects to the type of Jesus Christ and, perhaps, to reenact paradigmatic events from Christ's life. In general terms, "José Trigo, the most unfortunate of men" (29) is an archetypal figure of human suffering and, like Jesus, an outsider who satisfies a communal need for a scapegoat. More specifically, he is reputed to be almost as old as Christ at the time of his betrayal and crucifixion: "Some say that he was 32 years old." *Madrecita* Buenaventura contests this precise estimate of José Trigo's age, arguing, "You could just as well say that he was 32 as that he was 40" (20). But her objection does not diminish the coded significance of a number which we may assume was chosen deliberately for the purposes of characterization. A reference to "the calvary of José Trigo" (152) strengthens the analogy with Christ and is illustrated in a scene where José Trigo passes through the Campamento Oeste shouldering an empty coffin; the narrator's apostrophe, "You good scarecrow, carrying your own death around on your shoulders" (246), evokes clearly Christ's procession along the *Via crucis*.

Taken in conjunction with the identities of Pollux and Quetzalcóatl, these reflections of Jesus Christ build up a composite picture of an archetypal Everyman, an elusive hero with "a thousand faces" (514) who embodies, among other things, the promise of resurrection and regeneration. In this respect it is important to note José Trigo's association in name and appearance with the wheat crop that is cultivated throughout Central America. Described as "a stealthy man who was tall and slim ["espigado" < "espiga"= ear of wheat] with light brown hair [Cabello trigueño]" (492), he personifies cyclical processes of growth and renewal and fits into a structure of beliefs that assert the natural continuity of life and its transcendence of death. The renewed fertility of old land that has been cleared, burned, and sown with fresh seed in the Mesoamerican maize cycle is a potent illustration of this principle, which *madrecita* Buenaventura explains to the narrator with engaging simplicity: "Fire is excrement, Buenaventura told me, and fire is the cypress tree, and the cypress tree is death, return, and the flowers that come to life" (261). Coincidentally, Christianity affirms a similar belief, in terms that are directly applicable to José Trigo: "Except a corn of wheat fall into the ground and die, it abideth alone; but if it die, it bringeth forth much fruit" (John 12.24). By virtue of these associations, José Trigo represents the potential for renewal that is attributed only ambiguously to the dead Luciano, and he embodies an essentially humanist conception of suffering and its transcendence through love, solidarity, and sacrifice.

This positive spiritual dimension of the narrative sets *José Trigo* apart from other Mexican novels of city life written around the midpoint of the twentieth century. Certainly, there is no such promise of growth and renewal in *La región más transparente*. There, while the themes of death and resurrection are mentioned repeatedly, any positive prospects for the affairs of men and women are consistently denied (viz. Ixca's fixation on "the man who died in vain," p. 458). Indeed, Fuentes invokes the image of ashes—intimately connected, in pre-Columbian mythology, with rebirth—only to emphasize their failure to generate new life: "Our world has died for ever," Ixca assures Teódula. "It would make no difference if the ashes of your sons and of Celedonio were cast over the ground without a single tear being shed on them, without any hope of their having provided us with sustenance" (331). Holding this passage up against the story of a secondary character, Bernabé Pérez, who honored the memory of his dead father by casting to the winds "floral seeds" of which, according to the narrator of *José Trigo*, "many already sprouted" (378), we see how Fernando del Paso, using almost identical raw materials to Carlos Fuentes, nevertheless conveys a radically different vision of life and death in his novel of qualified hope and regeneration.

Symbolic Form, Totalization, and "Saying It with Flowers"

The concepts of resurrection and regeneration that I have privileged in my interpretation of del Paso's novel are mirrored comprehensively in the formal arrangement of *José Trigo*. The novel comprises eighteen chapters divided into two parts ("The West" and "The East"), plus a section entitled "The Bridge (An Intermediate Part)" located at the geometrical center of the book. The numbering of chapters in ascending order in part 1 and in descending order in part 2 has been interpreted almost universally as signifying a pyramidal form, with the "Intermediate Part" representing a flat plane atop the structure of *José Trigo* (Martínez, "Nuevas letras"; Mata, *Un océano de narraciones*). Against that critical consensus, the text sanctions an alternative reading which accords even more closely with the pre-Columbian world picture that informs the novel. Without denying the suggestiveness of the image of the text as pyramid, I find it much more productive to view the formal design of *José Trigo* as a set of wheels within wheels, revolving around the hub of "The Bridge," which offers both a mythical key to the exegesis of the story and a microcosm of the surrounding bounded whole.

A key episode in *José Trigo* is Luciano's visit to a fairground in chapter 7 of part 2. There, he relives the scene of his rival, Manuel Angel's amorous success with Genoveva, in an earlier ride on a Ferris wheel. At a psychological level, the "wheel of fortune" functions as a catalyst of Luciano's jealousy; at a symbolic level, it stands as a mise-en-abîme of the text: just as the novel comprises eighteen chapters, so the wheel has eighteen seats (cabriolés) of which any nine, when the machine is in motion, describe an ascending arc while the others trace a downward path. Furthermore, the wheel displays at its hub "a representation of itself in miniature" (359), which mimics exactly the position of the "Intermediate Part" in *José Trigo*.

The image of the Ferris wheel has many layers of symbolic significance in the novel, stemming from the cosmological value of the number eighteen. As anthropologists have long been aware, this was the number of months attributed to a year in the Aztec calendar. By virtue of this detail, *José Trigo* becomes a model of temporal progression and, in addition, an image of the sun as, according to ancient belief, it revolved around the earth. Luciano in fact envisions the Ferris wheel as a "circle of fire" (353) and thereby establishes a three-way analogy whose terms are the text, the wheel, and the sun. The narrative of *José Trigo*, which traces a path from West to East, may be seen to match the movements of the sun and other celestial bodies, as pictured by ancient Mexican cosmology. "The Mexicans," we are told, "thought of the world as a kind of Maltese cross, the east uppermost, the north on the right, the west below and the south to the left" (Soustelle 111); accordingly, on its daily course, a body like the sun or Venus would rise, traverse the skies, and then return to the underworld, following a circular trajectory of rise and fall. Fernando del Paso evokes that cosmological model quite clearly in his description of Manuel Angel and Genoveva's ride on the Ferris wheel. Wandering through the fairground, Luciano imagines

> the two of them up there on the wheel of fortune, Manuel Angel and Genoveva, and the wood and tinplate seat swaying in the air to the sound of a romantic waltz, in a ternary rhythm, it kept on going up and down, and below them everything was like a glass cabinet full of phosphorescent objects, and it thus reached the highest point, higher

than the Bridge, where, from an Olympian position, they could make out on either side the two encampments and, looking north-wards and southwards, the silken garment of the mighty, cosmopoli-tan city, splashed with lights, and the skyscrapers: extravagant light-houses that stood out in the distance. (353)

The two characters' movement through cosmic space effectively glosses the physical layout of *José Trigo,* with its clearly signposted correspon-dences in the physical environment and geographical setting of Mexico City. (A feature of the first edition of the novel was the reproduction, on the inner cover, of a section of a street map of the capital, with the area of Nonoalco-Tlatelolco highlighted in a rectangular box.)

Delving further into pre-Columbian cosmology, we discover that the ancient Mexicans ascribed particular and distinct qualities to each of the four quarters of the world: "fertility and abundance to the east, barren aridity to the north, falling-off, old age and death to the west (setting sun), and a neutral character to the south" (Soustelle 111). In keeping with this scheme, Fernando del Paso's novel, which plots a progression from west to east, juxtaposes the signs of death and fertility in what may be seen as a dynamic relationship of succession and renewal. The point is illustrated in an observation about the significance of plant life in the ancient Mexican worldview, which, given the novel's preoccupation with cereals (trigo and espigas) and flowers ("flowers which come to life," 261), is wholly perti-nent:

Maize and the garden plants are born in the occident, in the western garden of Tamoanchan where the earth goddesses live, the sources of life. Then they undertake a long journey under the ground (that of germination), praying the gods of rain to guide them on their road; at last they come up in the east, the country of the rising sun and of youth and plenty. (Soustelle 105)

In this tableau we find compelling evidence of the presence, at the struc-tural level of del Paso's novel, of that essential concern with natural regen-eration that I have interpreted as the thematic crux of *José Trigo.*

The structural profile that emerges from the present analysis of *José Trigo* combines dynamism, manifest in the relation between the novel's two main parts, with poise, reflected in the "Intermediate Part." The sec-tion entitled "The Bridge" mirrors the Olympian viewpoint attained by Manuel Angel and Genoveva at the highest point of their ride on the Ferris wheel, and holds a number of key antinomies in arrested suspense.

Through the visions of the first-person narrator and Nance Buenaventura, "The Bridge" effects a poetic *coincidentia oppositorum* that fuses cyclical and linear time and accommodates both positive and negative interpretations of human endeavor. The view of life that crystallizes in that section is ambivalent and enigmatic, and it is summed up in the narrator's rhetorical question, "What has the chaff to do with the wheat?" (265). Defeat and loss, hope and transcendence are all implied in the narrator's gnomic reference, which seems to offer an imminent explanation of the stories of Luciano, José Trigo, and all the other characters of del Paso's archetypal narrative.

The transcendental vision communicated in the "Intermediate Part" of *José Trigo* offers a distillation of the narrative that includes all of its elements in a grand totalizing gesture. Critical appreciation of del Paso's work has been marked from the beginning by an interest in the pretensions and strategies that characterize his novels. The author himself observed in 1978: "I have never tried to say all about everything, just all about something, about a microcosm, a small world endowed with its own dimensions and its own rules of play" (Sánchez Bardón and Goñi 49). In *José Trigo,* the "Intermediate Part" is the first instance, in del Paso's novelistic production, of "those narrative frames or containment strategies that," in the words of Fredric Jameson concerning the modernist novel, "seek to endow their objects of representation with formal unity." Jameson's adaptation of a Hegelian and Lukácsian conception of totality to the analysis of narrative is faithfully reflected in the microcosmic conception of *José Trigo,* whose organic form and mythopoeic synthesis identify it as typical of the tradition of high modernism (Jameson, *Political Unconscious* 52–56).

The totalizing strategies of *José Trigo* are numerous and include the cultivation of an encyclopedic range of reference, the saturation of narrative procedures, and a verbal proliferation that stretches the very limits of the linguistic system. A brief examination of the two chapters 8 may serve a useful purpose in highlighting the principal mechanisms that serve to create an *illusion* of totality in the pages of *José Trigo*. Needless to say, it is this *effect* of totalization, and not totalization itself, which distinguishes del Paso's prose from more conventional styles of writing.

Designated an "Oda o corrido, valona, tonada, inventario, romanza, aria," chapter 8 of part 1 sets out to explore the vastly varied and apparently unpromising subject of Mexican railways. The narrative begins by distinguishing between types of passengers—suicides, newlyweds, cattle thieves, etc.—who travel by train, for whatever purpose: "On a journey. On an outing to the country. On business. On summer vacation. On a trip heading in a certain direction. On an excursion with friends" (223–24). In increasingly complex patterns of sound and sense it accounts for the historical, social, political, and environmental impact of steam locomotion throughout Mexico, accommodating a potentially limitless range of inquiry within certain flexible poetic schemes, of which the anaphoric list is the most commonly used. The typology of passengers in the opening paragraph, for example, comprises no fewer than twenty-seven items relating to professional or civil status, juxtaposed in a deliberately incongruous manner so as to strengthen the narrator's claim to represent "*all* those men and women of *every* race [my emphasis], black or white, *huicholes, babispes, chochopopolocas, tarahumaras, acafes*. Who are travelers" (223). Strongly reminiscent of Ixca Cienfuegos's all-encompassing vision of Mexico at the conclusion of *La región más transparente*, this and other lists in *José Trigo* function by reproducing on the syntagmatic plane of the narrative a whole range of paradigmatic possibilities that do not appear to have been subjected to any process of selection. Consequently, to the extent that it eschews that normal requirement of literary decorum, del Paso's text conforms to Roman Jakobson's classic definition of poetic writing as the projection of the principle of equivalence from the axis of selection (the paradigmatic axis of language) onto the axis of combination (the syntagmatic axis of language) (Jakobson 358).

Many of the effects of the writing in the chapter under review derive from the prevalence of the figures of synecdoche and metonymy, which correspond to the paradigmatic and syntagmatic axes of language, respectively. At a certain point in the narrative, the concept of "the whistle of a locomotive" is introduced, and this generates several pages of associations in keeping with the proposition that

> The whistle of a train is the train itself [synecdoche].
> And, it is everything being carried on the train.
> And, it is all the places that are known to the train.
> And everything that has to do with the train [metonymy]. (230)

These claims acquire substance straightaway as the narrative apostrophizes, "You, woods of Guerrero, swamps of Tabasco, valleys of Puebla," and twenty-seven other landmarks of Mexico which together add up to a microcosm of the nation (239). An imaginative reading of the passage persuades the reader that s/he has completed a fictional journey to the four corners of Mexico, transported by a powerful narrative vehicle.

Turning to chapter 8 of part 2, we observe a renewed reliance on the figures of metaphor and synecdoche, along with numerous instances of paradigmatic overspill. The chapter is constructed on the image of "the river of time and the torrent of the centuries" (302), and it begins, "On the river of time and the torrent of the centuries sails a temple, as magnificent as a triumphal carriage" (281). The temple thus evoked refers to a famous landmark in Mexico City and stands synecdochically for a whole area whose history it condenses; the "triumphal carriage" is one of several alternative representations of the "temple-ship-aerostat-horse of fire" (283) and the paradigmatic vehicle, "infinite in its forms, as in its materials," "in which there travel all the centuries and beastly creatures, the wonders and spectacles, the monsters, stories and legends which have passed through the district of Nonoalco-Tlatelolco, the land of José Trigo" (281–82).

Together, temple and chariot serve as devices for narrating "the preposterous chronicle of Santiago Tlatelolco" (287). This is a literary document, modeled on famous texts by Hernán Cortés, Alfonso Reyes, Salvador Novo, and—once more—Carlos Fuentes in *La región más transparente,* which purports to record "everything that has happened in these parts in every century of their existence." The chronicle is entrusted to a pseudo-omniscient narrator who surveys the life of the capital city from pre-Columbian times through the colonial period down to the modern age, and seeks to evoke "the diversity, the abundance, the infinite number of things" captured at a representative moment of the capital's six-hundred-year history (297). A richly detailed description of the marketplace in colonial times is the centerpiece of his narrative. Cast in the form of a "farragosa recopilación" (301), which is reminiscent of the "chaffering allincluding most farraginous chronicle" composed by James Joyce in the "Oxen of the Sun" episode of *Ulysses* (345), it comprises an inventory of human types, foodstuffs, and miscellaneous objects that would have filled the "great market of America" (287) at any time in the late sixteenth and seventeenth centuries. The following extract (quoted in Spanish so as to preserve all the flavors of the original) describes multiple kinds of organic waste that would have congested the marketplace at the time:

> También percebes, almejas y palinuros muertos, entre altibajos de mareas con toda la basura y el desperdicio coetáneos del mundo: setas sépticas, cinturas escapulares de palomas, cartilaginosas aletas de elasmobranquios, quelas de crustáceos, gárbulas, carniza, vainas de habichuelas, trozos de bramante, ternillas, gañiles, rodelas de butifarras, collejas que ensalobran, encarroñan las aguas para siempre jamás. (300–301)

The passage is typical of del Paso's totalizing style and is remarkable on two counts: first, in respect to subject matter, it illustrates as if by design Severo Sarduy's conception of baroque space as "the space of superabundance and wastefulness" (181); second, as a formal enumeration of types of organic trash, it provides a very literal example of paradigmatic overspill onto the syntagmatic plane, or flow, of narration.

Perhaps not surprisingly, the strain of absorbing such an excessive amount of "waste" material causes the hitherto free-flowing narrative briefly to lose momentum and the narrator to reflect, "But the word becomes exhausted, giving way to stagnation, passivity, stillness." The question is now posed, "Just how long can the elegiac out-size chronicle of Tlatelolco, the detailed records and the farraginous inventory continue, without their remaining permanently incomplete?" (301). For a few seconds, the very legitimacy of the totalizing project hangs in the balance, as its paradoxical foundations are exposed to the objections of reason: no matter how exhaustive the inventory, some aspect of the phenomenal world will always elude representation, so demonstrating the futility, already acknowledged by Borges in "El Aleph" and elsewhere, of all attempts at the total description of "an infinite whole" (Borges 62).[12] Yet the totalizing impulse is not ultimately subject to rational constraints, being by definition an instinctive force and part of a general impulse toward artistic creation that seeks to give verbal expression to a maremagnum of thoughts, memories, perceptions, and other data that "flood" the consciousness of an author like del Paso; as long as that consciousness remains active, the totalizing impulse will continue unabated. So it is that the narrative insists on making one last effort, in a richly complex Spanish prose style:

un esfuerzo más [. . .], un último bogar por el cauce absorto de los siglos, por las olas de vértebras mordientes, agua eficaz, remos los juncos nupciales, arpa eólica la lluvia tañida por los cierzos, hojarasca cordial las hojas desprendidas de lunarios y almanaques, fuego estéril la soflama que ilumina historia y leyenda. (301)

It matters little that the final flourish covers only a page or two: what is important is the irrepressible vigor with which the narrative reaffirms its totalizing pretensions before the chapter comes to an end.

Baroque excess is one of a number of styles employed in the construction of "a world of words," which by the author's own account "ranges from simplicity—a relative simplicity, that is—to the most esoteric baroque discourse" (Carvajal ii–iii). True to this description, the narrative project of *José Trigo* entails an almost infinite variety of linguistic practices, governed by a poetics that has its origins, principally, in a combination of Symbolism and Mexican literary tradition. Along with *madrecita* Buenaventura, the presiding narrator is responsible for the regime of language that configures the world of *José Trigo*. That regime is fundamentally poetic, in the sense of Roman Jakobson's definition of "the set towards the message" (356). For, if many of the narrator's words have a common referential value sanctioned by usage, it is also the case that the objects and experiences which they evoke "are to be regarded as never having happened" (18). *Madrecita* Buenaventura's style further exemplifies the semiotic and poetic processes of the narrative, as conveyed in the following quotation, which I again preserve in the original Spanish:

> Manzanas incircuncisas, rosario, jaula, zancos: con éstas y otras palabras que sacó de su baúl mundo, comenzó la madrecita Buenaventura la historia siempre trunca o aun no comenzada, y siempre detenida en los momentos en que la realidad y el sueño se confundían: realidad de su mundo llanero y bajuno de atorrantes y descamisados, y sueño de mi mundo de piedras manantías que brillan al sol de la mañana cuando José Trigo, largo o languruto, desgarbado o desgarbilado, camina por las vías. (19)

Reading this passage, our attention centers immediately on the image of the "baúl mundo," which connotes a secret store of words accessible to the mythopoeic imagination. Once articulated by the centenarian *madrecita,* the words constitute a mode of narration that dissolves the boundaries between the external world of phenomena and the private realm of dreams, a process exemplified in the opening lines of the passage where five such words are cast in relief. At subsequent points in the narrative, the reader will discover their central role in the verbal economy of the novel: "manzanas incircuncisas" reappear in the story of Guadalupe and Dulcenombre (153); a rosary (rosario) figures in that of Eduviges (79); Atanasio "es paseado en una jaula" (406); and stilts (zancos) are mentioned in relation to an incident involving José Trigo and Buenaventura. Yet the phrase *manzanas incircuncisas* and the words *rosario, jaula,* and *zancos* are not perceived immediately as signposts of important themes in the narrative; rather, they are experienced as discrete and poetically arresting images with an imprecise but nonetheless powerful semantic charge.

Talking in 1966 to Juan Carvajal about his philosophy of composition, Fernando del Paso placed great emphasis on "the power of words," consciously echoing the title of an essay by Edgar Allan Poe that, among other things, celebrates "the physical power of words" demonstrated in the artist's capacity for "speaking a wild star into birth" (Poe 192–93). Poe's concerns in that essay anticipate to a large degree those of del Paso in *José Trigo* and point to a common grounding in symbolist aesthetics: readers of *José Trigo* are encouraged to dwell on the suggestive force and multiple associations of words, starting with those "discrete words" (palabras sueltas) (32)—generally nouns and noun phrases—that periodically interrupt the flow of the narrative. True to the principles of Symbolism, their enunciation enacts the creation of a fictional world: "Say to me things such as: 'carajo,' 'huevón,' 'ojos,' 'olvido,' 'vísperas,'" claims the narrator, "and I shall speak my world into existence with them" (21).

Of the various items which go to make up the verbal microcosm of *José Trigo,* place-names are a particularly fertile source of poetic and thematic effects. A place-name may be highlighted for purely aesthetic reasons: this is the case with the names of Binbaletas, Centauro, and "the station of La Polka, Alacranes and Anzaldúas," rural locations which the narrator mentions in his lyrical ode to Mexico for the sufficient reason that they have "the most beautiful names in the world" (235). In other instances, place-names are cited for their wealth of cultural associations. Thus, the "híbridos apelativos" of ancient districts in Mexico City—"el sitio verde de Nuestra Señora de Belén Tlaxoxiuhco, el lugar de la orilla de la muralla de Santa Ana Atenantitech" (285)—bear eloquent witness to the nation's history of cultural syncretism, while the names Crisantema, Naranjo, Fresno, and Laurel are exact toponymic references to streets in Nonoalco and *trouvailles* that enhance "the magic of the book" by evoking a universal order of myth identical to that surveyed by Sir James George Frazer in his monumental study, *The Golden Bough.* As Fernando del Paso explained,

> The main street of the encampments is Chrysanthemum, which means "flower of gold," and is essentially a golden bough which joins Ash, Orange, Cypress, and the other perpendicular streets like mistletoe, in the process binding together the legends of the world. (Carvajal iii)

The floral aliases of a character like María Patrocinio—Flor de mi vida (flower of my life), Azucena (madonna lily), Pensamiento (pansy), and Lirio del Valle (lily of the valley)—similarly combine universal resonances with highly specific local associations to do with poetry, the natural order, and renewal. Connections between flowers and poetry are documented in Nahuatl verse by Alfonso Reyes, who detected a veritable obsession with flowers (and to a lesser extent, stars) throughout pre-Columbian Mexican writing ("Visión de Anáhuac"). In a diachronic perspective, the narrator of *José Trigo* conforms to the type of the poet with "flowers on his lips" and gives renewed expression to a conception of language and poetry that has its roots in the cosmology of the ancient Mexican peoples (León-Portilla 27–28), replicating at yet further levels the myth of cyclical growth and regeneration around which *José Trigo* is structured and conceived.

Intertextual Relations, Cultural Contexts, and the Narrative Tradition

As accounted for above, *José Trigo* is a text that grows out of centuries of Mexican writing enriched by North American and European Symbolism and brought up to date in the modernist experiments of Carlos Fuentes. Overall, Fernando del Paso recapitulates the anthropological, historical, and literary production of several centuries, in a project that exceeds by far the bounds of normal academic coverage. Restricting our attention to Mexican narrative of the postrevolutionary period, we need to place further limits around a field that includes Mariano Azuela, José Guadalupe de Anda, J. Manguía Torres, José Revueltas, Agustín Yáñez, Juan José Arreola, and Juan Rulfo, all of whose work is anthologized to some extent in the summa of Mexican literature that is *José Trigo*.[13] For reasons of economy, I propose to concentrate on relations between *José Trigo* and a small selection of works by José Revueltas and Agustín Yáñez, which provide a sharpened focus on the issues of aesthetics and culture articulated in *José Trigo*.

With regard to Yáñez, the texts that offer the most tangible points of contact with *José Trigo* are *La tierra pródiga* (1960) and *Las tierras flacas* (1962). These two works represent the culmination of Yáñez's tireless pursuit of innovation in narrative form and technique initiated in *Al filo del agua* (1947). In them, narrative discontinuity and the schematic alternation of narrative with dialogue and/or interior monologue anticipate the architecture of several chapters of *José Trigo;* more specifically, in *Las tierras flacas* the performance of a "choir" of discordant voices that argue, interrupt, and cut one another off foreshadows the contrapuntal technique and theatrical form of presentation of the two chapters 3 of del Paso's novel. Additionally, Yáñez's prose style reverberates in many features of the writing of *José Trigo*. *Las tierras flacas* affirms the magical power of isolated words and some proper names, in terms identical to those used in certain chapters of *José Trigo* and elsewhere in the author's glosses on his novel. *Las tierras flacas* also emphasizes its own verbal status and advertises itself as a "world of stories" destined to be "transformed into legend" by the poetic procedures of narrative (Yáñez 302). In particular, Yáñez's novel presents an abundance of totalizing procedures that, viewed comparatively, are the forerunners of the baroque manner soon to be cultivated in *José Trigo*. Among many possible examples, the "extensive lists of valuable and intriguing objects" that are recited in the opening lines of the "Quinta estancia" of *Las tierras flacas* illustrate a totalizing intent bound up, as it will be in *José Trigo*, with the recuperation, through memory, of "stories and countenances that have fallen into total oblivion" (293).

In respect to narrative design, *Las tierras flacas* stands in a complex and ultimately revealing relation to *José Trigo*. At the same time, Yáñez's text both overlaps with, and diverges from, an earlier narrative model, *El luto humano* by José Revueltas, which is nearer to possessing the status of a master text after which *José Trigo* is fashioned. Given this plurality of intertextual relations, our comparison of the narrative profile of the works concerned must be three-sided and ready to acknowledge the greater importance of *El luto humano* as a precursor of del Paso's novel.

At the simplest level of narrative content, *José Trigo* and *El luto humano* share an almost identical storyline set in postrevolutionary Mexico and dealing with a conflict between organized labor and a reactionary government that employs *agents provocateurs* to intimidate a disaffected workforce whose ringleader is abducted and eventually murdered. A retrospective narrative interest in the barbaric *Cristero* conflict and its psychological legacy is also common to both works, as is a *dramatis personae* that includes two male protagonists cast in the roles of hero and villain, and a mismatched elderly couple: a vindictive, reactionary husband and a long-suffering spouse who seeks consolation in the arms of a younger man. The women concerned, Buenaventura and Cecilia, resemble each other further in being the bearers of ancestral memories, which they preserve inside the "nostalgic womb" of a *baúl* (*El luto humano* 67). These coincidences in the narratives of *José Trigo* and *El luto humano* are bolstered by a common thematic interest in human suffering, political injustice, betrayal, and solidarity.

Narrative coincidences between *José Trigo* and *Las tierras flacas* are less numerous than those just listed, but no less exact. Yáñez, for example, emphasizes the relationships of conflict between Jacob Gallo and his father, Epifanio Trujillo, and between the same character and his half-brothers, Jesusito and Felipe, thereby duplicating the antagonisms, clearly defined in *José Trigo*, between Luciano and the abusive Todolosantos, and

Luciano and Manuel Angel. What is more, in both *José Trigo* and *Las tierras flacas* these dominant configurations of character articulate extreme positions in a conflict between good and evil that centers on issues of social and political justice. With regard to the women characters, *madre* Matiana in *Las tierras flacas* is a double of *madrecita* Buenaventura in *José Trigo:* introduced early on as a "miracle-worker [. . .] healer, counselor, provider of consolation, midwife and officiator at burials" (90), she embodies the traditional folk wisdom, mythical beliefs, and ritual practices of her community, which assigns to her a set of functions almost identical to those performed by *madrecita* Buenaventura.

Of particular relevance to our study is the casting of characters in all three novels in the mold of Christian archetypes endowed with sharply defined moral significance. In *El luto humano* the murderous Adán, "son of God, father of Abel, father of Cain" (23), clashes with Natividad, "a son of the masses" (287), who is identified with Jesus Christ. Adán, personified in a string of paradoxes as "impotence full of energy, warm indifference [and] active apathy" (30), already bears responsibility for the deaths of Guadalupe, Valentín, and Gabriel. When offered the assignment of killing Natividad, he accepts with perverse relish: "Upon discovering that there was a means to that end, which entailed a clinical and treacherous lying in wait for his victim, [Adán's soul] was filled with an encouraging tranquility full of affirmation" (180). Mean, hateful, and lacking any redeeming virtue, his character clearly anticipates that of Manuel Angel in *José Trigo,* just as his relationship with Natividad prefigures that between the treacherous Manuel Angel and Luciano.

In the elaborate conceptual scheme of Revueltas's novel, Adán is both a type (a villain like Cain or Tezcatlipoca) and a symbol (of the evil inherent in mankind). His antagonist, Natividad, also displays archetypal characteristics which, in his case, are those of the virtuous hero. Natividad is characterized by a "frank, broad, magnificent smile" (176) signaling a strong and generous disposition that he places at the service of others: "Natividad longed to transform the earth and he envisaged a new and free man living on a new and free earth" (298). Like Luciano in del Paso's novel, he devotes his life to the labor movement, interpreting the popular will "as if he were powerful and many, constituted by hundreds of men and women and houses and wills" (247). Again like Luciano, he is betrayed and dies in circumstances that reenact Christ's Passion: "Natividad will die transfixed, crucified" (260). Steeped in archetypal resonances, his death causes widespread grief, but this is tempered with faith in Natividad's survival in the afterlife, where his followers believe he will be sustained by "a new and secret bread, nutritious, immortal, immortalizing":

> The masses shared out the bread of History and Natividad fed on that bread. How could he ever die? As in the ancient Egyptian rites, the masses gave an item of food, a loaf of daily bread, to the living dead. (287)

In *Las tierras flacas*, Miguel Arcángel wears the same mantle of exemplary virtue as Natividad, and while he certainly is not a member of the proletariat, he enjoys the popularity reserved for heroes. Through his various names—"Jacob Gallo," "Miguel," "the fantastic sobriquet of Archangel" (77), and the nickname "el Rey de Oros," meaning the King of *Oros*, a suit of cards (215)—he is associated in a wholly conventional way with "representations of heavenly wars involving invincible lieutenants and just causes" (77) and also with the biblical "struggle of Saint Michael against Lucifer" (218), which he enacts annually with other parishioners in a tableau performed at Christmas on his father's estate. In a complementary role he is also presented, obliquely, as a Messiah figure. However, he does not die like Luciano and Natividad, and ultimately he belongs to a category of archetypal heroes different from theirs. He is, nevertheless, imaged in the popular mind as "Miguel Arcángel, risen from the dead" (154) and thereby recovers some measure of likeness with Luciano and Natividad and their primary archetypal referent, Jesus Christ.

With this last remark, a gap may be seen opening up between *José Trigo* and *El luto humano* and, on the other hand, *Las tierras flacas*, a gap which becomes wider when we consider the range of cultural references and symbols that underpin each text. Expanding on our analysis of *El luto humano*, we note how throughout the narrative, Christian motifs such as the Crucifixion and the theme of immortality interweave with mythical motifs derived from other sources. In the following quotation, Natividad's death is pictured as a descent into the underworld, reminiscent of pre-Columbian accounts of the death of Quetzalcóatl:

> Natividad went down into the grave, as if a raging fire had been buried. The earth received him to combine his flames with the inner fire that she keeps blazing permanently in her heart. (287)

Other references in the novel to "pre-Cortesian animals" (22), "formless gods" (28), and the exodus of "the first tribe" (83) contribute further to the evocation of an ancient order of Mexican history whose legacy, represented as a "dark unconscious atavism" (225), Revueltas explores in the pages of *El luto humano,* thus creating a monument to cultural *mestizaje* that squarely anticipates Fernando del Paso's depiction of Mexican realities in *José Trigo.*

In *Las tierras flacas,* Yáñez likewise evokes an atavistic order in the polyfaceted figure of Matiana. A literary relative of Teódula Moctezuma in *La región más transparente, madre* Matiana symbolizes the continuing presence of pre-Columbian customs in modern Mexico. Yet there is no recourse to Aztec mythology in the elaboration of the storyline of *Las tierras flacas:* Christian mythology alone determines the shape of the narrative, thereby setting it apart from *José Trigo* and *El luto humano,* which share a well-defined hybrid character, part Christian, part Aztec. In this respect, *José Trigo* displays greater narrative complexity than *Las tierras flacas* and a denser figurative texture rooted in the peculiar cultural syncretism of Mexico.

These comparisons with two precursor texts add weight to the conclusion of Aralia López González regarding the place of *José Trigo* in the Mexican narrative tradition: "It is the product of a long process of development in [national] prose fiction and one of its high points." In effect, del Paso's debut novel elaborates on the canonical achievements of Revueltas and Yáñez, and on those of Rulfo, Arreola, and a budding Fuentes, too, bringing what I here call the "novel of hybridity" to a qualitative and historic climax. According to López González, "As the culmination of a process, [*José Trigo*] belongs to the period which stretches from 1940 to 1970," paving the way for other types of fiction that will dominate the Mexican literary scene after 1968 (140).

Beyond national boundaries, *José Trigo* carves out a place for itself in a continental narrative tradition that extends through Central America, to the River Plate and Paraguay. An affinity with the "transculturating pole" of Spanish American writing is revealed through a comparison of *José Trigo* with *Hijo de hombre* by Augusto Roa Bastos and two novels by Miguel Angel Asturias that are generally regarded as showpieces of narrative transculturation in the Americas at large. *Hijo de hombre* (1960) was published just one year after del Paso had begun work on *José Trigo.* In broad outline, Roa's novel tells a powerful story of suffering and redemption against the background of the Chaco War between Paraguay and Bolivia (1932–35) and an earlier peasant uprising of 1912–13. This dual temporal scheme projects a view of Paraguayan history as a repetitive process "oscillating tirelessly between rebellion and oppression" (229). Straightaway, we note a very precise similarity with *José Trigo:* del Paso's novel also incorporates a dual temporal perspective, focusing on two moments of contemporary Mexican history—the Cristero War and the railway strikes of 1959—which likewise configure a recurrent pattern of rebellion and defeat.

Regarding the political philosophies that are expressed in the two works, Roa's solidarity with the oppressed masses of Paraguay and his concern for "this American people, which has been the object of so much calumny" (229) come across more forcefully, perhaps, than the messages implicit in *José Trigo,* and are in fact more redolent of José Revueltas than of Fernando del Paso. *Hijo de hombre* and *José Trigo* nevertheless coincide very closely at the level of a moral and spiritual outlook that affirms the value of human life, measured partly in terms of a capacity for suffering and sacrifice. Both novels feature protagonists who embody an ideal code of dignified altruism and self-sacrifice on behalf of a class or group that is unjustly excluded from the political process. The characters concerned, Luciano and Cristóbal, pledge themselves to the collective struggle for greater freedom and improved living standards, goals for which they are ready to lay down their lives. As they pit their strength against the superior might of the state, they seem destined to share the fate of "innumerable and anonymous victims" (23) whose bravery and bloodshed are ignored in official historiography. Yet they and other unpretentious heroes like them live on in the popular imagination, which preserves the story of their exemplary exploits in legend and myth.

In *José Trigo* the death of a character does not signify ultimate dissolution, nor does it in *Hijo de hombre,* where Macario expresses the conviction that "Man has two births. One on being born [into this life], the other at death. . . . He dies but remains alive in others, if he has behaved properly towards his fellow human beings" (33). This belief is borne out by the figurative rebirth and regeneration of many of the characters of *Hijo de hombre.* Casiano Jara is an example: officially thought to have been killed in an explosion at Sapukai station in March 1913, he reappears two years later, "revived and back from the dead," out of the obscurity of his make-shift home—a railway carriage transported over "the parched and cracked plain" (108-9), which is reminiscent of the *furgón* occupied by Luciano and María Patrocinio in *José Trigo.* Casiano's son, Cristóbal, also exemplifies the promise of rebirth in two distinct ways. First, he actively rehabilitates the prostitute, María Encarnación, who under his tutelage experiences an "inconceivable regeneration" (175). And second, he is popularly believed to be immortal, despite having perished on a wartime mission that involved carrying precious supplies of water to troops cut off behind enemy lines. Ironically, the only survivor Cristóbal could help on reaching his goal was Miguel Vera, an enemy of the proletarian cause, but this does not detract from the value of his mission: a narrator assures us that "Cristobal's lorry did not drive through death to save the life of a traitor. Engulfed in flames, it still keeps on rolling at night, across the desert, following the trails, carrying water to slake the survivors' thirst" (223). The dignity of Cristóbal's mission thus remains intact, along with the integrity of the themes of revival and regeneration in *Hijo de hombre*.

Significantly, Roa Bastos inscribes these themes within a symbolic framework of mythical references, many of which derive from Christianity. A number of critics have examined Roa's use of Christian imagery in the novel, among them David Foster and Donald Shaw, who together have shown how Roa inverts conventional forms in order to convey a secular and humanistic outlook on life (Foster 38–64; Shaw, "Inverted Christian Imagery and Symbolism"). The presentation of Cristóbal Jara illustrates the author's practice in this regard. As his Christian name suggests, Cristóbal has the unequivocal status of a Christ figure. However, like Johnny Carter in "El perseguidor" by Julio Cortázar (see Fiddian, "Religious Symbolism"), he does not conform to conventional images of Jesus; instead, Roa portrays him as "the son of Man and not the son of God" (Shaw 77), a strategy signposted in the reversal, in his full name, of the initials "J. C.," which are shorthand for "Jesus Christ."

From Roa's presentation of Cristóbal, Shaw infers a profound disenchantment with orthodox Christian values and interprets the inverted Christian imagery of *Hijo de hombre* as a "technique" for diagnosing "modern spiritual despair" (73, 81). This means that, for Shaw, the patterns of imagery that structure Roa's text are devoid of local cultural significance. Indeed, Shaw insists that the function of inverted Christian imagery throughout modern Spanish American fiction is "to lift the novel in which it appears out of mere referentiality into a more universal relevance" (74). Other commentators such as Carlos Battilana interpret Roa's novel differently, as an encoding of historical and cultural conditions in Paraguay. In my reading of *Hijo de hombre* I opt for this line of approach rather than Shaw's, and I would contend that Roa's portrayal of Cristóbal has less to do with alleged universalist aspirations than with a desire to render as faithfully as possible striking peculiarities of the worldview of the *itapeños*, whose culture and history are the real subjects of the novel. Here, the word *culture* is meant to connote secular myths and traditions, on the one hand, and a set of religious beliefs and practices, on the other, including a liturgy— "The *itapeños* had their own liturgy, a tradition born out of certain events which, though relatively recent, had already acquired the status of legend" — and rites like the lowering of the figure of Christ from the cross on Good Friday: "a harsh, defiant, primitive rite, fermented in a spirit of blasphemous rebellion" which, Roa's narrator observes, "has earned the *itapeños* the reputation of fanatics and heretics" (13). Investigating the origins of the heretical rite of "el Cristo del cerrito," we find that they are something of a mystery to the narrator, who locates them, rather condescendingly, beyond the "simple understanding" of the *itapeños*. Yet his unconscious prejudice and mystification cannot obscure a basic truth, which is that "that strange belief [. . .] which essentially entailed a reversal [inversión] of conventional faith, a permanent outbreak of insurrection" (13) originates in the spiritual lives of the *itapeños* themselves: it is they who first developed it and they who preserve it in the fictional present. As far as the role of Roa Bastos is concerned, he simply fashions a novel reflecting their beliefs and mediating their cultural assumptions. But that is the limit of his creative involvement: authorship of the community's rites and customs, including their controversial "inversión de la fe," rests ultimately with the native *itapeños*.

Roa sharpens the local focus of his narrative by providing a historical perspective on the cultural traditions of Sapukai and Itapé post-1600. He records the subordination of the two communities to the authority "of a viceroy far away in Lima" (12), and he discusses at some length the colonizing role of the Jesuit missionaries:

> Three centuries earlier the Jesuits ran estates whose sphere of administrative influence stretched as far as the hill of Paraguarí. [T]here the Fathers had left intact the legend of the appearance of Saint *Tomé*, superimposing it skilfully and delicately, as was their custom, on the local Indian myth of *Zumé*, which had sprung up in the same place in times when the sun was still a lesser deity than the moon. The Indians acted as if they were believers [in the Christian saint]. But that was no longer of any importance now. (45)

This account of Jesuit guile and Indian resistance gives a penetrating insight into the connection between historical experience in Paraguay and the formation of a cultural identity based on a fusion between western (predominantly Christian) values and myths and the local cultural heritage of the Guaraní Indians.

I have already commented on the role of Christian references in *Hijo de hombre*. What we must now acknowledge is their coexistence with Guaraní motifs, beginning in the preface where a quotation from the Book of Ezekiel in the Bible stands alongside one from the *Himno de los muertos de los Guaraníes*. Crucially, the preface establishes no visible hierarchy of importance between the two sources, and invites the reader to adopt a bifocal view of the subject matter of the book, which subsequently refines and extends ideas contained in both quotations. So, while the words of Ezekiel prefigure essential themes and elements of the storyline, the *Himno de los muertos* echoes in an *estribillo* sung by María Rosa as she accompanies the statue of "el Cristo del cerrito" into the church at Itapé:

> In a broken, feeble voice, she began to sing that incomprehensible refrain from the Hymn of the Dead. Every so often she would stop and start again, through clenched teeth. Finally the ancestral song went silent on her lips. (26)

What is particularly noteworthy from the point of view of our study is the fact that the Guaraní hymn which María Rosa and her fellow *itapeños* ritually intone articulates a message of resurrection and regeneration. The excerpt that is reproduced in the preface envisages the reincarnation of spirits and lost voices: "It behooves me to make the voice flow through the bones again. . . . And I will make speech become flesh again," at the same time as it heralds the dawning of a new age "[a]fter this time is lost and a new time dawns" (9). Viewed in isolation, the excerpt tellingly sums up the Guaraní attitude to death and renewal; taken in conjunction with the Christian view of life after death, it is a striking illustration of the cultural syncretism of Roa's native Paraguay.

These observations permit an overall assessment of the relationship between *Hijo de hombre* and *José Trigo*. Not only do the two novels share a cyclical view of history, a belief in regeneration, and specific kinds of archetypal imagery. They also have a common foundation in a dual cultural paradigm that is typical of American syncretism. A further comparison of *José Trigo* with two novels by Miguel Angel Asturias reinforces this view of the affiliation of *José Trigo* with a continental tradition of narrative, whose cultural assumptions and forms of expression it reproduces with remarkable fidelity.

Hombres de maíz (1949) and *Mulata de tal* (1963) offer the greatest scope for consideration here. To begin with language, *Hombres* and *Mulata* are works of incomparable linguistic brilliance that illustrate their author's conception of the novel as "a verbal enterprise" (hazaña verbal).[14] *Mulata* unfolds a dazzling display of puns, associations, and playful distortions of the sound and form of words, features which translate directly into the linguistic extravagance of *José Trigo*. In addition to this material resemblance at the level of *parole,* the two texts share a common poetics of language based on a belief in "the element of mystery that is enclosed in words" (*Mulata* 227), which is an Asturian equivalent of the symbolist-derived mystique of language that informs *José Trigo*.

The use of mythical elements to organize the narratives of both *Hombres* and *Mulata* generates numerous coincidences with *José Trigo*. Some of these are limited to a single detail of characterization, as in the attribution of an identical archetypal referent to two characters in the authors' works. We might compare, for example, the description of Yumi as "the Infernal Christian Prince" in *Mulata* (275) with del Paso's characterization of Manuel Angel as a satanic prince in the fairground episode of *José Trigo*. Other coincidences involve a more complex arrangement of narrative themes, characters, and motifs, like those found in *Hombres de maíz*. *Hombres de maíz* displays the following parallels with *José Trigo*: It reenacts ancient myths of death and rebirth in a narrative that gives prominence to two male protagonists (Gaspar Ilóm and Nicho Aquino) cast in the role of the mythical god, Quetzalcóatl; it features secondary characters with referents in ancient Mesoamerican mythology, for example, la Piojosa, who, like *madrecita* Buenaventura in *José Trigo,* is an avatar of the Aztec goddess, Tlazolteotl; it explores themes of fertility and renewal, and incorporates imagery related to the local cult and cultivation of maize.[15]

Together, *Hombres de maíz* and *José Trigo* offer complementary representations of native America. Translating the rural dramas of Asturias (and Roa Bastos, Rulfo, and Revueltas) into a largely urban setting, *José Trigo* remains rooted in the cultural matrix out of which *Hombres de maíz* and other narratives reviewed in this section emerged. No less committed to technical experimentation than the novelists who went before him, del Paso may be judged to have chosen the option, when producing *José Trigo,* of "a transculturating modernization" available, according to Angel Rama, to the writers of Latin America after the rise of modernism ("La tecnificación narrativa" 69–71).

The relationship beween the literary cultures of Latin America and those of Europe and North America is fundamental to the scheme proposed by Rama and to the postcolonial preoccupations of a younger generation of critics as well. The universalist cast of Fernando del Paso's thinking about culture and politics calls for some consideration of the relation between *José Trigo* and a vast network of international forerunners and counterparts, whom the author has acknowledged on various occasions as his "literary forefathers." In an early roll call of literary mentors, del Paso cited Flaubert, Thomas Mann, Rabelais, Pavese, Faulkner, Pessoa, and Broch before adding "one name, the one that cannot be overlooked, the greatest: James Joyce, my teacher par excellence [mi maestro por excelencia]" (Carvajal iii). Some observations on Joyce provide a final perspective on the cultural status of *José Trigo,* a text which sustains rigorous comparison with either *Ulysses* or *Finnegans Wake.* Given the impossibility of accounting for all of del Paso's literary debts, these two pathbreaking novels by Joyce must stand as a serviceable synecdoche of a millenarian western tradition that is held conventionally to culminate in Anglo-American modernism and postmodernism. Their dual status as syntheses of the canon (from Homer through Dante, Shakespeare and Sterne, to Wilde) and as compendia of a history of political dissidence, cultural peripherality, and moral and religious heterodoxy (see Fiddian, "James Joyce and Spanish-American Fiction") further bolsters their claim to be read as parts standing for the whole of western literature.

Formal links between del Paso's and Joyce's work were first documented by Ramón Xirau (1967), Aida Nadi Gambetta Cruk (1974), and Dagoberto Orrantia (1975). In relation to *Ulysses,* the greatest area of overlap is the mythical design and archetypal projection of the narrative material of *José Trigo.* In a particularly close set of correspondences, characters in both *Ulysses* and *José Trigo* reenact a classic Oedipal drama that pits son against father in an atmosphere of varying degrees of hostility: Luciano defies Todolosantos, Guadalupe fears Nicanor, and Stephen Dedalus resents his father, Simon, and is obsessed with "the Father and the Son idea" (Joyce 16). Consistent with the archetypal basis of their experience, characters share an intuitive sense of being caught up in patterns of repetition that operate beyond the normal parameters of human understanding. Thus, as they yield to an incestuous longing for each other, Guadalupe and Dulcenombre feel instinctively that they have "already lived those moments in some former time" (156). They thereby bring to the fore themes of reincarnation and ancestral memory that also appear in a conversation between Molly and Leopold Bloom in an early chapter of Joyce's novel: Asked to explain the concept of "metempsychosis," Joyce's common hero remarks by way of illustration, "Some say they remember their past lives" (53). Along with a battery of allusions to a wide range of myths and legends—Christian, pagan, Hellenic, Amerindian—these archetypal themes are evidence of a common conceptual design in *José Trigo* and *Ulysses.*

A no less interesting and substantial set of correspondences can be posited between *José Trigo* and *Finnegans Wake.* And here it must be stated right away that I am not claiming any wholesale resemblance between the two books. As early as 1966, Fernando del Paso discounted that proposition when he declared that *"Finnegans Wake* is an unrepeatable experiment": a unique achievement ("It has value because there is no other work like it") which no other writer could hope to emulate (Carvajal iii). More modestly, I merely assert the existence of a number of points of coincidence that have relevance to a discussion of the issues of cultural identity and affiliation under the spotlight in this study.

The most palpable coincidences between *José Trigo* and *Finnegans Wake* are located in the areas of (i) a common thematic preoccupation with Oedipal conflict, incest, and guilt, (ii) the archetypal projection of some of the characters in sharply defined relationships of antagonism, and (iii) the presence of certain predominantly Christian motifs, the most important being the myth of resurrection, which acts as a vehicle for mediating a positive view of the place of humankind in the cosmos. Having remarked already on the place in Joyce's work of themes relating to the Oedipal complex, we can dispense with any further comment on that topic and pass immediately to a consideration of the two other areas indicated above. The first area involves the modeling of characters on archetypal antecedents who represent an essential and irreducible form of conflict. In *José Trigo,* Luciano and Manuel Angel exemplify such a pairing, their relationship being defined alternately as a form of sibling rivalry (Quetzalcóatl vs. Tezcatlipoca) and a confrontation between evenly balanced powers of good and evil (Christ and the Archangels vs. Lucifer). In summary, *Finnegans Wake* tells the story of a nuclear family composed of Humphrey Chimpden Earwicker (HCE)—who, like Luciano, is distinguished by a "Christlikeness" (33)—his wife, Anna Livia Plurabelle (ALP), their daughter, Issy, and the multifaceted siblings, Shaun and Shem (491). Described as "heavenlaid" twins (177), Shaun and Shem are compared on occasions to the archetypal pair, Castor and Pollux, and, more frequently, to the biblical types of Cain and Abel and Michael and Lucifer. "The Mime of Mick, Nick, and the Maggies" (219–59) exemplifies this allegorizing method, portraying Shem and Shaun, respectively, as Nick/ Nekulon/Lignifer and Mick/Makal in order to convey recognizable themes of duality, conflict, and complementarity.

Other analogies derive from the animating presence in *Finnegans Wake* of certain Christian themes and motifs including those of Eden ("a prefall paradise," p. 30) and the Fall itself as "retaled in bed and later on life down through all Christian minstrelsy" (3). These related myths coalesce in the collective story of the Earwicker family and, most pointedly, in the biography of Anna Livia Plurabelle, whose sexual initiation "in county Wickenlow, garden of Erin" is recounted in the famous section beginning "O tell me all about Anna Livia!" (196 ff.). In that section, a group of gossips wage a whispering campaign against ALP, accusing her of all sorts of sexual misdemeanors. Yet Anna Livia cannot be dismissed as a figure of wanton sexual indulgence, for she is also an agent of cleansing and purification who has the power to bring about "the regeneration of all men by affusion of water" (606). In so much, she fulfills a symbolic function identical to that which is attributed to *madrecita* Buenaventura in the imaginary world of *José Trigo*.

The promise of spiritual regeneration represented by Anna Livia brings us close to the notional center of *Finnegans Wake*, where the essential message of the text effectively resides. That message is generous and humane and implies an optimistic belief in the constant renewal of vital potential and the ultimate triumph of life over death. At its simplest and most direct, the message takes the form of a rallying call which H. C. Earwicker addresses to the whole-old world:

> Calling all downs. Calling all downs to dayne. Array! Surrection!
> Eireweeker to the wohld bludyn world. O rally, O rally, O rally!
> Phlenxty, O rally! (593)

With these words, Earwicker invites all-comers to celebrate the dawning of a new day and affirms the moral and poetic truth of the doctrine of resurrection which is the cornerstone of Joyce's metaphysics in *Finnegans Wake*. Throughout the novel, the motifs of daybreak and awakening are associated with the themes of regeneration and resurrection and provide a rhetorical accompaniment to the narration at moments of particular intensity: for example, at the end of I.iii, when the narrator imagines the return of a mythic hero who will "wake from earthsleep" (74); the conclusion of III.ii, which anticipates a time when "The silent cock shall crow at last. The west shall shake the east awake" (473); and in the vision of Tim Finnegan's return from the dead, "renanescent; fincarnate; [. . .] awike in wave risurging into chrest" (596).

From a formal perspective, it is interesting to note the consistency of Joyce's figurative language and the uniform burden of meaning that it discharges at climactic moments of the narrative. From a comparative perspective, our attention is caught by the extent to which *Finnegans Wake* resembles *José Trigo*, both in the joint respects of theme and tone and in that of imagery. The motif of the sun's passage along an east-west axis; the image of the phoenix in Joyce's homage to Dublin's "sphoenix spark" (473); the reference to Christ/Chrest as a type of resurrection—these items constitute the fine detail of a substantial likeness between two works that are united by a common set of concerns grounded in the same humanistic outlook and articulated in a similar, mixed cultural register.

The global diffusion of Roman Catholicism and Christian mythology goes a long way toward explaining the affinities that exist between *Finnegans Wake* and *José Trigo*. It is, perhaps, ultimately not surprising that a mid-twentieth-century narrative compendium of the cultural paradigms of Mexico should echo some of the basic concerns of an earlier landmark novel steeped, like the rest of Joyce's work, in the Catholic-agrarian heritage of Ireland—a country to which del Paso's observations concerning Mexico's history of spiritual colonization could be applied with some justification. No less pervasive an influence, or code, is the tradition of western humanism and its basis in universalist assumptions that have been embraced not only by James Joyce and Fernando del Paso but also by Leopoldo Zea, Frantz Fanon, and others. The categorical assertion, made by the narrator of *José Trigo*, that "What matters is the story of mankind" (11) articulates an ethical position to which del Paso, Zea, and Fanon each subscribed in the 1960s and 1970s and, in the cases of del Paso and Zea, up through the 1990s.[16]

As an inheritor of Borges's decentered model of cultural relations between different regions of the world, del Paso could rightfully claim for *José Trigo* the same inherent cultural value as *Finnegans Wake*. For one reason or another, this is something he has never actually done. Yet, if the above comparison is accurate, *José Trigo*, depicting the human condition in terms often identical to those used in *Finnegans Wake*, displays a semantic density that entitles it to be considered as no more and no less "universal" than Joyce's novel. Indeed, *José Trigo* can be viewed as exemplifying a genuinely Latin American universal that fuses the local and the continental with a more generalized message about humankind, Nature, the political order, and transcendence. In my analysis of relations between *José Trigo* and at least one canonical text from each of the Mexican, Latin American, and European narrative traditions, I have sought to validate all three projections of del Paso's multilayered text.

In his acknowledgment of the "unrepeatable experiment" of *Finnegans Wake*, del Paso could not overlook the unique linguistic and intertextual achievement represented by Joyce's novel-to-end-all-novels. Notwithstanding his denial of the iterability of *Finnegans Wake*, the experimental flair of Joyce's writing inevitably carries over into the prose style of *José Trigo*. As we saw earlier, del Paso exploits the linguistic system of his native Spanish relentlessly and to the point of exhaustion. A favorite strategy involves reproducing the entire contents of a paradigm, for example, the names of animals and insects (147–48), trees and flowers (375), the days of the week and months of the year (387), the letters of the alphabet (142 and 398), and the cardinal numbers (140). Not only is this a strategy already favored by Joyce in and after *Ulysses,* but many of the paradigms are exactly the same as those that are called into play in *Finnegans Wake,* including the days of the week (301), the cardinal numbers (589), the "allaphbed," and parts of speech. *José Trigo* also experiments with various modes of discourse, showing a particular penchant for parody and a pastiche of models ranging from the inflated style and archaic lexicon of Catholic sermons composed by a "verbose and soporific priest" of the *Cristeros* (413), to the rhetoric and invective of a crudely politicized press (149, 371), and the popular slang and wordplay of a cabaret compere who entertains an unruly audience with a string of puns (retruécanos) (334) and double entendres (albures calambureros) (337). From a higher register, del Paso reworks an equally wide range of models that, in addition to those already surveyed, include the virtuoso rhetorical exercises of Juan José Arreola in "palimpsestuous" texts such as *Confabulario* and *La feria*[17] and the unique narrative style of Juan Rulfo. The re-creation, in the stories of *El llano en llamas,* of a peasant mind-set and of conventions of popular speech and storytelling is the starting point for a "Rulfian pastiche" wrought, with conscious artistry, in chapter 4 of part 1 of *José Trigo* (Carvajal iii).[18]

The profusion of intertextuality and pastiche in *José Trigo* is reminiscent of Joyce's practice in both *Ulysses* and the *Wake* and follows the totalizing programs of those two quintessentially modernist works. At the same time, those features of the writing of *José Trigo* suggest a link with postmodernism as theorized by Ihab Hassan, Fredric Jameson, and others. Blanca Merino Juti, in an unpublished doctoral thesis of 1994, considered *José Trigo* a postmodern novel. It goes without saying that such a reading is fundamentally at odds with the picture of *José Trigo* that I have built up in the preceding pages. I believe that the combination, in del Paso's novel, of an overarching figurative design, a humanist message and master code, and a totalizing aesthetic that seeks to reconcile opposing interpretations of fictionalized experience conforms to a modernist practice of narrative. Yet Merino Juti's reading opens up alternative possibilities of classification that are not to be dismissed out of hand. If pastiche, a dissenting historiography, and self-referentiality are typical of a postmodern aesthetic as characterized by Hal Foster, Julio Ortega, and Ricardo Gutiérrez

Mouat, then the picture of *José Trigo* elaborated above might be adjusted to accommodate a certain number of postmodern features within a dominant modernist frame. This makes for a more complex understanding of *José Trigo,* as a text informed by two competing artistic paradigms. In the context of del Paso's work as a whole, the tension between modernism and postmodernism, resolved in *José Trigo* in favor of the former, foreshadows further relationships that I will trace in subsequent chapters, along with the processes of interaction between texts of different origins and cultural affiliations.

3

Palinuro de México

The Body, the Nation, and the Book of the World

> I went to live in London in order to confirm and reaffirm the
> western, European, and Judeo-Christian components of my cul-
> ture, my way of life, my traditions, both past and present.
> **Fernando del Paso, "Mi patria chica, mi patria grande"**

> Palinurus: your blank and maritime
> face offers images of sleeplessness
> to the calm of night. Naked and prostrate,
> you will repeat your death perpetually in the sand.
> **Silvina Ocampo, "Palinuro insomne"**

Begun as early as 1967, but composed for the most part between 1971 and
1975 (Ruffinelli, "Entrevista" 46), *Palinuro de México* repeats the paradigm of *José Trigo,* but with a difference. Like *José Trigo, Palinuro de
México* is a book of Joycean pedigree and proportions, modeled in this
instance on the example of *Ulysses,* and comprising an extravagant, multifaceted narrative infused, in Jorge Campos's words, with an "ambition
of totality" (iii). Del Paso's declaration that "I wanted to write a good
book, a book full of life, an extensive poem about love and death, about
the human body" (Sánchez Bardón and Goñi 49) gives an indication of the
ethical pretensions and thematic scope of the novel, which encompasses
philosophical, medical, sexual, political, psychological, historical, and literary concerns.

As a means of dealing with this vast agenda, *Palinuro de México* utilizes
a multiplicity of narrative modes including the satirical, the dramatic, the
epic and mock epic, the burlesque, the picaresque, and the pornographic.
In respect of form, the material of the narrative is mediated through a

complicated structure of voices that compete and intertwine, sometimes merging imperceptibly, sometimes doubling up in unexpected reversals. There are four principal narrative voices in the book: those of Palinuro and Palinuro *desdoblado* observing and addressing himself at various removes; that of Cousin Walter, articulated in chapters 9, 12, and 22; and the voice of *abuelo* Francisco, apparently speaking from the afterlife, in chapters 21 and 25.

As part of its program of prolixity, the novel exhibits an obtrusive intertextuality, with quotations, imitations, and reformulations of work by writers as varied as William Shakespeare, Jonathan Swift, Lewis Carroll, François Rabelais, Francisco de Quevedo, Jorge Luis Borges, Octavio Paz, Virgil, Cyril Connolly, Henry Miller, and sundry surrealists. Literally, *Palinuro de México* is all of the following: a tale of two cities (in this instance, of the capitals of Mexico and England), a book of the nation, and a concerted dialogue with world literature. Quite consciously, *Palinuro de México* sets out to summarize the entire western tradition, which it claims unproblematically as its own heritage. With a confidence bordering on hubris, the text stakes out for itself a place in canonical territory alongside some of the most famous landmarks in the history of western culture.

Notwithstanding its tendency toward extravagance, the centrifugal impulse of del Paso's narrative is kept in check by an overarching view of the human condition which, in summary form, acknowledges the physical vulnerability and limitations of the human subject yet expounds a message of affirmation of life, including a spiritual belief in rebirth and immortality. Embodied at the narrative level in a design that incorporates archetypal motifs common to such works as *Ulysses* and *Rayuela* as well as del Paso's own *José Trigo*, that affirmative vision pervades the entire novel, constituting the crucial factor of differentiation between *Palinuro de México* and del Paso's earlier novel, where the myth of resurrection was articulated in several instances yet contradicted by the historical and ideological messages encoded in the narrative. With greater internal consistency, *Palinuro de México* matches the blueprint of the book that Palinuro's Cousin Walter would wish to write: "as sickly, fragile and defective as the human organism yet at the same time, if this were possible (although it is clearly impossible), just as complicated and magnificent" and "a Dionysian book which might affirm life triumphantly in all its darkness and horror" (499–500). In its range of tones, del Paso's novel veers accordingly between extremes of somber realism and pathos, on the one hand, and joyful celebration and affirmation, on the other.

Narrative Strands and Themes: Eros, Thanatos, and the Novel of '68

Every work of fiction aspires to the condition of totality, to be a self-contained universe, to take control of its own time.
Carlos Fuentes, *Casa de guardar*

The novel of '68 . . . has perhaps still not crystallized as a literary type.
José Luis Martínez and Christopher Domínguez Michael, *La literatura mexicana del siglo XX*

The expansive vision of *Palinuro de México* is conveyed to the reader through a number of interwoven narrative strands that embody aspects of the character of Palinuro and the principal spheres of his existence. There are five such strands, or codes, each one providing a vehicle for the treatment of certain thematic concerns and an occasion for the utilization of a specific narrative mode and method.

The first strand of the narrative provides information about the character of Palinuro and the personality traits that are attributed to him. Over a number of chapters it builds up an identikit picture of a twenty-year-old medical student from Mexico City whose interests include medicine, sex, literature, art, music, and politics. A cultured young man, Palinuro also possesses a lively sense of fun and mischief that can manifest itself in riotous forms of behavior. At the same time, he is characterized by a certain innocence and naiveté; the description of Palinuro as "above all, a dreamer" (253) refers to a deeply embedded character trait, also connoting political idealism and a commitment to social justice.

Through such descriptions and successive accounts of his involvement in narrative incident, Palinuro is endowed with the inner personality and external behavioral identity of a *homo fictus* (Forster 78–79), who is much more clearly defined than the spectral and elusive José Trigo of del Paso's earlier novel. The youthful Palinuro nevertheless lacks precise physical features, even of the spectral sort attributed to Artemio Cruz in the well-known novel by Carlos Fuentes. And like the other characters in *Palinuro de México*, he is a contradictory and plural being irreducible to a stable ego. When Walter reasons, "Though we are not one, neither are we two, but ten, or a thousand, who knows how many, and between the lot of us we do not make up that one which we *are not*" (179), he articulates a theme, drawn from the Borgesian repertoire, that is central to the novel and that calls into question conventional ideas about individual personality and, with them, the notion of literary character. No longer conceivable in terms of discreteness and unity, "character" in *Palinuro de México* implies double, multiple, and contradictory personalities, as it does in a wide range of twentieth-century fiction including Joyce's *Ulysses, Cumpleaños* and *Cambio de piel* by Carlos Fuentes, and *Lapsus* by Héctor Manjarrez.

Any specificity that might be read into Palinuro's character is further attenuated by the workings of allegory. As "Palinuro of Mexico" he is a metonym for the life of the nation: "And just as in ancient times there was a Rufus of Ephesus and a Xenocrates of Aphrodisias," he proclaims, "so will I one day become so famous that future generations will link my name with my country of origin and call me 'Palinuro de México'" (96–97). More precisely, Palinuro stands for Mexican youth at a conjunctural moment in the nation's history. In a 1978 interview with Ildefonso Alvarez, del Paso remarked, "Palinuro is a character of our times. [. . .] Palinuro is a student who dies during the student riots of 1968 in Mexico City" (Alvarez 15). However, in the ellipsis sandwiched between these two statements, the author refers to Palinuro as "a character who perhaps can be found not only in Mexico but in many other countries," thereby conferring on him the status of an Everyman figure who transcends specifics both of place—as indicated in the remarks to Ildefonso Alvarez—and time—as the text itself makes clear in the comment that "Palinuro lived simultaneously in several periods" (552). In the overall framework of *Palinuro de México,* this transcendent function is inseparable from a wider pattern of myth and archetype that holds the protean material of narrative together. It thus illustrates both the element of complexity inherent in Palinuro's character and the versatility of his role in the narrative economy of del Paso's novel.

The second strand of narrative material in *Palinuro de México* is concerned with Palinuro's family background and his relations with members of his family. The first two chapters of the novel summarize the history of Palinuro's family over at least four generations, evoking the charmed atmosphere of the Porfirian mansion in Mexico City where Palinuro was born and raised with his cousin, Estefanía, his parents, Clementina and Eduardo, an assortment of aunts and uncles, the most eccentric being Aunt Luisa, and his maternal grandparents, Altagracia and Francisco. Depicted as a microcosm of harmony and prosperity, the home is the perfect setting for a family romance where Palinuro would typically be mesmerized by his Uncle Esteban's "conversations about the marvels and horrors of the art of Hippocrates and Avicena" (18) and listen spellbound to stories told by "the greatest and most memorable of grandfathers" (34).

Of all Palinuro's immediate family ties, the one that has the most profound effect on his character and development is his relationship with his mother, and it is this relationship which receives the most intense and detailed attention in the narrative. In chapter 17 we read how Palinuro's early childhood was a time of emotional security and wholeness, recalled, in adulthood, as an *illud tempore*:

> On those nights or only on that single night when his mother came into his room and said Mamma wants to know if her little boy cleaned his teeth properly, and he surrendered to her his breath smelling of warm mint; Mamma wants to know if her little boy washed his hair properly, and she buried her face in his hair; Mamma wants to know if her little boy washed his thighs properly, and she sunk her face into his flesh as in a mound of perfumed sand and the two of them fell asleep, making a kind of love for which they as yet had no name. (285–86)

Like the mother in Freud's "Third Essay on Sexuality" (1905), Clementina regards her son Palinuro "with feelings that are derived from her own sexual life; she strokes him, kisses him, rocks him and quite clearly treats him as a substitute for a complete sexual object" (Freud 145). For Palinuro, the attachment is also a source of gratification and a vehicle for "teaching the child to love," also in keeping with the Freudian scenario (Freud 146).

The knowledge Palinuro acquires in his childhood years about his parents' sexuality causes him distress and confusion. He graphically represents his mother as "a vulva with two legs" and his father as "a penis with two hands" (370). His imagination stirred by primal phantasies, he cannot help but visualize sex between his parents as naked aggression, and taking sides with his mother, he becomes locked into an Oedipal conflict that is still unresolved when he reaches puberty. At that stage of his development, Palinuro's feelings toward Clementina become consciously sexual and erotic, bearing out his Cousin Walter's description of puberty as a period when "everything around you: your mother, words, foodstuffs, become tinged with sexuality and your genital tubercule which started to grow in length from the first weeks after your conception [. . .] continues to grow in length, confirming that you are a male" (274). In a tangible illustration of that phallocentricity, Palinuro masturbates "with mamá Clementina's hand cream" (137), demonstrating the "incestuous fixation of his libido," which he must repudiate, according to Freud (151), if he is to effect the passage from boy to man. In the event, the death of his mother prevents Palinuro from immediately resolving his Oedipus complex and burdens him with a guilt complex that casts a shadow over his relations with women; he eventually attains release from its restrictions only through the mediation of Estefanía.

In its depiction of Palinuro's relationship with his mother, del Paso's narrative thus traces an evolution away from complete symbiosis with *mamá* Clementina to a prolonged state of acute Oedipal anxiety. The lyrical and, at times, elegiacal treatment of precious years spent in the protective embrace of the family gives way to a scenario of adolescent trauma and frustrated potential that compares with the blight inflicted by mother-son relations as described in the work of other Mexican writers of the mid-twentieth century, especially in *Pedro Páramo* by Juan Rulfo and *Cumpleaños* and *Zona sagrada* by Carlos Fuentes. Relevant points of comparison in the broader frame of Spanish American prose fiction include Juan Carlos Onetti's *Los adioses*—mentioned by del Paso apropos the theme of incest in conversation with Ignacio Trejo Fuentes—and García Márquez's *Cien años de soledad,* which offers both a deterrent evocation of the charm and destructiveness of incest and an exploration of the family romance similar to the perspective offered in *Palinuro de México.*

Within *Palinuro de México* there is an alternative treatment of the theme of incest, found in the strand of the narrative that explores Palinuro's relationship with Estefanía. Partly by virtue of sidestepping the Oedipal trap and partly because it subsumes Palinuro and Estefanía's sexual activities under a wider exploration of eroticism, this strand of the narrative succeeds in portraying one of those "incestuous bonds" which, according to del Paso, "could be wonderful if our society had not made them into something horrific" (Trejo Fuentes 9). In a utopian discourse that has its immediate origins in Marcuse and other icons of 1960s and 1970s counterculture and, further back, in the heterodox program of surrealism, del Paso asserts the marvelous beauty, the life-enhancing powers, and the liberating potential of erotic love, even within the bounds of the family.[1]

Dealt with in approximately a third of the novel's twenty-five chapters, Palinuro's relationship with Estefanía provides the context for an intense and playful treatment of the erotic, regarded by del Paso as inseparable from monogamous, romantic love. The conventional cast of the author's attitude on this point is made clear in an interview with Ignacio Trejo Fuentes, when del Paso insisted he believed that "love only exists within a relationship of a certain permanence and depth, a love that should be inseparable from eroticism." An accompanying statement that "As far as I'm concerned, the overriding significance and the importance of love and eroticism are enormous" (Trejo Fuentes 8) reaffirms that point of principle and paves the way for an uninhibited celebration of the body's erotic potential and for the enumeration, on repeated occasions, of an almost infinite catalog of forms of lovemaking bound up with a range of emotions.

A noteworthy example of erotic writing is found in chapter 4 of *Palinuro de México,* which, in the author's own approving words, "oozes love and eroticism, physical passion," and "immense affection" (Trejo Fuentes 8). The chapter unfolds along two dominant axes: the articulation—affectionate, empassioned, contradictory—of Palinuro's feelings for Estefanía; and the description, given directly by Palinuro in a series of observations, enumerations, and recollections, of his cousin's character and physical attributes. While the first of these two axes comprises a mixed register in which conventional terms of amorous idolatry such as "pure," "angelic," and "goddess" give way to epithets expressive of a lesser enthrallment such as "damnable," "whore," "hypocrite," and "perfidious," the second evolves through a systematic account of the properties of parts of Estefanía's body into a detailed anthology of orifices exploited scandalously for sexual ends. As Palinuro explains, this

> is not just talk for talk's sake, since the love that Estefanía and I had for each other, and not only because we loved each other but because we loved our love, led us into all possible encounters: naked, sweating, with blood open to the fluttering of wings, and for the short duration between going to the cinema and the hours that Estefanía spent adorning her breasts while on high the moon swelled in envy like a Dutch sponge, we explored all the orifices born of heaven, both to Estefanía and to her cousin, the moon. (76)

The subsequent list of openings and surfaces that Palinuro either penetrates or bathes in semen functions accordingly as a figure of the lovers' erotic imagination and sexual prowess. But, more significantly and controversially, the writing of this part of the chapter gestures toward puritanism and pornography in ways that are quite deliberate and ultimately parodic in intent.

At the level of authorial intention, the emphasis placed in *Palinuro de México* on the body and its various functions, and, as part of that agenda, the untrammelled expression of the erotic dimension of the characters' lives, are meant to challenge the historically embedded puritanism of western societies, particularly the tradition of Christian denial of, and contempt for, the body. The medical officer who escorts Palinuro around a hospital and announces forthrightly that "Saint Augustine perverted the thought of mankind for over a thousand years, you know: we wish to free it of original sin" (403), speaks for a multitude of dissenting figures, ranging—within the twentieth-century literary canon—from James Joyce (in texts such as *Ulysses* and the letters to Nora Barnacle), and several surrealists including Georges Bataille, to Octavio Paz and Julio Cortázar (in *Rayuela, Libro de Manuel,* and other works). These and several other authors line up behind Fernando del Paso in support of his repudiation of philosophical and religious doctrines that would impoverish the physical and erotic dimensions of human (predominantly male) experience.

At its most extreme, del Paso's opposition to conventional standards of moral (and literary) propriety takes the form of a deliberate cultivation of obscenity. As acknowledged by the author himself, "*Palinuro de México* contains some chapters that are frankly obscene, where it could be said that I had recourse to a technique of 'commotion'" (Trejo Fuentes 8). Valid as a gloss on sections of the narrative that deal with bodily matters in general, del Paso's statement also applies to those sections which represent most precisely the sexual/erotic dimensions of the characters' lives. However, the self-styled obscenity of parts of *Palinuro de México* has serious implications, particularly in regard to an assessment of the relation of those parts of the novel to pornography. Speaking some time after the publication of his novel and expanding on a quotation already cited, del Paso maintained, "The chapter titled 'Unas palabras sobre Estefanía' oozes love and eroticism, physical passion, an immense affection, and, it goes without saying, irony, because I had in mind to make a caricature of pornography—and therefore a criticism" (Trejo Fuentes 8). Yet, if we posit momentarily a functional similarity between the arts of parody and caricature, arguments about the resistance of pornography to parody place a question mark over the aims and actual results of del Paso's project.

According to Susan Sontag, "Pornography isn't a form that can parody itself. It is the nature of the pornographic imagination to prefer ready-made conventions of character, setting, and action. Pornography is a theatre of types, never of individuals. A parody of pornography, so far as it has any real competence, always remains pornography" (51). On this view, an exercise in the imitation of pornography of the sort conducted by del Paso in parts of *Palinuro de México* is contaminated at source. The accounts of Palinuro and Estefanía's lovemaking would match exactly the conventions of pornography as described by Annette Kuhn:

Pornography speak[s] both to and from a masculine position, [. . .] usually privileging the male organ over the female and equating it with ejaculation. [. . .]

[Pornography insists on] the moment of penetration in male-female intercourse. [. . .]

Pornography is preoccupied with what it regards as the signifiers of sexual difference and sexuality: genitals, breasts, buttocks. (20, 35, 37)

More controversially, those accounts would reproduce the offensive assumptions on which the practice of pornography rests.

Against such a view, and seen from a perspective that assumes good faith on del Paso's part, the instances of erotic writing under consideration would belong to another order of literature altogether, setting themselves apart from conventional pornography in at least the following respects: the images conveyed of Palinuro and Estefanía's physical exertions are exaggerated, often to the point of absurdity, and, in any case, range far beyond the standard repertoire of physical acts and positions depicted in works of pornography; the presentation of the protagonists is playful, not mechanistic, and the tone of the writing is often humorous and very different from the "affectless" tone of pornography documented by Sontag in her enumeration of the features of pornographic writing (55). Significantly, the chapters of *Palinuro de México* that represent the protagonists' sexual acts do so from a perspective that incorporates the point of view of Estefanía, even though her voice is subsumed under a first-person plural form articulated by Palinuro. And, finally, the criticism, made by Angela Carter about pornography, that its "principal and most humanly significant function is that of arousing sexual excitement" (12) does not apply to *Palinuro de México,* where the chapters featuring erotic subject matter fulfill a variety of functions, both in the context of the narrative as a whole and as self-contained exercises in imitation.

Assessing the results of del Paso's critically motivated caricature of pornography, the evidence suggests a high degree of consistency between the author's intentions and the range of meanings that can be read into his text. But what is also demonstrated is the vulnerability of the position of any male author who intervenes in the arena of sexual politics, where the intentions behind a literary work are especially likely to conflict with the expectations of readers who are highly sensitized to the implications of a subject as controversial as pornography. Issues of pornography aside, the treatment of themes of love and eroticism in the strand of the narrative under review advances a cause—that of reclaiming the body from the discourses of repression—already pursued, in Mexican writing, by Octavio Paz in *Conjunciones y disyunciones* (1969) and, in a very different idiom, by Gustavo Sainz in *Gazapo* (1965). Where del Paso breaks new ground is in the elaboration of a utopian scenario of incest, independent of the regime of Oedipal prohibitions that has exercised so profound an influence on the organization of western societies and the theoretical apparatuses that have served to legitimate them.

Turning to the fourth strand of the narrative of *Palinuro de México*, we find an emphasis initially on themes relating to the motif of the double, dramatized in the relationship between Palinuro and Walter. The character known synonymously as "Walter the learned, Walter the knowledgeable" (171), "Walter who had read everything" (159), and, more disparagingly, "Walter the know-all" (167) is also the focal point for the discussion of a vast repertoire of other themes from the areas of philosophy, medicine, and culture.

Partly an ironic cipher of the author, partly a complex example of more or less objectionable forms of dilettantism and pedantry, Walter stands out as a tragicomic figure of hyperbole and contradictoriness ("I am a knot of contradictions," he admits to Palinuro, p. 517) who is a direct literary descendant of another Walter—the temperamental father of Tristram Shandy in Lawrence Sterne's famous novel of 1759–67. In the context of Palinuro's family, Walter is bound to Palinuro in a relationship that is effectively fraternal and, figuratively, that of twins: as he puts it, "More than cousins, Palinuro, we are fraternal twins" (501). Harking back to *José Trigo* and exploiting the same archetypal motif as Carlos Fuentes in *Terra nostra*, Walter compares himself and Palinuro to the Dioscuri: "We shall take turns to talk and shine, like Castor and Pollux" (52), repeating the assertion on a later occasion: "If it's true that you swallow your words and I spit them out, that's because we are condemned to shine alternately, like Castor and Pollux" (501).

As symbolic twins and "cuates" (a term deriving from the name Quetzalcóatl and denoting an indivisible bond of male friendship), the two men provide a sharply defined illustration of the category of the double. Recalling once again the networking of characters in *José Trigo* (cf. the relationship between Luciano and *el albino*) and the light-hearted twinning of Huberto Haltter and Humberto Heggo in *Lapsus* (1971) by Héctor Manjarrez (a Mexican author ten years younger than Fernando del Paso), Palinuro and Walter coexist as partners whose experiences crisscross and double up like reflections in a mirror. In chapter 3, Walter performs the narrative function of an exact double of Palinuro: identifiable, in an anonymous first-person narration, by a reference to a "diamond patterned vest" that he borrows from Palinuro and by certain peculiarities of thought and speech, Walter is nonetheless turned inside out by his normally diffident cousin, who on this occasion displays the qualities of assuredness and articulacy that are normally Walter's trademark.

More generally, the cousins' lives are governed by a principle of complementarity that decrees Walter should act and appear as Palinuro's "other." Within this subcategory of the double, Walter functions as an alter ego who compensates for the opportunities and achievements that Palinuro is denied "by an irony of fate" that placed "more money, more books and more opportunities within his [i.e., Walter's] grasp" (169). To his moral credit, Walter appreciates the good fortune that made it possible for him to live (as did the author) for several years in England, where he never forgot Palinuro and would often "speak to [him] out loud" from famous landmarks in London (488). In doing so, he performs roles of complementarity and compensation that carry strong echoes of Oliveira and Traveler in Julio Cortázar's *Rayuela*. The question that Walter—a genuine Traveler, who has chosen a life of exile in Europe—retrospectively asks, "Where were you at that moment, cousin? Where were you as I walked past the National Gallery in London?" (498), echoes precisely those themes of the double and simultaneous experience that characterize Cortázar's version of the semimystical theory of the *figura,* reprised from, among other sources, Jorge Luis Borges.

Despite his tangled connections with Palinuro, Walter evinces sufficient intellectual personality and fullness of self to be considered a fictional entity distinct from Palinuro. He is, in fact, older than his cousin, more cosmopolitan than the naive and idealistic student who is just twenty years old. What sets Walter apart from Palinuro, as it does from all the main characters in the novel, is his particular outlook on life, summed up in the phrase "tragicomic sense of life" (486). True to the spirit of contradictoriness that he embodies, Walter combines two extreme and equally plausible points of view on the human condition and the world. The first is a pained awareness of "the poverty and fragility of human life" (160): concepts documented in a vast catalog of diseases, barbarous medical acts, and forms of physical suffering that are at one and the same time expressions of Walter's "liking for the sad and the cruel" (159) and stark evidence of "our human wretchedness" (182). Notwithstanding its basis in real experience, that awareness is assimilated to a philosophical and ethical conviction that "At the end of the day, the world [. . .] is not such a bad place" (183). Associated with attitudes of optimism and good humor, this second pole of Walter's outlook is synonymous with a sense of wonder at the undeniable marvels and mysteries of life.

Of the various themes that concern Walter, those of the body and of language and consciousness are especially indicative of his philosophical cast of mind. Already discussed in connection with Palinuro and Estefanía's shared eroticism, the theme of the body as considered by Walter intersects with thoughts, *inter alia,* about "ownership of our bodily organs" (269), the problematical integrity of the body, and its vulnerability (su integridad amenazada) at every instant of a person's life (272). With quasi-religious fervor Walter defends "the sacred symmetry" of the body (504) against accidents, disease, and political assaults including torture and mutilation, and he celebrates the splendor of "the marvellous form of Man, writ large" (516). Through the deliberate use of capital letters, Walter promotes the view of the body as a microcosm of creation and "copy of the universe" (516), thus affiliating himself with a tradition of thinkers from Paracelsus to Scotus Erigena, Swedenborg, and Bohme who consistently posited "strange links between the highest and the lowest, the celestial and the terrestrial" (171). This mystical notion, entertained by Borges in "Los teólogos" and other writings, places the highest conceivable value on the human form and opens out sublime perspectives on its powers of transcendence—a theme that acquires its ultimate significance in *Palinuro de México* at the level of archetypal design, as discussed below.

Walter's ideas on language and consciousness express equally affirmative sentiments, despite their origins in the nominalist tradition of essentially skeptical philosophers like Hobbes and Fritz Mauthner. Echoing that tradition Walter insists, first, on the equivalence of language and memory and, second, on the ties of memory to imagination. Then he underlines the crucial significance of language in our construction as human beings engaged in and with the world. Language, Walter argues, provides the most conclusive proof that human beings are more than physical systems:

> I mean, matter pure and simple we are not. [. . .] And do you know why? Because we are made of words and so are things; because we are but memory, and things exist and acquire the status of truth when they allow themselves, tamely, to be clothed in the fabric of the world of words. (183)

In the terms of this argument, language constitutes consciousness and endows the world of objects with authentic and "truthful" existence, thereby demonstrating humankind's capacity for entering into a constructive, creative relationship with the circumstantial world.

Walter's own flexible and dynamic use of language is but one instance of this capacity and a trait that Palinuro is proud to "inherit" from him in particular (539). The examples that the text immediately provides of Palinuro's verbal skills are examples not of empty rhetoric but of rhetoric used to promote personal and collective causes involving issues of solidarity—with protesting students, for example—and social and political justice in a country where the rich and powerful effectively monopolize resources and the state has no compunction about authorizing the armed forces to repress popular demonstrations with tanks, machetes, and rifle butts, as happened in Mexico City in the summer of 1968. In this context, words relate conscientiously to a world of referents and events that have compelling and immediate significance for the fictional characters of the narrative. Temporarily overriding questions of its relation to memory, consciousness, and play, language addresses a number of urgent political issues in which all the parties involved in the novel's circuit of communication—author, narrators, characters, and readers—have a stake.

The political dimension of the fictional world portrayed in del Paso's novel is delineated most fully in the fifth strand of the narrative, which traces Palinuro's exploits with friends and fellow students, including his involvement in the public disturbances that hit Mexico City in 1968. Turning yet again on the body, this strand combines a scabrous treatment of base physiological functions, reminiscent of the carnivalesque scatology of Rabelais and Quevedo, with a grisly attention to details of torture and other forms of physical abuse whose closest analogue in Mexican fiction is Salvador Elizondo's *Farabeuf* (1965). The shift from the Rabelaisian to the Elizondan perspective is a most effective vehicle for addressing the contemporary political situation and for denouncing the violent repression of the student movement by the Mexican military and police acting on the orders of President Gustavo Díaz Ordaz between July and October 1968.

A climate of political unrest and general expectation is registered as early as chapter 5 with the mention by Palinuro of students who "take to the streets to demand an end to poverty, ignorance, and hunger" and his question-cum-invitation to an alter ego, "Will you come and protest with me?" (95). Later, a third of chapter 23 is given over to a tirade against political stagnation, institutional corruption, and police brutality, with Palinuro adopting a rhetoric of denunciation and misplaced confidence, as in the following excerpt:

They are afraid of us, [. . .] they are afraid that we might fuck up their Olympics, they accuse the ill-intentioned agents of exoticism of trying to strip Mexico of its prestige before the attentive eyes and ears of the world, and meanwhile, *I* have seen them, *I* have seen how they manhandled the students and put hoods over their heads and then the soldiers delivered eloquent blows with rifle butts to their ribs and shouted the order to get ready, take aim and fire the salute to the Motherland, because anything is possible in a state of peace. (542)

Ironically, the testimony given by Palinuro turns out to be a prefiguration of his own death from injuries received in a violent confrontation with troops in the Zócalo of Mexico City on the night of 27–28 August 1968. That particular tragedy, recounted in chapter 24 of *Palinuro de México*, provides a dramatic climax to the narrative and constitutes a uniquely powerful and imaginative contribution to Mexican literature on the theme of Tlatelolco.[2]

Entitled "Palinuro on the stairs, or the art of comedy," chapter 24 is unique in casting the events of Tlatelolco and the sacrifice of Mexican youth that occurred there in the dramatic form of the commedia dell'arte. Expanding on Héctor Manjarrez's momentary reference to the commedia dell'arte near the end of chapter 2 of *Lapsus,* Fernando del Paso elaborates a full-scale dramatic narrative that combines historical reality and fantasy, archetype and allegory, in a contrived mosaic of modes and dramatic levels that is explained at the beginning of the performance, in italics:

(Reality is at one remove, toward the rear of the stage. Reality is Palinuro, who started out dragging himself through Charon's Cave, and never got to his feet again. Reality is Palinuro beaten up, on the dirty stairway. It is the bureaucrat, the concierge, the drunken doctor, the mailman, the police officer, Estefanía, and me. This reality is played out in the center of the stage. Dreams, memories, illusions, lies, harmful desires and imaginings, together with the characters from La Commedia dell'Arte: *Harlequin, Scaramouch, Pierrot, Colombine, Pantalone, etc.: these all make up a fantasy. The fantasy, which freezes reality, re-creates it, treats it comically and with pathos, and either imitates it or prefigures it, occurs only in space and not in time. The place allocated to it is the front of the stage.)* (548)

In this two-dimensional space, Palinuro appears both as himself and as Harlequin; Estefanía doubles as Colombine, Walter assumes the character of Pierrot, and a phalanx of protesting students appear simply as "Student

Number One," "Student Number Two," etc. Their principal antagonists are Capitano Maldito and Pantalone, representing the Mexican police and military, who intervene directly in the "simple" storyline of "Palinuro on the stairs . . . Palinuro knocked down by a tank: that's all there is to it! Simple as that!" (551).

At the beginning of the first act, an authorial voice identifies "the date on which events took place" as "Wednesday 28 August," adding disingenuously, "The year [. . .] could have been any year belonging to a familiar past or an invisible future. Let us say—but this is just a manner of speaking—that it is 1968" (552). Thereafter, a plethora of place-names, proper names, incidents, and slogans all specific to the Mexican situation provide constant reminders of the play's historical frame of reference, at the same time that they confirm its fidelity to the events and chronology of the student movement as reflected in chronicles such as *Días de guardar* by Carlos Monsiváis (1970) and the remarkable 1971 volume compiled by Elena Poniatowska under the title "La noche de Tlatelolco: Testimonios de historia oral."[3]

A particularly famous episode, the Silent Protest (la Manifestación Silenciosa) of 13 September 1968, is the model for an "Interlude" sandwiched between acts 3 and 4 of "Palinuro on the stairs, or the art of comedy." Documented in vivid detail by Monsiváis (258–75), this episode links up with other fictional versions of the Silent Protest in works by Arturo Azuela (*Manifestación de silencio,* 1979), Jorge Aguilar Mora (the central chapters of *Si muero lejos de ti,* 1979), and Marco Antonio Campos (*Que la carne es hierba,* 1982). In general terms, Azuela, Aguilar Mora, and Campos adopt an approach that is close to a documentary of lived experience. However, such an approach and aesthetic bear little similarity to the method adopted by del Paso. His "Interlude" transcends the mode of documentary writing, first, through its witty imitation of the commedia dell'arte and, second, through its theatrical use of the visual media of mime, pantomime, and cartoon, which paradoxically attain unexpectedly high levels of verisimilitude in the representation of conflict and repression, even as they render strange those same experiences:

HARLEQUIN PRODUCES ANOTHER BANNER
"Soldier, don't shoot: You too are of the People!"
(Nevertheless, a sign pops out of the barrel of Pantalone's rifle saying, "Bang!" Harlequin takes out another banner.)
HARLEQUIN'S BANNER
"Ouch!"

(He falls down without making a sound. Columbine goes over to Harlequin, strokes his hair, and takes out yet another banner.)
COLUMBINE'S BANNER
  "Farewell!"
DOTTORE TAKES OUT A BANNER
"Sit tibi terra levis . . . which is to say, may the earth rest lightly on you."
(Capitano Maldito and Pantalone lay into Columbine, Pierrot, and Scaramouch with their rifles, their drums, their trumpets, and their fists. Banners of different shapes, sizes, and colors fly through the air, reading, "Wham!" "Smash!" "Bam!" "Crash!" "Take that!" and others: "Ooh!" "Ah!" "Ouch!" (605)

In this passage, techniques of defamiliarization and a language of quotation and onomatopeia achieve a degree of graphic representation equal to that of the most conscientious of documentaries.

Other features of the expressive system of "Palinuro on the stairs, or the art of comedy" include popular *fantasías* and allegory, which create effects of satire and pathos. An example of a *fantasía* is the patchwork interlude, in that part of the play entitled "The Second Floor," in which Capitano Maldito, sleepwalking and wielding a cudgel, beats the stuffing out of a Harlequin figure that is suspended from the ceiling "dressed up as a fat *piñata*" (571–72). Here, traditions of puppetry, the commedia dell'arte, and Mexican popular culture combine to convey a scenario of violence that is made all the more menacing by a reference, carried over from a preceding part of the chapter, to the Big Bad Wolf of the children's song "Jugando al escondite."

The most obvious allegories in the play are the figures of Death and the madre-Patria. The first of these presides over the action of "Palinuro on the stairs," where it appears in an almost infinite number of guises: as a rag-and-bone woman, as the author, and satirically as "Death-His-Most-Serene-Highness-Mr.-President," who is presented as possessing a monstrous ego ("Yo, el Señor Presidente"), soaking up the adulation of fawning subordinates, and giving the order to shoot Mexican students on "the night of a certain Tuesday, 30 July" (581–83). In the context of Mexican writing of the period, the cutting edge of del Paso's satire in this section is matched most closely by René Avilés Fabila in *El gran solitario del palacio* — a novel with which it shares both a sharpness of tone and a very precise set of targets that include the personality and institutional figure of President Gustavo Díaz Ordaz, the complicity of groveling aides (depicted most contemptuously in the opening lines of chapter 6 of *El gran solitario del palacio*), and the worn-out rhetoric of the Partido Revolucionario Institucional, exemplified in "the oratory of the President, sublime on all counts," which in Avilés Fabila's version of events is dependent on electronic prompts, grotesque histrionics, and subliminal threats for its impact on a shamefully passive audience (Avilés Fabila 48). Notwithstanding the fact that it is constructed on a smaller scale than *El gran solitario del palacio*, Fernando del Paso's satire of President Díaz Ordaz in "Palinuro on the stairs, or the art of comedy" scores as many points per page as Avilés Fabila in his novel, and it fully exploits the presentation of the president as the personification of death and corruption.[4]

Compared with the figure of Death, "The voice of the motherland, our poor, unfortunate motherland!" (617) is a less original but no less eloquent allegorical cipher. Identified at the level of plot with one of Palinuro's neighbors ("the woman who lives in number fifteen"), the voice speaks for all those mothers who lost a son or daughter in the indiscriminate repression of the Mexican student movement of 1968. Through her plaintive cry, "Oh, my children, oh, my children!" (617) she clearly evokes the widely represented Mexican type of La Llorona—featured in a popular film of that title made in 1933, for example, and subsequently granted a double mention in *Noticias del imperio* (175, 551). In the contemporary sphere, the voice of the wailing woman chimes in with that of another mother, mentioned in *Que la carne es hierba* by Marco Antonio Campos, "who had gone onto a balcony to say that her son had been killed" (80). Acting as part of a chorus, it laments the wasted lives and crushed dreams of Mexican youth whose collective idealism and sacrifice are personified in characters like Palinuro and, from *Que la carne es hierba*, Fernando— a victim, at nineteen, of the state's intolerance of a younger generation's "rare and beautiful dream" (72). Also found in other Mexican writing of the moment (most powerfully in Poniatowska 164), this elegiac mood is particularly strong in *Palinuro de México* and *Que la carne es hierba*, where it signals a common sensibility and shared perspective on suffering that are grounded in humanism.

Human sentiment and values inevitably provide the driving force behind the political chapters of del Paso's novel, where they take the form of an ethical imperative to bear witness to intolerance and repression and to keep alive the memory of injustice: "It's simply a matter of not forgetting," Palinuro bluntly tells an interlocutor, agreeing with Pablo of *Que la carne es hierba* that the tragedy of 1968 "must not be forgotten" (Campos 101). This injunction is similar to the declaration made by Felipe, the writer in

El gran solitario del palacio: "It's a matter of denouncing and making a protest: some of us choose not to remain silent in the face of repression" (118). Valid for the entire body of writing known as "Tlatelolco literature," Felipe's declaration serves especially well as a motto for del Paso's satirical project in "Palinuro on the stairs, or the art of comedy." Beyond the limits of that chapter, the mood of levity and satire couples with a range of humanist concerns voiced elsewhere by Elena Poniatowska, Marco Antonio Campos, and Rosario Castellanos, and produces a tonal amalgam that ultimately distinguishes *Palinuro de México* from all other major works of Mexican literature of the time.

The Nation and Beyond: Archetypes, Intertexts, and the "Mexicanization" of *Ulysses*

> In general terms [and in contrast to the United States of
> America], the mind-set of this America of ours seems to find in
> European culture an attitude to all that is human which is more
> universal, more basic, and more akin to our own sensibility. [. . .]
> The American mind is called on to perform the noblest function
> of complementarity: that of establishing syntheses.
> Alfonso Reyes, "Notas sobre la inteligencia americana"

Taken en bloc, the main strands of the narrative of *Palinuro de México* address themes and issues whose cultural referents belong to a variety of spheres ranging from the local and the national (for example, the immediate political realities of 1968 in Mexico City) to the universal (for example, matters to do with Oedipal anxiety, the body, and the double). The generic variety of the writing (satirical, picaresque, parodic, etc.) further emphasizes the many sides of del Paso's text, the surface texture of which displays little apparent uniformity or unity. The multiple modes and agendas of *Palinuro de México* nevertheless achieve a perceptible resolution at the level of narrative structure, where they fit into an orchestrated design whose principal characteristics are repetition and symmetry, and a systematic exploitation of archetype and myth that grounds the text firmly in the realm of the universal.

The division of the text into two main parts translates its overt preoccupation with doubleness into formal terms and allows for patterns of repetition as shown in the incorporation of references to an autopsy or to a narrative voyage in both halves of the novel, and the allocation, in each part, of a complete chapter to Walter and a section of another to the members of Palinuro's larger family; in most cases, the reprise that activates a repetition allows for an expanded treatment of a character or theme already mentioned in the first part of the novel. While the design of *Palinuro de México* is admittedly not as symmetrical as that of *José Trigo,* it exhibits a similar degree of deliberate contrivance and consistency with the principal thematic concerns explored in the book.

The attention given in the opening pages of part 2 of *Palinuro de México* to the themes of death and rebirth offers a reflection in miniature of a wider structure of archetypal themes and motifs that holds the entire narrative of *Palinuro de México* together. In its recounting of Palinuro's life and death, the narrative reproduces a standard pattern of human experience comprising initiation and loss of innocence, degradation and isolation, death and apotheosis, rebirth and resurrection. In summary outline, Palinuro—lover, medical student, and political agitator—is initiated into the major biological and sexual mysteries of life; he becomes estranged from his closest friends and dies heroically in a confrontation with security forces in the Zócalo of Mexico City in October 1968. The chapter entitled "Palinuro on the stairs, or the art of comedy" relates with considerable pathos the agony and death of Palinuro and concludes by celebrating his apotheosis "in the burning dawn of the world" (621). That poignant episode, reminiscent of José Clemente Orozco's painting *The Man of Fire,* would seem to complete the narration of the trajectory of Palinuro's experience, the *historia* of his life having come literally to a dead end. However, there remains the final chapter, where Palinuro's grandfather, Francisco, exhorts him in the closing pages: "Come and see how my Homeric breast is full of love for you. [. . .] Come and see yourself being born" (646). Through this apostrophe at the end of the *relato,* the narrative of *Palinuro de México* anticipates Palinuro's acceding to a second birth and thereby promises him a resurrection that had been denied his literary antecedent and namesake, Palinurus, in books 5 and 6 of Virgil's *Aeneid.*

At the same time as it rounds off Palinuro's archetypal trajectory, *abuelo* Francisco's Homeric exhortation evokes a general matrix of classical European literature and mythology that provides a source for numerous details of narrative incident and motif in del Paso's novel. The chapter that relates "Palinuro's Travels around the Advertising Agencies and Other Imaginary Islands" carries echoes of the heroic peripluses of Virgil's Aeneas and Homer's Ulysses, complete with references to "trials, tests, interrogations and examinations that awaited [Palinuro] in life" (210). The topos of the descent to the underworld is featured in that section of

chapter 11 which recounts Palinuro's voyage to THE ISLAND OF SPON-
SORED ADVERTISEMENTS. There, in a biting satire of consumerism, Fernando del Paso describes how Palinuro descends to "the hell of torments
suffered by all those who in life had appeared in commercial advertisements declaring I Use Such-and-Such a Product, I Prefer This Other One,
I Consume Another. . . . And he saw there . . . how all those who had ever
recommended a type of food or drink were force-fed through a funnel
with those very same products until they burst" (213–14). The same motif
of the voyage of discovery underlies Palinuro's tour of a hospital in chapter 18, where he witnesses monstrous suffering, and it is also the subtext
of a visit to some underground burial chambers in chapter 23. In the
second of these "adventures," Palinuro is chosen as "the hero whose assignment it was to crawl at midnight through the tunnel . . . that linked an
empty tomb with a section of the old communal grave of the Panteón de
Dolores" (544–45). The final paragraph of the chapter establishes a parallel between Palinuro's underground adventure and the journey of Quetzalcóatl "through Mictlán, the land of the dead" (548), as well as evoking
the Virgilian source for this topos, in the *Aeneid*.

Other episodes in *Palinuro de México* correspond to the ancient rites of
Bacchus, Priapus, and Dionysus. In his role as Palinuro's double, Walter
recalls a visit to a cantina, telling his story with humorous hyperbole that
debases the mythical referent but does not weaken the analogy as such:

> Oh, Estefanía, what a bender we went on that afternoon when I
> walked through the boiling springs of mythology in the warmth of
> a ritual of alcoholic consumption . . . ! Pepes's cantina was like a
> temple. (64)

In addition, chapter 20 recounts an outrageous prank that Palinuro carries
out in the company of his fellow medical students, Molkas and Fabricio.
Baptized "La Priapíada," the operation involves the theft of some male
genitalia from a morgue and their indecent exposure to shocked female
customers at a department store; this juvenile episode is followed by a
contest at *la Española* cantina to discover which of the patrons boasts the
biggest penis, in a second lighthearted homage to Priapus.

Two motifs in particular acquire their fullest significance in the light of
references to classical western literature and mythology. The first of these
is the motif of the unquiet grave and the treatment of "the souls of the
unburied" (162) by the guardian of the morgue known to Palinuro and his
fellow medical students by the nickname "Charon." Already assimilated

into contemporary Latin American fiction through the medium of Gabriel García Márquez in *La hojarasca,* the motif of the unquiet grave derives most notably from Sophocles' trilogy about Antigone and her brother, Polynices, whose corpse was condemned to remain outside the walls of Thebes "unburied and denied the tribute of tears" (García Márquez quoting from *Antigone* in the epigraph to *La hojarasca* 7). A second route of transmission is from books 5 and 6 of the *Aeneid,* where the character Palinurus is also denied a decent burial. Identified in part as a dreamer who allowed himself to be beguiled by sleep at the helm of Aeneas's ship, Palinurus is encoded no less precisely as an archetype of the anguish provoked by a higher authority's refusal to grant a decent burial. This was certainly the construction put on him by Cyril Connolly, who depicted Virgil's Palinurus in *The Unquiet Grave* as "an archetype of frustration" (3), in the process providing Fernando del Paso with a richly detailed blueprint for the delineation of the character of Palinuro and the outline of his experience in the narrative of *Palinuro de México.*[5]

The other motif that reveals its most pointed significance within the broader context of mythological reference in the novel is the comparison of Palinuro and Walter to Castor and Pollux, the sons of Zeus. In Greek mythology, Castor and Pollux achieved a unique kind of immortality whereby each spent alternate days on Olympus and in Hades. In *Palinuro de México,* besides illustrating the category of twins, Castor and Pollux function, as they had in *José Trigo,* primarily as types of immortality and, by implication, as symbols of resurrection who confirm the promise of rebirth held out to Palinuro at the novel's close.

The structural and thematic coherence of *Palinuro de México,* together with its mythical and archetypal scaffolding, narrative exuberance, and message of life sacrificed and then restored, endow del Paso's novel with a composite profile redolent of other texts, both European and American, of which the most canonic and relevant examples are James Joyce's *Ulysses,* Cortázar's *Rayuela,* and, occupying a position of intermediary between those two texts, *Adán Buenosayres* by Leopoldo Marechal. It is my contention that *Palinuro de México* (1977) stands in a relation of direct descent from *Ulysses* (1922), with which it shares numerous features of note; the relation is also mediated via Marechal's novel (which was published in 1948) and via *Rayuela* (1963), both of which can be regarded as source texts of *Palinuro de México.* A checklist of the major properties of Joyce's master text indicates the extent of similarity between the members of this family of texts, at the same time as it confirms *Ulysses* as the prototype of the class:

1. *Ulysses* narrates the secular Odyssey of twentieth- century urban man.
2. It projects contemporary events against a backdrop of mythic and Shakespearean parallels.
3. It cultivates a tone that is mock epic and parodic.
4. While stressing the debasement of traditional standards of heroism, it seeks to redefine heroic values and behavior in the contemporary world.
5. The narrative of *Ulysses* traces a search for psychological and/or spiritual wholeness, and it concludes with a message of affirmation.
6. It incorporates elements of family romance.
7. Among its repertoire of themes are sexual and bodily experience, issues of nationalism and colonialism, history, culture, and morality.
8. *Ulysses* is a laboratory for experimentation with innovative techniques of narration and structure, and a showcase for the display of an almost infinite variety of styles and registers.
9. *Ulysses* aspires to represent a total reality.

This is a paradigm that holds, with local variations, for each of the Spanish American novels under consideration. The example, and indeed the influence, of *Ulysses* is perceptible, first, in *Adán Buenosayres,* which matches the above typology on all nine counts. A battery of themes, narrative situations, episodes, and specific narrative devices identify Marechal's novel quite clearly with Joyce's, as has been noted in a number of comparative studies (de Sola, Gordon, Fiddian). Differences between the texts are also substantial, although they have often been overstated. Marechal himself went to considerable lengths to distance his novel from *Ulysses,* arguing that the only points of convergence between the two books were at the levels of narrative technique and derivation from "the same Homeric source" (Marechal, *Las claves* 20); more crucially, he insisted that *Adán Buenosayres* possesses a spiritual dimension entirely absent from Joyce's novel. While no one would contest the centrality in *Adán Buenosayres* of religious (specifically, Roman Catholic) and spiritual concerns expressed in the course of Adán's nocturnal wanderings and in the pages of his "Cuaderno de Tapas Azules," their denial in *Ulysses* betrays both a blindness to the moral vision enshrined in Joyce's novel—which promotes values of love, charity, and compassion ultimately indistinguishable from "the sweet laws of compassion" subsequently invoked by Adán (853)—and a willful misprision of a precursor text that is symptomatic of psychological and cultural tensions present in some areas of Latin American literature after Joyce. Given the perceptible differences in tone and structure between *Adán Buenosayres* and *Ulysses* (differences accentuated all the more by Marechal's free acknowledgment of the importance of Dante and Quevedo to his literary project), it would surely have been sufficient for Marechal forthrightly to state that his borrowings from *Ulysses* had been limited to an amount of narrative raw material which he then assimilated to a vision and sensibility that were all his own. Yet Marechal felt the need to deny the contribution of James Joyce to the making of *Adán Buenosayres* and in so doing provided a copybook example of the anxiety of influence analyzed by Harold Bloom in a pivotal study of intertextual relations (Bloom 1973).

A possible reason behind Marechal's disavowal of the incontestable may have been his discomfort with Joyce's rebellious political attitudes and heterodox religious views, which would have been difficult to reconcile with his own ex-Peronist's reactionary instincts. Another reason is the perception of Joyce as a synecdoche and symbol of a European aesthetic that was felt in some quarters of Latin America around the midpoint of the twentieth century to be extrinsic and even alien to Latin American culture. Marechal wrote his defense of *Adán Buenosayres* in the mid-1960s, when the influence of James Joyce on Spanish American literature was both active (as demonstrated in the work of Salvador Elizondo and Carlos Fuentes) and a matter of often heated debate. The essay "Las claves de *adán buenosayres*," in which Marechal argued the independence of his novel vis-à-vis *Ulysses,* was the centerpiece of a publication that also contained contributions by Julio Cortázar and Graciela de Sola and, significantly, an essay by Adolfo Prieto that took issue with an interpretation of *Adán Buenosayres* published by Noé Jitrik in 1955. Recapitulating the main points of Jitrik's argument, Prieto wrote:

> Jitrik assumes that the lesson of modernity implicit in the adoption of Joyce as a starting point is compromised in *Adán Buenosayres* as a result of Marechal's prejudices and personal weakness. According to this view, the author's prejudices were threefold: Catholicism, nationalism, and the highly subjective delineation of the characters and "key" episodes [in the narrative of *Adán Buenosayres*]. (33)

Prieto went on to defend Marechal against such attacks, claiming that he had no need whatsoever to learn the "lesson of modernity" that was implicit in Joyce's work and pointing to names within the Spanish literary tradition—Quevedo, Gracián—that could just as readily be regarded as influences and precursors of Marechal. Prieto's position raises all sorts of issues to do with cultural exchange. My point in reproducing his views here is to document the connection, made in cultural debate at the time, between Joyce and a definition of modernity felt to be impertinent to Latin American culture and, in the opinion of hardline skeptics such as Manuel Pedro González, likely to be a hindrance to its progress.

What is pointedly missing in Prieto's essay, and in Marechal's own defense of his novel, is a full-scale celebration of the achievement represented by *Adán Buenosayres*. While the novel demonstrates a spirited appropriation of Homeric and biblical materials and their assimilation to an Argentinian narrative project unified by Catholic beliefs and enlivened by the spirits of comedy and satire, the role of *Ulysses* as mediator and example seems to have inhibited a more wholesome acknowledgment of Marechal's creative achievement. Certainly, the impression derived from a reading of his and Prieto's essays is of two authors who are on the back foot and unable, for whatever reason, to argue the dialectics of cultural appropriation with greater confidence and equanimity. Yet implicit in their stance and in Marechal's novel itself is a statement of differentiation from a donor culture that had provided material for adaptation in a non-European context. Through its negotiation of the influence of *Ulysses* and its domestication of Greek and Christian myths, *Adán Buenosayres* points to ways that an American text might absorb European source material and refashion it in line with the demands of a local sensibility. Notwithstanding the defensive position adopted by one of Marechal's principal apologists and by Marechal himself in a satellite text, his novel anticipates more confident practices of absorption and transformation that will be found in the work of later authors such as Fernando del Paso in *Palinuro de México*.

In point of fact, *Adán Buenosayres* bequeaths a considerable legacy to del Paso, both through the medium of the Joycean paradigm and through the more direct channel of del Paso's firsthand acquaintance with Marechal's work. The nine categories listed previously form the bulk of that legacy, the only substantial point of divergence being the comparative weakness of the message of affirmation articulated in *Adán Buenosayres*, in relation to category five. At the level of detail, references in *Adán Buenosayres* to police torture (526), Castor and Pollux (197–98), and the dissection room (288); a satire of consumerism and sundry human vices in the "infernal descent" of chapter 7; and themes of memory and the grave (582) and the regenerative cycles of nature (632), constitute a fictional world that is the province of both *Adán Buenosayres* and *Palinuro de México*. Two further details cement the relation between the two novels:

the name and associations of Adán's beloved uncle, Francisco—clearly a prototype of Palinuro's grandfather of the same name—and Marechal's own invocation of the myth of Palinurus in the narrative reference to "that ocean over the sound of which you may have discerned the ancient voices of Jason or Ulysses, and on the bed of which, strewn with corals and sponges, there lies to this day the skull of Palinurus—he who fell asleep one night beneath the stars" (575).

Moving on to *Rayuela,* we encounter a text affiliated with several cultural and aesthetic traditions and one that has assimilated the lessons of *Ulysses* into a densely woven fabric from which it is not always easy to tease out individual threads. No less problematically, *Rayuela* is a supremely ironic text that resists univocal interpretation and constantly dismantles its own structures of meaning, seeking to generate a provisional sense that is fluid, open, and figural. Confronted with this model of elusiveness, existing comparisons of *Rayuela* and *Ulysses* have been understandably cautious and circumspect in acknowledging fundamental differences in the conception and circumstances of production of two works separated by several decades of change. Nevertheless, Lida Aronne Amestoy's view of *Ulysses* and *Rayuela* as books that "epitomize two successive stages in the Odyssey of the twentieth century" (31) still holds, bolstered by the explicit mention of *Ulysses* in a passage where Morelli, the author's alter ego, traces the roots of the comic novel back to *Ulysses* (*Rayuela* 454).

Of the nine properties of the Joycean novel identified in our typology, the sixth is lacking in *Rayuela* while the rest of points 1–7 are integrated firmly into its structure. Horacio Oliveira's grappling with the inauthenticity and spiritual emptiness of his life, first in Paris, then in Buenos Aires, is presented as the periplus of a "Hodious Hodysseus" (Hodioso Hodiseo) (450) who also refers to himself mockingly as a "Prodigal Son" (449). Returning to a girlfriend in Buenos Aires who is an ironic counterpart of Penelope in the myth of Ulysses, Horacio-Odysseus subsequently assumes the role of Orpheus (238 and 372) when he goes down into the morgue of a madhouse with Talita, his best friend's partner. Constantly subverted by irony and ridicule, the mythical pattern that subtends Horacio's experience eventually culminates in Oliveira's quite genuine reconciliation with Traveler and Talita at the end of chapter 56. Visualized as the crossing of "a bridge from one man to another" (313), the reconciliation exemplifies the abandonment of worn-out modes of behavior and the embracing of a new humanist ethic based on a revised definition of love, solidarity, and the very Joycean virtue of *caritas*, embodied most wholesomely in *Rayuela* by *la maga* whom Oliveira thinks of as "a good Samaritan" (238).[6]

The spiritual search that configures the narrative of *Rayuela* is bound up with a commitment to collective renewal mirrored in Oliveira's belief that "the problem of reality has to be viewed in collective terms, not merely as the salvation of a chosen few" (507). This, in turn, is inseparable from a sense, also strong in Joyce, of the interrelatedness of human affairs, manifested in patterns of symmetry, repetition, and coincidence that approximate to the status of *figures* and are invested with the power of transcendence. Elaborated most fully in Morelli's notebooks, the concept of the *figura* links *Rayuela* with a number of authors and texts, ranging from *Ulysses* to Borges and Fernando del Paso in *Palinuro de México*.

As well as matching the *Ulyssean* blueprint on all but one of points 1–7, *Rayuela* follows the example of Joyce's systematic experimentation with nonrealist techniques of narration and narrative structure; Cortázar's practice in this regard is consistent with his assessment of "the symphonic enterprise of *Ulysses,* a sort of technical showcase [from which] there derive, either by direct influence or by coincidence, the most significant branches [of nonrealist fiction in the twentieth century]" ("Situación de la novela" 233). Cortázar's fascination with problems of language, his parodying of a range of styles and registers, and his generally playful treatment of language are also part of the Joycean heritage, further enriched, in *Rayuela,* by techniques borrowed from surrealist writing and poetics.

Finally, the aspiration of *Rayuela* to represent a totality through an "accumulation of fragments capable of suddenly crystallizing in a total reality [. . .] which an alert eye would be able to look at through a microscope, there to perceive a large-scale polychrome rose, and to read it like a figure, an *imago mundi* which existed outside the microscope in the form of a living room decorated a la Provençale, or as a gathering of aunts having tea with Bagley biscuits" (533) identifies Cortázar with a family of modern authors, exemplified by Joyce and Borges and including Spanish American writers of the 1960s and 1970s such as Carlos Fuentes, Mario Vargas Llosa, and Fernando del Paso, who were all promoters and practitioners of the "total novel." Though differing in their understanding of this multifaceted concept, the last three authors mentioned share a common debt to James Joyce and a view acknowledging his immense contribution to the phenomenon of the "total novel."[7]

The connections thus documented between *Ulysses* and *Rayuela* help to explain the continuing impact of Joyce on a younger generation of

Spanish American authors including Fernando del Paso and his compatriots Gustavo Sainz (in a novel like *Obsesivos días circulares,* 1969) and Jorge Aguilar Mora (in *Si muero lejos de ti,* 1979). Through *Rayuela,* *Palinuro de México* receives a mediated version of the Joycean paradigm, as well as a specific set of preoccupations and narrative materials that are absorbed directly into the body of del Paso's novel. The most essential elements of the Joycean paradigm that are relayed via *Rayuela* are the mythical structure of the periplus, the quest for renewal represented as a resurrection, reflections on death involving references to the mythological figure of Charon (*Rayuela* 493, 503), and the impulse toward the representation of a total reality. More directly, *Palinuro de México* echoes *Rayuela*'s questioning of the major tenets of western religious and philosophical orthodoxy and repeats many of its linguistic subversions in a spirit akin to Cortázar's repudiation of the *Diccionario de la Real Academia Española* as "undeniably a necropolis" (*Rayuela* 279).

A crucial connection between the two books derives from the inclusion, in both *Rayuela* and *Palinuro de México,* of a narrative sequence set in a hospital or mental asylum that stands as an allegory of the state and/or the human condition. In *Rayuela,* Horacio goes to work in a mental institution in Buenos Aires where distinctions between madness and sanity, and between the world of the asylum and the exterior world of sociopolitical contingency, operate only imperfectly. In an equivalent chapter of *Palinuro de México,* Doctor Palinuro is shown around the wards of a "residence for the sick" by a man who identifies himself at the outset as the "deputy medical director of the hospital" (379) and then confesses at the end of the tour, "I too am a patient. . . . The illness from which I suffer is an illness of the mind, doctor" (427). At the chapter's close, Doctor Palinuro's guide confirms that the hospital is "a symbolic and consequently wretched copy of life" (426), with no dividing line between the wards and the world at large. Conceived in part as a Swiftian satire, the chapter also taps the spirit of *Rayuela,* including the irony of the mention, in fragment 53 of Cortázar's novel, of political instability and undercurrents of violence in Argentinian society in the late 1950s. Just as del Paso, in the pertinent chapters of *Palinuro de México,* implicitly denounces the moral and political sickness affecting Mexican society around 1968, so Cortázar, in the relevant fragments of his novel, views the involvement of the military in Argentinian public life a decade or so earlier as nothing short of political madness.

The complicated set of intertextual parallels and affinities detailed here should suffice to demonstrate the links between *Palinuro de México* and a narrative tradition deriving ultimately from James Joyce's *Ulysses*. Making all reasonable allowances for other influences including those of surrealism (transmitted through the works of Miguel Angel Asturias and Octavio Paz, as well as via Cortázar), Sterne, Swift, Lewis Carroll, and Borges, the relation with Joyce emerges as the dominant genealogical feature of *Palinuro de México*. In del Paso's novel, the Joycean paradigm gives birth to a strongly affirmative text that combines the experimentalism of earlier Mexican "*Ulysseses*" such as *Al filo del agua* (1947) and *La región más transparente* (1958), with the moral outlook of Joyce's novel, and acts as a springboard for the assimilation of *Palinuro de México* to an undifferentiated community of world literature. For that is the ultimate goal and frame of reference of the novel, as becomes clear in the expansive closing pages where Palinuro's grandfather calls on him to summon innumerable authors and characters of world literature to witness the glorious event of Palinuro's second birth:

> Inform Flash Gordon.
> Tell Domingo Gonsales to come back from the moon.
> And Multipliandre to come back from the future.
> Inform the time traveler of H. G. Wells.
> Tell Saint-Menoux and Héctor Servadac.
> Ask Remedios la Bella to descend wrapped in a moon beam.
> Tell Lieutenant Gulliver Jones to come back from Mars on his
> flying carpet.
> Tell Cyrano de Bergerac to bring you a jar in which to store
> Mamma's tears.
> And inform the spirit of Faust as it traverses dimensions of space
> (647).

The infinite spatial and temporal perspective envisioned by Grandfather Francisco is a fitting climax to a chapter that pretends to encompass "All the roses, all the animals, all the town squares, all the planets, all the characters on earth" (622), and bespeaks a total assuredness about the right of *Palinuro de México* to membership in a universal culture.[8]

It is instructive to compare *abuelo* Francisco's untroubled assumption about the relationship between the local and the universal with the attitude of the eponymous narrator of *Adán Buenosayres* on the subject of the imitation of foreign models in Argentine literature. The subject features in the account of Adán's descent to the multitiered hell of Cacodelphia, specifically in that section where Adán stumbles across his literary friend,

Pereda, emprisoned in a "false Parnassus" (890), and defends him against a female tormentor, whom he addresses in the following terms:

> Has it not been claimed that an onerous spirit of imitation of foreign models has been weighing down on our national literature? Don't deny it: that claim has been made! And when a man such as Pereda takes it upon himself to defend the right of *criollo* culture to accede to the universal realm of art, he is subjected to levels of ridicule and abuse that are tantamount to suffering the discomforts of hell. Well, Madame, I take my hat off to our champion. (892)

Essentially, Adán defends Pereda as the champion of local culture (*lo criollo*) who has refused the influence of foreign models and deserves praise for that; Adán also claims that the local has every right to ascend to the level of universal art, and he laments that Pereda should be consigned to hell for his attempts to scale the heights of universal culture. For the purposes of this analysis, what is most interesting about Adán's attitude is (i) its defensive character and foundation in a protectionist mentality, and (ii) its assumption of a hierarchical and quite artificial opposition between the local and the universal. Within a couple of decades, these assumptions would be challenged in Spanish American culture by writers such as García Márquez, who in 1950 openly advocated the incorporation of external, modernizing influences into Spanish American fiction ("¿Problemas de la novela?" 269), and Octavio Paz, who in the same year famously declared that Latin Americans were "for the first time in [their] history, the contemporaries of all men" (Paz, *El laberinto* 340). What is more, under closer scrutiny the prejudices of Adán/Marechal are seen to be nothing other than the symptoms of a negative ideology. When he comes to write *Palinuro de México* in the late 1960s and early 1970s, Fernando del Paso will show that he has clearly transcended Marechal's anxieties concerning influence by foreign models; he will also show that, as far as he is concerned, the local/universal opposition is an outmoded construct that has no useful role to play in debates about culture in Latin America.

The carnivalesque litany of names and titles reeled off at the close of *Palinuro de México* is one instance of del Paso's dismantling of the local/universal opposition. At a more pervasive level, that dismantling is illustrated in the appropriation of the myth of Palinurus for political and ideological purposes that prioritize national imperatives and concerns. *Palinuro de México* takes a minor figure from Virgil who is an icon of distraction and frustration, and expands his semantic range by transforming him into a symbol of political victimization in contemporary Mexico. Palinuro's additional status as, firstly, a type of lost innocence and by the end of the novel, of the promise of rebirth further enhances his profile and permits him to exercise a stronger appeal than Virgil's Palinurus. Del Paso's Palinuro also outstrips the range of significance and archetypal resonances of Adán in *Adán Buenosayres* where the protagonist of Marechal's novel— charged with representing, by synecdoche, important spiritual, psychological, and artistic currents in 1930s Argentina—is invested with considerably less local specificity than Palinuro of Mexico, with the result that he radiates little of the transcendent power of del Paso's protagonist. Measured against Marechal's novel, *Palinuro de México* shows signs of a greater assertiveness and maturity of attitude symptomatic, in part, of the political and cultural environment of Latin America from the 1960s on. On a more personal level, and in psychoanalytical terms, del Paso's free acknowledgment of a multiplicity of "literary father-figures" (Carvajal iii) sets him off as an Oedipus without a complex who is equally at home with authors of European origins—Virgil, Rabelais, Joyce—as with the representatives of a particular American tradition—Borges, Paz, Cortázar. Inscribing himself in a community of authorial relations that is supranational and all-inclusive, he personifies freedom from the anxieties of influence and their associated structures of paternalism and dependency.[9]

Modernism/Postmodernism: Between Paradigms and Politics

> From dependent and imitative, always behind the latest international slogan of the new, Latin America now becomes the precursor of the postmodernist simulacrum in the simulations and dissimulations already contained in the colonial signature that feigned obedience to the European code, while diverting its icons toward alternative messages.
>
> Nelly Richards, "Cultural Peripheries: Latin America and Postmodernist Decentering"

On the subject of its relation to the cultural movements of modernism and postmodernism, *Palinuro de México* shares the dual affiliation of *Ulysses, Rayuela,* and other precursor texts that straddle those two movements. Until the mid-1980s, it was customary to view *Ulysses* as an archetypal product of high modernism (Bradbury and McFarlane; Levitt; and McHale); since then, refinements in the conceptual models used to characterize postmodernism have produced a more nuanced picture of Joyce's novel and its position in literary history. In a lucid analysis, Brian McHale argues the presence of both modernist *and* postmodernist elements in *Ulysses*. Elaborating on existing critical opinion, McHale formulates the view of Joyce's novel as "double, two differentiable texts placed side by side," in which a modernist "norm" established in the first half of *Ulysses* is then exceeded and parodied in the second; these strategies of excess and parody constitute the principal postmodernist element of Joyce's novel, further exemplified in the succession of "disparate discourse worlds" that make up the narrative of the second half of *Ulysses* (McHale 42–58).

The critical consensus about *Rayuela* has undergone a similar evolution, with the orthodoxy of a neohumanist approach exemplified by Graciela de Sola and Lida Aronne Amestoy giving way to the deconstructionist and postmodernist assessments of critics such as Julio Ortega, Jaime Alazraki, Dominic Moran, and Neil Larsen. Writing in 1988, Ortega represented Cortázar as an author who had moved beyond the epistemological and ethical paradigms of both modernism and surrealism to recuperate the iconoclastic potential of an earlier avant-garde whose most radical possibilities had been suppressed and excluded from the modernizing projects of both movements. Referring to *Rayuela,* Ortega observed, "This novel is not just concerned with reforging a critical community with the reader"—as modernist writing had sought to do—"but also with the necessity of transcending the modernist autonomies of the work of art and the corresponding role of the artist as officiating priest, solitary demiurge of his work but likewise guardian of public speech" (198–99). In more precise detail, the use of collage and the transgression of boundaries between disciplines or discourses (for example, literary/journalistic) figure among a repertoire of features of the text of *Rayuela* that match Ortega's model of postmodernism—a model put together with elements taken from a range of sources including Hutcheon and, most pertinently, Hal Foster.

Subsequently, Jaime Alazraki investigated the subject of "La postmodernidad de Julio Cortázar." Discriminating among the critical positions of Douwe W. Fokkema, Hans Bertens, and Linda Hutcheon, Alazraki aligned himself with Hutcheon (who had already claimed the Argentine author for postmodernism in two influential books of 1988 and 1989), and reaffirmed Cortázar's postmodernity on the grounds of (i) his cultivation of textual self-reflexiveness "as a means of sharpening and problematizing the perception of history," (ii) the transgression, in Cortázar's work, of "generic boundaries" (essentially, the blurring of the conventional division between the critical and the creative), and (iii) the presence, in some of Cortázar's writings, of a "process of assimilation and transformation of popular forms [implying] a critique of the art of the academy" (Alazraki 361, 363).

More recently, Dominic Moran and Neil Larsen have expressed dissenting views on the usefulness of relating Cortázar's work to postmodernism. In a brilliant doctoral thesis completed in 1997, Moran applied Heideggerian and Derridean modes of analysis to a vast corpus of Cortázar's fictional production and emphasized the indeterminacy of texts such as *Rayuela* along with their problematic relation to western metaphysics. Around the same time, Neil Larsen reconsidered *Rayuela* from the point of view of a reader possessing a "spontaneous and intuitive sense of the postmodern" and concluded by dismissing the novel as nothing less than a "relic" (58–59). Notwithstanding the rational skepticism of the first commentator and the provocative iconoclasm of the second, I believe that the attribution of Cortázar's work to the category of postmodernism is a valuable refinement to our understanding of the place accorded to novels such as *Rayuela* and *Libro de Manuel* in literary history. Yet it is important to stress that such an identification in no way renders obsolete or untenable the attribution of a text like *Rayuela* to modernism: features including the visionary dimension of that novel, its impulse toward totalization, and its incorporation of a residual humanist ethic anchor *Rayuela* incontestably in the modernist domain and provide a clear illustration of the ambivalence of Cortázar's novel, which combines aspects of a modernist outlook and design with a postmodernist poetics.

A similar diagnosis applies to *Palinuro de México*. Like *Ulysses* and *Rayuela* before it, *Palinuro de México* is assimilable to modernism on the basis of its unreconstructed humanist message, its universalist aspirations, and the totalizing sweep of its narrative arrangement, which is typical of "the resolving urge of modernism" (Hutcheon, *Politics* 99). On the other hand, del Paso's novel displays postmodernist traits of stylistic and modal plurality, narrative indeterminacy, and a multifarious intertextuality that avails itself of "established reputations" (prestigios ajenos) in order to render "a homage to literature through the medium of literature itself" (Trejo Fuentes 7). The refusal of *Palinuro de México* to resolve its constitutive dualities marks it out as a work of transition in the evolution of Spanish American fiction from a modernist paradigm, which flourishes in the 1960s and persists well into the mid-1970s (*Terra nostra* appears in 1975), to a more fully developed strain of postmodernist writing that subsequently comes to predominate in the 1980s and 1990s.

A final consideration regarding *Palinuro de México* stems from the connection between the category of the postmodern and that of the postcolonial. While certainly not synonymous, the postmodern and the postcolonial are homologous, laying claim to common areas of interest as indicated by Elleke Boehmer: "In short, postcolonial and postmodern critical approaches cross in their concern with marginality, ambiguity, disintegrating binaries, and all things parodied, piebald, dual, mimicked, borrowed, and second-hand" (244). The decentering processes that are fundamental to postmodernism also characterize postcolonial discourse, which critiques the authority of a center traditionally invested with power in order to promote the interests of "marginal" cultures and their traditions (see Richards). In *Palinuro de México,* the exploitation of the classical myth of Palinurus and its incorporation into a local narrative of political protest situate the text squarely within the category of the postcolonial. While not representing any radical subversion of the western canon, the adaptation of the myth of Palinurus in del Paso's novel involves the recuperation of a relatively minor figure from classical Roman literature and the full realization of its potential in a contemporary Mexican setting. As already noted, the considerable complexity and the monumental scale of the elaboration of this raw material in *Palinuro de México* are indicative of an attitude of untroubled confidence regarding the European tradition, an attitude which del Paso could discern in the work of any number of contemporary Spanish American writers from Octavio Paz, Augusto Roa Bastos, and Julio Cortázar to Carlos Fuentes, Gabriel García Márquez, and younger writers of subsequent generations. Striking up a confident postcolonial attitude in *Palinuro de México,* del Paso will develop its decentering perspectives, along with those of postmodernism, to an unprecedented degree in his next novel, *Noticias del Imperio* (1987).

4

Noticias del Imperio and the New Historical Novel

> The past is not over and done with; the past must be reinvented
> at every turn to prevent it from becoming fossilized in our hands.
> **Carlos Fuentes, *Valiente mundo nuevo***

> Was I such an extraordinary human being that nobody was able
> to understand or forgive me? Where is my beauty, my youth? Are
> not sixty years spent in darkness, in death, wearing this night-
> marish crown, sufficient for me to be granted a pardon?
> **Empress Carlota, in Rodolfo Usigli's *Corona de sombra***

Noticias del Imperio is a landmark text in del Paso's literary production. Written over a decade during which the Mexican press followed its progress continuously, the novel received immediate critical acclaim on publication in 1987, accompanied by an unprecedented level of commercial success.[1] In terms of its constituent literary features, *Noticias del Imperio* displays numerous continuities with del Paso's two earlier novels: formally, it is as ambitious and elaborate as either *José Trigo* or *Palinuro de México;* the multiple styles and voices that sound throughout *Noticias* carry strong echoes of the discursive variety of *José Trigo,* which had comprised a Bakhtinian plurality of modes and registers, including parody and pastiche; like the preceding texts, *Noticias* gives prominence to certain archetypal motifs; a profuse and highly conspicuous intertextuality is another mark of continuity, featuring a particularly intense dialogue with James Joyce and surrealism; a poetics of resuscitation, or recovery through the word, identifies *Noticias* as a narrative in the mold of both *José Trigo* and *Palinuro de México;* no less significantly, the presence of a totalizing consciousness refers back to preceding novels by the author, as does the articulation of an attitude of moral concern vis-à-vis the subject of *Noticias.* Yet, for all these points of contact with the earlier novels, *Noticias* diverges radically from both *José Trigo* and *Palinuro de México.* It aligns itself with certain principles of deconstruction and a postcolonial view of relations between the nations of Europe and their former colonies, and it incorporates a postmodern aesthetic and epistemology that together inter-rogate categories such as those of History and the Subject—categories essential to the ideology of humanism which had underpinned the narra-tives of *José Trigo* and *Palinuro de México*. In its attitudes, specifically, to history and to the representation of historical events in works of fiction, *Noticias* displays many of the characteristics of the mode of writing com-monly labeled "postmodern historiographic metafiction." In these re-spects, and in its thoroughgoing critique of discourses of power and hier-archy, *Noticias* emerges as a classic text of the 1980s which contests the cultural paradigms that had long held sway throughout Mexico, Latin America, and the West generally.

Given the dramatic swerve away from many of the assumptions on which the two previous novels by del Paso had rested, this chapter will concentrate on those aspects of *Noticias del Imperio* which constitute the most significant shifts of emphasis and innovation in the aesthetic and ideological construction of the text. A brief survey of the narrative content of *Noticias* prepares the ground, in section ii, for a detailed examination of the many-sided critique of imperialism that is conducted in the text. In section iii, attention shifts from the theme of history to the theory and practice of historiography that underpins *Noticias;* issues treated include the inscription of the referent, the function of archetypes, the challenge to totalizing models of consciousness, and the place of morality in the narra-tive representation of history. In a final section, I compare *Noticias* with other Mexican and Latin American novels on historical subjects, identify-ing features that are common to a number of works and, through a differ-ential lens, highlighting aspects of *Noticias* that may be considered distinc-tive; an approach through intertextuality helps to define the place that del Paso's third novel occupies in a number of literary contexts ranging from contemporary continental writing to the author's fictional production as a whole.

Noticias del Imperio and the Narrative of Empire

> If there is a history bathed in blood, outrages and injustices,
> that is the history of Europe.
> Gabriel García Márquez, *El general en su laberinto*

The subject of *Noticias del Imperio* is the short-lived empire of Archduke Maximilian of Austria and Princess Charlotte of Belgium, who between

1864 and 1867 reigned as emperor and empress of Mexico. From a perspective beginning in the 1830s and concluding in 1927, the narrative also traces the evolution of the entire political order of Europe both at home and overseas in parts of Africa, Asia, and the Americas. In terms of formal organization, the text of *Noticias* comprises twelve monologues of Princess Carlota that make up the odd-numbered chapters, alternating with eleven chapters, each of which is subdivided into three sections containing material presented by a coordinating narrator; that material provides observations on historical events viewed from a number of perspectives; the coordinating narrator stands outside the realm of the mimesis occupied by the characters of the novel and makes various kinds of diegetic utterances which, as well as passing judgment on individuals and events, also foreground the discursive conventions of narration and historiography.

The binary pattern that governs the organization of the novel's twenty-three chapters throws certain contrasts into relief. Of these, the dominant opposition is between the Americas and Europe, with France and Mexico offering a particularly pointed contrastive pairing; divergent perspectives on political issues are conveyed sharply through the novel's binary structure. The ternary pattern that is common to all of the even-numbered chapters also brings out certain contrasts of theme and ideology, and it is mirrored at the macro level in the attention that the narrative devotes to three principal players in the story of Mexico's brief empire. Thus, the monologues of Carlota present the reader with a reconstruction of events from a perspective of all-embracing madness, whose temporal point of reference is the year 1927, when Carlota finally died after enduring sixty years of mental estrangement and physical reclusion in the castle of Bouchout in Belgium. The circumstances under which Maximilian of Austria accepted the Mexican throne, his installation, early policy initiatives, the decline in his political fortunes, and his death by firing squad on El Cerro de las Campanas, Querétaro, on 19 June 1867 are related in the even-numbered chapters, through a variety of narrative forms (ranging from monologue and dialogue to the imitation of court tittle-tattle) and several narrators (e.g., a typesetter, a street vendor, and an anonymous soldier). These chapters, which are in the hands of the coordinating narrator, follow a chronological progression that is consistent with narrative modes of history.

The life and political career of a third protagonist, Benito Juárez, is also dealt with in the even-numbered chapters, through the medium of dialogue and in the author-narrator's discourse, which culminates in an imaginative re-creation of the scene of Juárez's agony and death on 18 July

1872. The place of this event in the narrative scheme of *Noticias* underscores the equality of status conferred on the three main protagonists in Fernando del Paso's fictional history of Mexican affairs between 1861 and 1872: occupying the opening ten pages of the final even-numbered chapter, the narration of Juárez's death is placed alongside a slightly longer section—entitled "El último de los mexicanos"—which is devoted to Carlota, and then matched by a ten-page section in honor of Maximilian that seeks to perform an act of reparation via an ingeniously conceived "Ceremonial para el fusilamiento de un Emperador" (etiquette for the shooting of an emperor). The climactic gathering together of the three characters at this point indicates the importance of their interrelationships within the narrative design and overall structure of meaning elaborated in *Noticias*.

The triple focus on Carlota, Maximilian, and Benito Juárez lends particular acumen and depth to the novel's explorations of four themes: the experience of empire, the concept of history, the critique of ideologies connected with the foregoing, and ethical issues left unresolved in the Mexican conscience after the deaths of Maximilian and Carlota. The first of these areas seems almost too obvious to require comment. Yet the preponderance in the critical bibliography devoted to *Noticias* of studies whose main interest is in metafictional and poetic dimensions of the text (see, e.g., Menton 81–94; González, "*Noticias del Imperio* y la historiografía postmodernista") has resulted in the comparative neglect of the theme of empire in del Paso's novel, overlooking what from the perspective of literary history is one of the most important aspects of *Noticias* vis-à-vis Spanish American novels of preceding decades, namely, its restoration of an ultimate referent: the historic empire of Maximilian. Sent by Napoleon III, French, Belgian, and Austrian troops arrived in Mexico in 1862, spent several years fighting against Republicans loyal to the constitutional president of Mexico, Benito Juárez, and eventually abandoned the emperor to his fate in Querétaro before returning to Europe in 1867.[2]

A precise focus on imperialism is established in *Noticias* in Carlota's opening monologue:

> I am Maria Carlota of Belgium, empress of Mexico and America. I am Maria Carlota Amelia, cousin of the queen of England, Grand Master of the Cross of Saint Charles and Vicereine of the provinces of Lombardoveneto, which were taken under the wing of the two-headed eagle of the House of Habsburg through the mercy and clemency of Austria. I am Maria Carlota Amelia Victoria, the daughter of Leopold, the prince of Saxe-Coburg and king of Belgium. [. . .] I

am Maria Carlota Amelia Victoria Clementina Leopoldina, the niece of Prince Joinville and the cousin of the count of Paris, sister of the duke of Brabant who was king of Belgium and conqueror of the Congo. (13)

In these lines, the incremental list of titles and family relationships serves most visibly to confer status and identity on Princess Carlota. At the same time, by asserting her connection with the most powerful royal families and imperial dynasties of Europe, it also presents Carlota as a synecdoche of them and invites the reader to construe her as a symbol of European imperialism.

Mention of the conquest of the Congo at the end of the quotation draws attention to the most violent actions and consequences of empire, which are expanded on in the following chapter where a narrator who possesses almost encyclopedic knowledge of the history of European colonialism cites "the military alliances, the imperialist expeditions, and the colonial wars" exported by Napoleon III to areas of North Africa, Indochina, Russia, and Syria (40), and anticipates the account, in a later chapter, of "unspeakable atrocities" (633) committed by Leopold II in the colonizing of the Congo and the plundering of its rich rubber reserves. Mindful of the suffering of "millions of human beings whose tragedy goes unacknowledged because it cannot be quantified" (635) and whose plight recalls that of "the wretched of the earth" championed by Frantz Fanon in a seminal text of 1961,[3] the author-narrator acknowledges the effects of imperialism on subjugated peoples in general and establishes the global coordinates within which the imperial adventure of Maximilian and Carlota was framed.

Significantly, a substantial part of the second chapter of *Noticias* is devoted to an imaginative re-creation of powermongering in mid-nineteenth-century Europe. Del Paso shows a particular interest in exploring the mind-set of the political classes of the time: the assumptions, interpretive schemes, and ethnocentric prejudices that lay behind the overt practices of colonialism and empire radiating from power centers such as London, Paris, and Vienna. The foundation stone of the worldview of those classes was the absolute conviction of their role as bearers of the values of civilization, including "the principles of morality and justice" (595) proclaimed by Napoleon III at the inauguration of the Universal Exhibition of 1867 in Paris. A corollary of that exalted self-image was a haughty contempt for "those poor countries in Spanish America [and elsewhere] that live in a permanent state of revolution" (49) and whose perceived backwardness and instability rendered them vulnerable to military invasion and colonial occupation.

At an abstract level, the assimilation of non-European territories to the European order is guaranteed by the mental operation (itself the effect of ideology) that domesticates the Other by means of comparisons with the already familiar. Examples of this hermeneutical operation abound in the three-part correspondence—which is entirely fictional—between two French brothers, Alphonse and Jean Pierre, over the time that the latter spends with the French troops in Mexico. A privileged vehicle for the transmission of news from the empire, the letters sent home by Jean Pierre convey information to his civilian brother about the conduct and social customs of the occupying forces, among whom it becomes fashionable to compare Mexican cities with those of Europe. According to Jean Pierre, "It is widely held that Xochimilco is the Venice of America, San Angel the Aztec Compiegne, Cuernavaca the Fontainebleau of Mexico, the city of León the Manchester of the New World, [. . .] the Castle of Chapultepec the Schönbrunn of Anahuac," etc. (402–3). A particularly interesting comparison is that made by a European powermonger at a fancy-dress ball held in the Tuilleries before Maximilian and Carlota depart for Mexico. Wearing the attire of a Venetian nobleman and addressing a guest disguised as a Roman senator (who is ultimately revealed to be Prince Richard Metternich), the character remarks, "We'll transform Mexico into a new Liberia" (51)—a statement which effectively condemns Mexico to a double alienation, forcing it into a category of territories whose erstwhile identities have been erased and overwritten with a name coined by a foreign power.

In this conscientious depiction of the ideological, linguistic, psychological, and political workings of empire, the presentation of Maximilian is a major concern. The novel acknowledges the political considerations that persuaded Maximilian to overcome initial reservations and to go ahead and accept the title and role of emperor of Mexico. It also takes account of psychological and ideological factors that may have influenced Maximilian, and it delves into the complex and contradictory character of a historical figure who could be considered the victim of circumstances that he was ultimately unable to control and who, on the other hand, was undeniably the architect of his own tragic destiny. As the narrator explains, Maximilian had always dreamed "of one day becoming an emperor on a grand scale: another Rudolph II, who surrounded himself with dwarves, painters, and silver-nosed astronomers; another Maximilian I, paragon of nobility, patron of the arts, a man of the Renaissance; [. . .] finally, another Charles V of Germany and I of Spain who, after he had governed half the globe, retired to a monastery where he could build clocks, eat ostrich eggs and contemplate his own burial casket" (198).

Benito Juárez's 1861 decision to suspend payments of the interest on Mexico's foreign debt gave Napoleon III an excuse to send an occupational force to Mexico. It also gave Maximilian the opportunity to make his private dream come true. Once in Mexico, Maximilian would be able to devote himself to the affairs of state and embark on a civilizing mission involving economic projects (for example, the development of the cotton and sugar industries) and the fine arts, thereby demonstrating the profoundly humanitarian orientation of his imperial regime. For, as the section entitled "El Emperador en Miravalle" informs us, such was the conception that Maximilian had of his role and of that of the administration around him. However, it is not difficult for readers today to see the extent to which Maximilian was acting out the combined programs of two ideologies that were prevalent in Europe in the second half of the nineteenth century: the ideology of liberal humanism, with its commitment to progress, education, sensibility, and the like (see Davies), and that of enlightened despotism, founded on a philosophy of paternalistic control. Underpinning both of these is a philosophy of history that the narrative of *Noticias del Imperio* identifies with European imperialism of the nineteenth century and traces to the work of Fichte and Hegel, among others.[4]

That attribution takes place in the second section of chapter 6, during a conversation between Benito Juárez and his secretary about the ideology of the Habsburg dynasty:

The Germans are a people fed on dangerous theories of racial superiority and mastery of the world. Have you read Fichte, Señor Secretario? A great philosopher, certainly, but one who instilled in the minds of German autocrats the idea that, following Bonaparte's betrayal of the ideals of the French Revolution, the Germans were better equipped than the French to lead humanity to the fulfillment of those ideals. The absurdity of this is clear from the fact that shortly after Fichte, Hegel deified the State, but really only succeeded in deifying tyranny. . . . What I ask myself is: how can a person like the Archduke, who you claim is essentially "liberal," reconcile the idea of the State as a social contract based on popular consensus, with the mystical conception of the State? It would seem impossible, don't you think? And yet it is possible, and I'll tell you why: because people like that are capable of betraying everything for the sake of ambition, and that includes betraying themselves. (157)

Beginning as a generalized discourse on the subject of the Habsburg Empire (156), the passage evolves into a series of criticisms of individual members of the dynasty and makes no exception of Maximilian in its blanket denunciation of the tainted practitioners of theories of world mastery.

The main obstacle to Napoleon III and Maximilian's political designs on Mexico was Benito Juárez, who is called upon in the novel to communicate a set of pungent observations about empire, relations between the Americas and Europe, and the subject of history. More precisely, Benito Juárez embodies anti-imperialist and anti-Eurocentric attitudes that are consistent with the postcolonial thinking of a later age and formally identical to views expressed by Fernando del Paso while he was writing his novel.

The essence of President Juárez's political stance is distilled in conversations that he has with his private secretary. In the following excerpt, the two men discuss Maximilian's ambition to found an empire stretching from Mexico to El Cabo de Hornos:

"Just imagine, the immodesty of it: What Bolivar could not achieve, an Austrian has the temerity to set as his goal."

"Quite so, Señor Presidente. . . ."

"But that attitude merely reflects the eternal arrogance of the Europeans. The idea that the people of Japheth are destined to govern the world, 'to share out the islands of nations,' as it says in Genesis, if I remember correctly.[5] Since time immemorial, they have claimed the right to draw and redraw the political map of the continents . . . including their own. The right to divide the world up among themselves: take the Treaty of Tordesillas, the Treaty of Utrecht, and so on. Have you, Señor Secretario, ever stopped to think why the Near East came to be called 'near' and the Far East 'far'?"

"Because they are near and far, Don Benito. . . ."

"Near and far in relation to where? Well, in relation to Paris, Madrid, London, and Vienna. The point is that they are neither near nor far in relation to themselves. Do you understand what I am saying? History has been measured with one yardstick: the rod of iron with which the European has subjugated other nations. . . ."

"You are right, Don Benito." (327)

The passage denounces a secular attitude of arrogance toward non-European peoples and exposes the geopolitical pretensions of generations of architects of European foreign policy. In respect of the latter, Benito Juárez's thoughts duplicate those of Fernando del Paso in the course of the speech that he delivered in Caracas on accepting the Premio Rómulo Gallegos for 1982. Referring to the arbitrary process whereby "the continent of Latin America [. . .] has often disappeared from view over long periods, and reappeared only when the greed or animosity of a European country has been awakened," and with the military and naval conflict between the United Kingdom and Argentina over the Islas Malvinas in mind, del Paso commented:

> One of its reappearances on the map occurred just a few weeks ago, with the outbreak of the war of the end of the world. The end of the world is exactly that: its end, not its beginning, because, just as man is the measure of all things, so for many centuries European man wielded the rod of iron with which he measured the history and geography of our planet. That is how he came to discover America, without giving any thought to the fact that America had been discovered originally by the Americans. That is how he gave the "Far" East its name: on the grounds that it is far from Europe, from the Meridian of Greenwich, and from the metre rule made of platinum which [. . .] is preserved in the [Conservatoire National des Arts et Métiers] in Paris. ("Mi patria chica" 159)

In a broader context, the fictional Juárez's remarks also chime in with the pronouncements of two influential critics of imperialism, Antonio Gramsci and Gabriel García Márquez. Gramsci discusses western naming of the East in *Prison Notebooks:* "Obviously East and West are arbitrary and conventional, that is historical, constructions, since outside of real history every point on the earth is East and West at the same time. . . . Japan is the Far East not only for Europe but also perhaps for the American from California and even for the Japanese himself, who, through English political culture, may then call Egypt the Near East" (447). The link with García Márquez revolves around a shared image and argument in the Colombian author's speech on accepting the 1982 Nobel Prize for Literature in Stockholm in December 1983. On that occasion, García Márquez took advantage of a unique opportunity to plead the cause of the peoples of Latin America before a captive European audience. Emphasizing the magnitude and number of difficulties faced by his fellow Latin Americans, the author of *Cien años de soledad* commented:

If these difficulties hold us back, [. . .] it is not hard to appreciate that the mental talents of this side of the world, in ecstatic contemplation of their own cultures, have found themselves without a valid means of interpreting us. It is understandable that they should insist on measuring us with the same yardstick that they apply to themselves, without recalling that the ravages of life are not the same for all, and that the search for one's own identity is as arduous and as bloody for us as it was for them. To interpret our reality with the aid of schemas that are alien to us only has the effect of making us even more unknown, even less free, even more solitary. (*La soledad de América latina* 8–9)

Masterful in its initial irony, the excerpt exploits the paradigmatic image of the yardstick to argue a geopolitical thesis identical to that formulated by Fernando del Paso in the fictional dialogue of Benito Juárez and his secretary and in the text of "Mi patria chica, mi patria grande."

The theme of relations between Europe and America receives considerable attention in that section of the narrative which introduces Benito Juárez to the reader. Treated under several aspects, the Europe/America theme establishes further links with the work of other intellectuals from Martí through Carpentier, of whom the most important in this connection is the veteran Mexican essayist Leopoldo Zea. As early as chapter 2, the narrator-author of *Noticias del Imperio* uses Juárez and Napoleon III, known as "Mostachú," as contrasting terms in a study of political personalities, ideologies, and reputations. In alternating paragraphs, Benito Juárez's humble origins and early commitment to liberalism are contrasted with Mostachú's aristocratic connections and his youthful credentials as "a kind of socialist à la Saint-Simon" (31). Adopting a more explicitly judgmental tone, the narrative then records the most controversial steps taken during Juárez's tenure of the presidency to reduce the power of the Catholic Church and liberalize religion in Mexico:

As a consequence of his audacity, Juárez came to be considered by Mexican and European conservatives and, needless to say, by the Vatican and Pope Pius IX—who would eventually establish the dogma of Papal Infallibility—as a sort of Antichrist. And because he was not white and of European stock, because he did not match the archetype of the fair-skinned Aryan who represented the highest form of humankind according to Count Gobineau in his "Essay on the Inequality of Human Races" published in Paris in 1854, and, finally, because he was not even a half-caste *mestizo*, Juárez, the shifty Indian, was viewed by the monarchs and champions of the Old World as completely incapable of governing a country which seemed inherently ungovernable anyway. (32)

On this account, an Old World cocktail of racist prejudice and ethnocentric arrogance was simply waiting to be stirred up by the *zapoteca*-speaking, dark-skinned Benito Juárez, provoking a flurry of accusations which, viewed objectively, were disproportionate to any harm done to European interests in Mexico and which hypocritically ignored the far more substantial political failings of Louis Napoleon, including his abuses of the political system and people of France after 1851.

The contrasting perceptions of the "instability," "degeneracy," "corruption," and "weakness" of the Mexican people (33), on the one hand, and the values of French "order" and "civilization" (42), on the other, evoke the standard nineteenth-century opposition, which dominated both European "Orientalist" and Spanish American thinking of the time, between *civilización* and *barbarie*. Happily, at various levels of Fernando del Paso's narrative, that opposition is reversed and shown ultimately to rest on a prior assumption of European superiority. One of the most loaded binaries in western thought is thus dismantled, as part of a critical project that coincidentally overlaps with that of Leopoldo Zea in *Discurso desde la marginación y la barbarie* (Discourse from the site of marginalization and barbarism).

The backbone of Zea's 1988 book is a critique and history of British, Russian, and Spanish imperialism, including chapters on the philosophical (largely Hegelian) underpinnings of Eurocentrism, and the clashes between native and Hispanic civilizations in Spanish America. Essentially, Zea sets out to argue the relativity of the terms *bárbaro* and *barbarie* and to assert the rights of people living on the margins against the claims to hegemony of those grounded in the center. Of particular interest to this study are some brief remarks made by Zea in a section subtitled "La barbarie europea y América," about the French invasion of Mexico and the contemporary reaction of Gabino Barreda, author of an "Oración cívica" delivered in Guanajuato on 16 September 1867. On that historic occasion, Barreda told his audience: "In this conflict between European backwardness and American civilization, in the head-on clash between the principles of monarchy and republicanism, in the final struggle of fanaticism against emancipation, Mexican republicans were ranged alone against the entire world." Barreda further depicted "the aggression of the Europe of Napoleón III" as "the very negation of the civilized values now embodied in America." Over a hundred years later, Zea depicted that episode of Mexican history in similar terms, as a popular rejection of "the aggressive civilization of Europe" (*Discurso* 55–56).

Zea's and Barreda's appropriation of the term *civilización* for America and the attribution of backwardness and *barbarie* to a European power are open to several interpretations, which are largely dependent on historical point of view. From the perspective of the moment of its enunciation, Barreda's reversal is a fascinating instance of a rhetorical "fighting back" on behalf of a people who had gained their independence from Spain some fifty years earlier and who now saw their national territory, already eroded by North American expansionism, invaded by a no less alien imperial power. From the perspective of Zea's and del Paso's later re-creation of the Mexican experience of occupation, Barreda's rhetorical turning-of-the-tables anticipates postcolonial strategies of contestation and decolonization of the mind, which Zea had advocated several decades before the composition of his and del Paso's texts in such essays as "North America in the Spanish American Consciousness" (1947) and "Colonization and Decolonization of Latin American Culture" (1970). There are, admittedly, grounds for arguing that the continuing deployment of the terms *civilización* and *barbarie* in an adversarial relationship preserves intact a hierarchical code that deserves to be completely dismantled. Against that view, and at least as far as the novel by del Paso is concerned, the reversal of the assumptions on which the "civilización-barbarie" opposition was originally constructed serves to lay bare the fundamental asymmetry of a scheme that was heavily distorted by ethnocentric prejudice, and it does so in a way that is entirely consistent with the anti-imperialist thesis put forward in the pages of *Noticias del Imperio*.

Turning back to Benito Juárez, it is evident that his characterization is enhanced by contrasts with a number of historical figures, including the emperor Maximilian and former Mexican president López de Santa Anna, besides Napoleon III. Juárez's rejection of pomp, his reverence for the law, and his professed "respect and admiration for life" (328) contribute to the portrait of a man of strong moral principles who believed in absolute values and felt a peculiar, almost reverential sense of responsibility before history. A crucial document in this last regard is the letter that Juárez sent to Maximilian on the emperor's arrival in Mexico City. As the narrator informs us:

> The letter had been written in the city of Monterrey, and in one of its final paragraphs it contained the following: "Sire, men are free to trample on the rights of others, seize their property, take the lives of

those who defend their nationality, and depict their virtues as criminal and one's own vices as positively virtuous; but there is one thing which cannot be touched by human perversity, and that is the terrible judgment of History. *She will pass judgment on us all.*" (261)

The letter expresses the view of history as the ultimate arbiter of the morality of human conduct. Taking the place of divine authority, history becomes the agent of ultimate judgments—a Transcendental Signified whose universal status is signaled by the initial capital *H* in the president's script. Awe of "the terrible judgment of History" inspires Benito Juárez up to the moment of his death and sticks in the mind as a powerful and defining feature of his characterization.

The view of history as external agent is also articulated by Carlota in the closing paragraphs of her first monologue, where she holds history to be responsible for her husband's death: "History, which left you stretched out and bleeding to death on the Cerro de las Campanas with your waistcoat on fire and left you hanging by your feet from the dome of the Chapel of San Andrés" (27). Carlota's recriminations against history thus conceived are but a small element in her overall characterization, which involves a broader and more complex identification with history and empire, as well as a critique of the related notion of the sovereign subject.

The character of Carlota in *Noticias del Imperio* is a creative amalgam of a precise historical referent and a fictional consciousness described variously as "poetic" (Inés Sáenz 172), "oracular" (Roberto González Echevarría 183), "omnipotent" (Vicente Quirarte 141), and "hallucinatory" (Claude Fell, "Historia y ficción" 85). Sometimes lucid, sometimes mad, Carlota's mental state crystallizes in a discourse of contradiction and desire reminiscent of Breton, Joyce (cf. Anna Livia Plurabelle in *Finnegans Wake*), and Carlos Fuentes (cf. la Dama Loca of *Terra nostra*). As far as ideological implications are concerned, Carlota's madness places a question mark over the category of the sovereign subject, which she literally personifies. Throughout her monologue she insists on her status as princess and empress. Her dominant position in the structure of the narrative, and her insistent use of the first-person form of the verb, are the outward signs of a subjectivity that is self-assured and in command. Yet the contradictions and instability that typify Carlota's discourse point directly to a rift in her consciousness and, beyond that, to fissures in the ideology of the subject.

The statement "History and I, Maximilian, who are both alive and mad" (27) confirms this view, while adding further dimensions to Carlota's character. Essentially, the pattern and duration of the empress's life make her a metonym of the experience of a hundred years: "I am [. . .] the widow of a century that died of old age, the widow of an empire that was left orphaned" (410). By virtue of her fabulous memory and obsessive recall, Carlota embodies "the living memory of a century, frozen in an instant" (362), and she seeks tirelessly to re-create and make sense of events that occurred between approximately 1840 and 1927. In the context of del Paso's fiction, Carlota is the latest instance of a totalizing consciousness that had presided over the narratives of both *José Trigo* and *Palinuro de México*. There is, however, a significant difference between Carlota's narration and the totalizing operations of earlier works. In *José Trigo* and *Palinuro de México,* the panoramic vision of narrators and characters such as *abuelo* Francisco had sought to encompass a field of cultural landmarks that were devoid of explicit political meaning, whereas in *Noticias* Carlota's consciousness is identified precisely with the political and territorial ambitions of empire and the mind-set of imperialism. Through the inherent extravagance and mobility of her range of reference, Carlota offers a hyperbolic and parodic representation of the Hegelian view of European expansion already discussed in relation to Emperor Maximilian, investing her with a key role in the novel's repudiation of the ideology of empire.

Two quotations from Carlota's concluding monologue illustrate forcefully the political connotations of her character. In the first quotation, Carlota expresses the desire to be Mexican and insists on presenting herself as "Mamá Carlota, mother of all Indians and of all *mestizos,* mother of all the whites and *cambujos,* of all the blacks and *saltapatrases*. I am Mamá Carlota, mother of Cuauhtémoc and La Malinche, of Manuel Hidalgo and Benito Juárez, of Sor Juana and Emiliano Zapata. Because I am as Mexican [. . .] as them all" (664). The passage begins as a fantasy, with Carlota casting herself in the image of the archetypal Mother of the Nation. She claims to offer a racial synthesis of the Mexican people, and then names a string of national celebrities, all of whom she assimilates to her archetypal persona. On a personal and psychological level, Carlota's fantasy undoubtedly expresses a desire for children and family of her own, in a vein of feeling with which the reader can readily empathize. At the same time, on a more controversial political level her words bespeak the attitude of indiscriminate possession and control of a sovereign toward the subjects of her realm: through the workings of her imagination Carlota seeks to subsume all *mexicanos* under a single totalizing principle analogous to the Hegelian paradigm of all-inclusive consciousness. The negative implications of this characterization are reinforced in the conclusion to her discourse, where Carlota boldly lays claim to Mexican nationality. Given her European stock and upbringing, Carlota's self-identification as Mexican is both logically preposterous and, from an ideological perspective, as reprehensible as European imitations of Mexican custom and dress dismissed earlier by Benito Juárez as pretentious and "absurd" (318).[6]

The second quotation takes the form of a list of territories that Carlota promises to Maximilian. Ranging over the entire geography and history of Latin America, the list is a striking hyperbole of imperial possession:

> I am going to give you Mexico. I am going to give you America. I am going to give you the Pico de Orizaba so that you can see Hernan Cortés arriving, from its peak. I am going to let you have Florida, so that you may go there with Ponce de León in search of the fount of eternal youth and so that you may drink of its waters and remain thirty-five years of age forever. I am going to let you have the Amazon so that you may sail up it with Orellana and the tyrant, Aguirre. I am going to give you Patagonia, Maximilian, so that you may see Ferdinand Magellan sailing past. (665)

Here, tenderness blends with extravagance in a discourse that figures the voracious territorial appetite of imperialism. In addition, there is undeniable hubris in the assumption that so many American landmarks are Carlota's to give away—a point also established earlier by Benito Juárez in a rhetorical question to his secretary: "How can it be that a foreign usurper can handle an asset belonging to the nation and give it away to another foreigner?" (319).

Carlota symbolizes both the excesses and the deficiencies of the ideology of empire whose agency she shared with Maximilian during their time in Mexico. On a wider view, that ideology is synonymous with the "concept of history and of the future of mankind" mentioned in a much-quoted passage from *Noticias del Imperio:* "Not only does Carlota survive Maximilian, Juárez, Napoleon, Eugenia [de Montijo], and all the rest, but she also outlives an entire age, an entire concept of history and of the future of mankind and the picture that man had of himself and of the Universe" (630). Attesting to a paradigm shift that was complete by the time of Carlota's death in 1927, the narrator-author of *Noticias* underlines the centrality of imperialist ideology in the European mind-set of the nineteenth century and provides the crowning confirmation of the role of Carlota as both emblem of empire and vehicle of the narrative demystification of the assumptions of European (and, subsequently, North American) imperialism in the postcolonial world.

Noticias del Imperio and the Making of History

> The habitually insoluble quandary of the historian [is this]: how
> to live in two worlds at once; how to take the broken, mutilated
> remains of something or someone from the "enemy lines" of the
> documented past and restore it to life or give it a decent inter-
> ment in our own time and place.
>
> Simon Schama, *Dead Certainties (Unwarranted Speculations)*

The systematic interrogation of the nineteenth-century paradigm of history and the human subject referred to in the last section extends to other
areas of *Noticias del Imperio,* including most crucially the activity of
making—or writing—history. Along with a handful of other Latin American texts of its kind and time, *Noticias* participates in the widespread
critical reassessment, begun in Europe and taken up by North American
scholars in the 1970s, of the concepts and categories of history, representation, narrative, and historiography. Roland Barthes, Paul Ricoeur,
François Lyotard, Fredric Jameson, and Hayden White are just a few of
the most prominent figures in this area of study, which has been mapped
comprehensively by Robert Young in an authoritative critical account,
White Mythologies (1990). Reflecting, and reflecting on, the main currents of the "history debate," *Noticias* implicitly and expressly poses essential questions concerning the nature and representation of historical
experience, and provides answers that are largely consonant with poststructuralist and postmodernist thinking.

At the base of del Paso's conceptual inquiry is the fundamental distinction between history as a field of experience and "sequence of raw empirical realities" (Hutcheon, *A Poetics of Postmodernism* 92) and history as
a discursive system of knowledge and representation, otherwise termed
"historiography." With reference to the first of these categories, and in
answer to the question "Whose history?" the narrative of *Noticias* acknowledges and accommodates a broad spectrum of subjects of history,
including not only celebrated personalities like Maximilian, Richard Metternich, and the empress Eugenia de Montijo, but also an innumerable
cast of common folk represented, in the novel, by figures such as a blind
street vendor who vividly registers the presence of French troops on Mexican soil through the heightened senses of hearing, touch, and smell; a
priest who is compromised by the confession and seduced by the charms
of a Mexican woman who uses her position as a French officer's lover to
acquire military intelligence; and a member of the firing squad that shot
the emperor Maximilian, who is haunted by the idea that his may have

been one of the rifles loaded with live ammunition on the morning of the execution. In spite of their anonymity, these characters are often individuated as fully as their more famous counterparts, and they illustrate the abandonment, advocated by Michel Foucault and others, of "unitary, closed, evolutionary narratives of historiography as we have traditionally known it," in favor of a postmodern historiography containing "histories (in the plural) of the losers as well as the winners, of the regional (and colonial) as well as the centrist, of the unsung many as well as the much sung few" (Hutcheon, *A Politics of Postmodernism* 66).

In its representation of the historical field—broadly speaking, relations between Europe and Mexico in the mid-nineteenth century—and the historical process—the rise and fall of the empire of Maximilian and Carlota—the narrative of *Noticias* acknowledges the determining influence on events of political decisions originating in Europe and recognizes the role of accidents, oversights, mistakes, and the unforeseeable in shaping the course of history. A matter of repeated interest is the implication of written discourse in the historical process. Referring to the complex negotiations that preceded Maximilian's acceptance of the Mexican crown, the narrator remarks, "In 1862 and 1863 and at the beginning of 1864, dozens, indeed hundreds of letters criss-crossed Europe and traveled back and forth to America. [Some] were transported normally, by mule, stage coach and in the ships of the 'Royal Mail Steam Packet Company,' while others went by special delivery. [S]ome were straightforward, others misleading and written in a secret code[;] they were concise or interminably long and full of optimism, and were carried by private or royal messengers" (193). A similar sense of the historical field being swamped by written documents is conveyed by Carlota who, in a two-page listing of types of writing connected with Maximilian's political career, remarks in exasperation that enough material was produced to "carpet the road from Vienna to Querétaro" (609). Taken together with the aphorism, delivered in a tone of mock seriousness by a typesetter, that "Through these twenty-eight letters whole empires and reputations are created and then destroyed" (330), Carlota's hyperbole adds flesh to her earlier vision, redolent of Bakhtin, of the world as a carnivalesque "fiesta delirante" (115) in which is acted out "the madness of history" (638).

With regard to the text's conception of history as a discursive system, the author-narrator states his—and the text's—position in principle near the end of the book. The context in which this occurs is the final section of direct commentary, in the first person, on the life, death, and ultimate place in history of the emperor Maximilian and his wife. Aware that the narrative situation is ripe, and indeed that it calls for a conclusive judgment in the form of "one final page" about the empire and the emperor and empress of Mexico, the narrator admits that such a page,

> which ideally would contain that "Judgment of History"—in capitals—about which Benito Juárez spoke, would never get written, and not only because the madness of history did not come to an end with Carlota, but also because, in the absence of a "Universal History" based on truth (which is logically impossible and, in the final analysis, undesirable), there exist many histories which are both particular in scope and subject to change, depending on the temporal and spatial perspectives from which they are "written." (638)

So, at the end of the narrative investigation of the story of Maximilian and Carlota, the only conclusion available to the narrator is, paradoxically, that the story of Maximilian and Carlota admits of no conclusion: the most that can be asserted about it is that it remains open to continuing interpretation and, in some particularly intractable areas, locked into a chain of unending speculation.

Essentially, the narrator's position involves the rejection of a view of historiography that belonged to the nineteenth century, founded on the notions of objective truth and a "Universal History." Exponents of that view of history sought to integrate the disparate data of the historical field in a coherent narrative form for which they made claims of objective truthfulness and which they invested with the formal properties of uniformity and closure (see White, *Metahistory* 88–92 and White, *Content of the Form* chapter 2). "Universal History" is identified in an early chapter of *Noticias* with the novels of Walter Scott and the work of Maximilian's "dear friend and tutor," César Cantú (195), author of a monumental *Storia universale* published, in thirty-two volumes, in Turin between 1836 and 1847. In dismissing the orthodoxy of Scott and Cantú, the author-narrator of *Noticias* rejects a paradigm of historical knowledge and representation that is outmoded, and replaces it with a view of multiple (hi)stories: "histories which are both particular in scope and subject to change, depending on the temporal and spatial perspectives from which they are 'written'" (638). This relativistic view is typical of the postmodern era, which is characterized by a "questioning of the universal and totalizing in the name of the local and particular" and by a recognition that "Any certainties we do have are [. . .] 'positional,' that is, derived from complex networks of local and contingent conditions" (Hutcheon, *Poetics*

12). The conception of history as a discursive system that is able to provide only approximate and provisional versions of historical experience aligns del Paso's text quite clearly with postmodernist and poststructuralist positions.

The word *written* (escritas) in the above quotation calls attention, with a degree of self-consciousness that is also typically postmodern, to the discursive status of historiography. In part an ironic reflection on the position of a narrator who is himself engaged in the activity of writing (a) history, the quotation marks signal above all else the constructedness, and reliance on convention, of all forms of historiography. Embracing this as a fundamental point of principle, *Noticias* emphasizes the precariousness of the writing of history and explores some of the problematical implications that follow from that initial premise. Foremost among these is the verbal and textual condition of all elaborated histories. While in no way denying the primary reality of lived, empirical history, the narrative of *Noticias* conceives of that reality as a material that is destined to become discourse, either oral or written. The inclusion of both oral and written (hi)stories in the text of *Noticias;* the image of propaganda posters superimposed on one another, as in a palimpsest, on the walls of public places in Mexican towns and cities; the saturation of the text with vocabulary belonging to the field of verbal communication ("noticias," "informe," "resumen," "historia," etc.); and the conscientious critiquing of the textual tradition concerned with the story of Maximilian and Carlota, are all graphic illustrations of the permeability of lived and recorded history, and reminders of "not only the inevitable textuality of our knowledge of the past, but also both the value and the limitation of the inescapably discursive form of that knowledge" (Hutcheon, *Poetics* 127).

A no less radical implication of the theory of historiography put across in *Noticias* is the denial of the privileged status of history as a site of the truth. According to the author-narrator of del Paso's novel, the pursuit of a single authoritative truth about a historical character, incident, period, and so forth inevitably runs up against the insoluble contradictions and patchiness of the historical field. As the author-narrator remarks about his own investigations, "Some of the things which history tells us happened to Maximilian and Carlota can be corroborated; others cannot" (264). Further barriers preventing access to a (notional) truth about the past derive from inconsistencies and disagreements in the textual field. Whether it is made up of totally divergent interpretations, or of variations in successive accounts by the same author (namely, the case of E. C. Corti, discussed by

Juan Bruce-Novoa 429–31), the field of textual data stubbornly resists attempts at homogenization and remains receptive instead to the free play of new and always provisional accounts of historical experience.

The view of historiography adopted in *Noticias del Imperio* assumes a freedom to invent, which places history on the same footing as fiction. The conventional distinction handed down from Aristotle between historical narratives and fictional narratives collapses in the face of Carlota's invitation to her dead husband, "Let's reinvent history all over again" (76), and the fears attributed to Benito Juárez of the "harm [that] would be inflicted on him by the words [. . .] made up by the people whose job it would be to discomfit him by telling the story of his life" (624). At a more immediate level, the license to invent is exploited, consciously and overtly, by the author-narrator of *Noticias,* who intervenes in the textual carnival of writing about the emperor and empress to make his own, ironically knowing, contributions to historiography on the subject.

Finally, the theory of history-writing subscribed to in the novel acknowledges the vulnerability of textual histories to ideological prejudice. A striking example of the manipulation of the data of history is the board game, "invented by Mr John Wallis, of 'The History and Chronology of the Universe'" (446), which the author-narrator imagines having been played on a single occasion in the imperial palace by Louis Napoleon, his wife, Eugenia, and the infant prince, Lulú. In a vividly depicted drawing room scene, the narrator explains why the game should have failed to find favor with the emperor:

> Lulú had enjoyed himself tremendously, but Louis Napoleon took against it because it presented the history of mankind from an English point of view: starting with Adam and Eve, certainly, but ending with Queen Victoria and Prince Albert in the middle of the board where they were crowned as angels and decked with laurel leaves. (446)

It comes as no surprise to the reader that Louis Napoleon should wish to replace Wallis's Anglocentric strain of Christian universalism with an alternative white mythology culminating in his own apotheosis:

> No, he would commission a game that would begin, certainly, with Adam and Eve who were part of the universal heritage, but which would end with him, Louis Napoleon, and Eugenia and the little prince, crowned in glory. And it would have to include all the impor-

tant dates of French history, especially those of his own dynasty: 18
Brumaire, Austerlitz . . . (446–47)

Not far removed from the educational games of Wallis and others,[7]
European-authored histories of Maximilian and Carlota's reign display
equally virulent ethnocentric prejudice against a people presided over by
Benito Juárez, whom they accused of judging and executing the emperor
Maximilian in barbaric disregard for the proprieties of law and the decen-
cies of civilized society. Echoing President Juárez's own documented stric-
tures concerning the racism and arrogance of European observers, the
author-narrator's views on the distortion of history reinforce the postcolonial orientation of *Noticias* and clear the way for the writing of a correc-
tive counterhistory more in tune with the attitudes and experience of the
Mexican people.

In practice, many of the insights into the nature and workings of historiography detailed here are incorporated into the textual fabric of *Noticias*
through an array of formal and narrative procedures that contribute significantly to the novel's aesthetic definition. With respect to the forms of
narrative representation generally available, according to Hayden White,
to the historian and, by implication, to the writer of historical fiction
(White, *Content of the Form* 42–47), *Noticias* employs (1) the chronicle
(in sections of chapters 6 and 18), (2) direct discourse as commentary, and
(3) historical narrative in the third person, interwoven with (4) the eccentric discourse of Carlota, which destabilizes and ultimately undermines
truth claims made at other levels of del Paso's multilayered narrative. The
indeterminacy that results from this formal mélange is reinforced by a
secondary cast of narrators whose accounts and opinions are invariably
contradictory, provisional, and incomplete: the cast includes narrators
who profess to have no interest in the truth, correct themselves on important points of information, and admit to being understandably prejudiced
against the French and Austrian invaders.

With regard to plot, the narrative structure of *Noticias* conforms most
closely to the tragic mode of emplotment discussed by Hayden White in
Metahistory. Borrowing from genre criticism in aesthetics and literary
studies, White distinguishes among types of dramatic action and identifies
as characteristic of tragedy a spectacle or process comprising conflict
(agon), the frustration of aspiration and intent, and a final resolution; the
specific nature of the resolution, and the fact that it is approached "from
the standpoint of the agent who sees deployed before him a world which

is at once a means and an impediment to the realization of his purpose" (95), determine the tragic character of an action, which White defines dialectically, in opposition to the reconciliations typical of comedy:

> The reconciliations which occur at the end of Comedy are reconciliations of men with men, of men with their world and their society; the condition of society is represented as being purer, saner, and healthier as a result of the conflict among seemingly inalterably opposed elements in the world; these elements are revealed to be, in the long run, harmonizable with one another, unified, at one with themselves and the others. The reconciliations that occur at the end of Tragedy are much more somber; they are more in the nature of resignations of men to the conditions under which they must labor in the world. These conditions, in turn, are asserted to be inalterable and eternal, and the implication is that man cannot change them but must work within them. They set the limits on what may be aspired to and what may be legitimately aimed at in the quest for security and sanity in the world. (9)

In broad outline, the story of Maximilian, and parts of that of Benito Juárez, match the blueprint of tragic emplotment described here. During his first year in Mexico (summarized in chapter 10 of the novel), Maximilian's fortunes follow an upward curve; from that point on, a process of deterioration sets in which sees him becoming more and more isolated and then sliding to an inexorable military and political defeat. The overall trajectory of Maximilian's experience thus closely resembles White's "pattern of Tragic rise and fall" (126), and it stems furthermore from a flaw in the emperor's character that does not prevent him from experiencing a partial anagnorisis in the final days of his life.

The tragic basis of Maximilian's frustrated quest for personal and political fulfillment is corroborated in the text and further reinforced by diegetic comparisons with the martyrdom of Jesus Christ. In one of her apostrophes to her dead husband, Carlota expressly laments "your tragedy" (77); elsewhere, the author-narrator announces, "This book is based [. . .] on the tragic fate of the ephemeral emperor and empress of Mexico," and she uses phrases such as "the tragedy of Querétaro" (584) and "the tragedy of the Cerro de las Campanas" (587) to refer to Maximilian's emprisonment and execution at Querétaro.[8] Comparisons of Maximilian with Jesus Christ evoke a complementary scenario of archetypal suffering. The first instance of this occurs in Carlota's opening monologue where she complains that upon their arrival in Mexico, she and Maximilian "were given a crown of thorns and shadows." A few sentences later she goes on to recall the dashing figure of Maximilian in a painting at the age of thirty-five, "resembling a Christ who was forever youthful and forever handsome" (21). The comparison appears in its fullest form in chapter 20, in the song invented by del Paso to suggest the persistence of Maximilian's death in popular memory. In the "Corrido del tiro de gracia" (Corrido about the coup de grâce), an anonymous voice reconstructs the scene of Maximilian's execution on El Cerro de las Campanas:

> Como Cristo en el Calvario
> parecía el Emperador.
> Juárez fue el Poncio Pilatos,
> y López lo traicionó
> (The Emperor looked like
> Christ on Calvary Hill.
> Juarez acted as Pontius Pilate,
> and Lopez betrayed him) (576)

The Christ-motif is then repeated three times in the paragraphs of prose that alternate with the stanzas of the corrido, forcefully emphasizing the image of Maximilian as a martyred Christ.

In the context of del Paso's evolving narrative production, this body of material would appear to place Maximilian squarely alongside Luciano—the charismatic representative of the railway workers who is betrayed and murdered in the storyline of *José Trigo*—and Palinuro—another tragic victim of archetypal violence and injustice. However, in *Noticias del Imperio* del Paso reveals the comparison of Maximilian to Christ to be an imaginative construct. In the pages that follow the "Corrido del tiro de gracia," he remarks:

> At that time, as at many others, it was not uncommon to liken a martyr's suffering to Calvary. If the man who could have been Maximilian's father, the Duke of Reichstadt, who died in his bed, was described by Catule Mendès as "the little Jesus of the Tuilleries who became the Christ of Schönbrunn," it is easy to understand the impact on people's imagination of the shooting of a European prince before whose portrait the Mexican Indians used to make the sign of the cross. (586)

The author-narrator's commentary functions quite clearly as a demystification,[9] and in so much is entirely consistent with the ironic, postmodern epistemology of *Noticias*. It points toward the constructedness of all cultural phenomena and in the process undermines any attempt at providing a totalizing explanation for the narrative of Maximilian and Carlota's lives. Notwithstanding the presumption, made by Hayden White in his commentary on Paul Ricoeur's philosophy of history, that the "symbolic content of narrative history, the content of its form, is the tragic vision itself" (White, *Content of the Form* 181), the unmasking of the Christ analogy as a popular fabrication detracts from the hypothesis of a tragic principle governing the narrative content of *Noticias*. Viewed in the round, the stories of Maximilian and Carlota are no more reducible to a single tragic paradigm than the varied conceptions of history represented in the novel are susceptible to resolution in the madhouse of Carlota's mind. This may explain the inclusion in the text of an alternative characterization of the life stories of both Maximilian and Carlota as grotesque melodramas (561, 638) palliated, in places, by fantasies of family romance (490–91).

The presence of deconstructionist and self-referential strategies in the historiographical project of *Noticias* helps to explain the novel's ready admission to the high-profile category of postmodern historiographic metafiction. Stella Clark and Alfonso González argue that view of *Noticias* in terms that I find broadly acceptable. However, the novel's deep-seated resistance to forms and ideologies of totalization rests uneasily with too hard and fast a categorization of it as a postmodern historiographic metafiction. Indeed, closer inspection of the ideological and aesthetic construction of del Paso's text reveals a clearly defined stratum of non-postmodern elements that are in fact consistent with some of the assumptions of nineteenth-century historiography as described by Hayden White, and grounded in the same humanist ethics that we have uncovered in the two preceding novels by del Paso. This residue of humanist and modernist elements opens up a fissure in the apparently uniform texture of the novel and ultimately constitutes a major ground for distinguishing *Noticias* from the countless other postmodern historiographic metafictions produced by Latin American authors in the last quarter of the twentieth century.

A step-by-step review of the motive forces behind the writing of *Noticias* helps to isolate those characteristics that are specific to del Paso's project. In schematic terms, the narrative of Maximilian and Carlota (not forgetting Benito Juárez, Col. Miguel López, and other Mexican protagonists) is motivated, first, by political and ideological considerations of the kind already alluded to in preceding pages. At bottom, the aim of the author of *Noticias* is to contest white mythologies that misrepresent the history of Mexico and to replace them with counternarratives that are self-conscious, keenly argued, and free of the animus and arrogance of contemporary European historiography. Second, in addition to the political impulse of postcolonial discourse, the narrative of *Noticias* responds to an aesthetic impulse that emphasizes the "grandeur" (638) and "magnificence" (644) of Carlota's extraordinary life, evoking a range and intensity of experience that flatly contradict the empress's disavowal of "the trivial story of my madness and loneliness" (492). Last, and definitely not least, the narrative plays host to a moral impulse that turns on issues of conscience, guilt, and reparation. On the fourth page of the novel, Carlota informs her dead husband of her daily efforts to "put my house and my conscience in order" (16), and she assures him of her personal forgiveness, in a stream of utterances that culminate in the following: "And just as I forgive you everything that you did to me, so I forgive all our enemies and I forgive Mexico" (16). Carlota subsequently qualifies that generosity of spirit and shows a more subtle and critical awareness of the various factors and parties involved in the imperial adventure of 1864–67. Detailing some of the positive aspects of Maximilian's character and conduct, she exclaims, "Oh, Maximilian: sometimes I think I'll never forgive the people of Mexico" (606). But the memory of some of his personal faults and more conspicuous military and political failures leads her to the view that "You were a traitor to your new Fatherland. And for that reason, Mexico will never forgive you." She also anticipates that his defeat in "the Battle of Mexico" is something for which "you will never be forgiven by your Austrian compatriots" (607).

The welter of recriminations that are articulated here form part of a wider and more complex field of feeling that includes rancor (acknowledged by Carlota in chapter 17), remorse (as suffered by Benito Juárez on his deathbed), and a generalized guilt that permeates the cast of the narrative. Carlota admits to being embarrassed by the amount of "Mexican blood [that] had been spilt on our account" (550) and complains about the number of Mexican dead who weigh on her conscience (551). The soldier in the firing squad responsible for executing Maximilian hopes to God that he was given blank ammunition, "so that I should not have to spend the rest of my days feeling guilty about having killed the Son of God, Maximilian" (578). Yet so pervasive is his malaise that he suspects that "If by a miracle my memory were to go blank, I am certain that my bad conscience would make me invent everything all over again" (575). Most crucial of all, the author-narrator detects a collective guilt in the Mexican psyche over the way that the nation treated Maximilian and Carlota, and he proposes an act of reparation which might assuage his and the nation's conscience as well as belatedly do justice to the emperor and empress.

The author-narrator spells out his view of the situation in the middle section of chapter 22, entitled "The Last of the Mexicans." At this point, the narrative of the historical process—the *historia* of *Noticias del Imperio*—has advanced as far as Maximilian's execution and Carlota's descent into madness, while the discursive account—the *discurso*—is poised to assess "the political and ethical responsibility of [the emperor and his wife]" (641). The author-narrator opens his account by surveying the assessments offered by other Mexican writers, among whom the most significant is Rodolfo Usigli in *Corona de sombra* (1943). Reviewing some of the assertions made in the prologue to that play, the author-narrator cites Usigli's opinion that "The blood of Maximilian and the insanity of Carlota deserve better from Mexico," and he concurs with him:

> And this would appear to be the case, that that death and that insanity, because they are magnificent, deserve better from Mexico, from the makers and writers of its history and its literature; more than anything else, they deserve to be considered as the mitigating factors of greatest importance by any author who ventures, and is obliged, to form a personal assessment concerning the characters in the tragedy. (642)

The emphasis in this passage is on the writer's obligation to give Maximilian and Carlota their due, through equitable consideration of the behavior of each of them in the larger tragedy of Mexican involvement in the Habsburg Empire in the mid-nineteenth century. Attenuating factors such as Carlota's mental instability and the dignity displayed by Maximilian when facing the firing squad should, in the author-narrator's view, be accommodated in any final judgment.

Taking a further cue from the prologue to *Corona de sombra*, the author-narrator agrees with Usigli that "History tells us that only Mexico has the right to kill its dead, and that they belong forever to Mexico," and then elaborates:

> The problem is not that we have killed Maximilian in Mexico, nor that in Mexico we may perhaps have driven Carlota mad: the problem is that we did not actually bury either of them in Mexico. Which is to say [. . .] that neither of them, neither Maximilian nor Carlota, was committed to this soil which has been fertilized by the remains of all our heroes and all our traitors, in equal measures. (643)

In a nutshell, the author-narrator's thinking boils down to the proposition that two outsiders who came to grief in Mexico should be integrated fully into the national pantheon of heroes and villains. He stresses the benefits of accepting Maximilian and Carlota as Mexican, "if not Mexican by birth, then Mexican by death," and in a sentence that carries distinct echoes of both *Palinuro de México* and *The Unquiet Grave*, he proposes that "maybe that's the way we should proceed, so that they may terrify us no longer: the souls of the unburied always protest about the fact of having been abandoned" (643). After a short parenthesis, he pleads with his compatriots to show "a little goodwill" and to assist in the imaginative recuperation of two lost souls who, in the words of Usigli, "deserve better from the imagination of Mexico and its people" (644).

The author-narrator's exposition is couched for the most part in terms of equity and desserts, needs and benefits, with recourse to emotive language limited to the references to "terror" and "abandonment." Overall, his discourse evokes a wholesome scenario of reparation that holds out the prospect of a just and fair settlement for Maximilian and Carlota, and the restitution of equilibrium to the secretly troubled national psyche. The means to the projected end—namely, the general exercise of goodwill (un poco de voluntad)—may be substantially different from the path envisaged by Carlota in an earlier chapter, but the motivation is ultimately the same: "We need to forget what they did to us. They, the people of Mexico, need to forget what we did to them" (492–93).

Given the restrained tone of the narrative in the middle section of "The Last of the Mexicans," the reader is taken somewhat by surprise when, at the beginning of the penultimate paragraph, the author-narrator suddenly exchanges the indicative for the optative mood and embarks on a flight of wishful thinking:

> Ah, if only we could invent for Carlota a madness that would be never-ending and magnificent. [. . .] If only we could translate imagination into the mad woman of the house, the mad woman of the castle, the mad woman of Bouchout and release her, insane and unfettered, insane and with wings, to fly freely over the world and over history, truth and tenderness, eternity and sleep, hatred and untruth, love and agony. (644–45)

Introduced by the mildly exclamatory "Ah," the two sentences contained in this quotation express the author-narrator's fundamental sympathy toward "the mad woman of Bouchout" and his desire to effect an imaginative compensation for the suffering endured by "poor Carlota."

The concluding paragraph of the section under review sums up the author-narrator's feelings about Maximilian, who it now becomes clear is the referent of "The Last of the Mexicans." Matching symmetrically the consideration just shown to Carlota, the paragraph begins simply and directly: "If only it were possible, too, for us to invent a death for Maximilian that would be more poetic and more imperial." It continues in a familiar vein, "If we were just a little more compassionate toward the Emperor and resolved not to let him die that way, abandoned on a hill covered in dust and nopals, on a grey and barren hill with stones all around." The desire to invent and the invitation to show compassion are identical to the thoughts and sentiments expressed in connection with Carlota. However, the material that follows projects the narrative toward a very different horizon, where documented history is no longer merely a pretext for imaginative re-creation (as it is throughout Carlota's monologue) but a starting point for a complete and deliberate rewriting of recorded history.

The author-narrator's revisionary thoughts evolve in two stages. He first elaborates on his evocation of the circumstances of Maximilian's execution and requests an unprecedented degree of identification from his readers:

> If we were to kill him, instead, in the most beautiful and majestic square in Mexico . . . if we took his place for just one moment and put ourselves in his shoes and got inside his body and his head.

Having set the imaginary scene, the author-narrator then muses,

> And, fully aware that we are a Prince and a Sovereign who has always shown good humor and courage and never lacked a certain style and flair, who has always loved formality and ostentatiousness, pomp and circumstance, and all kinds of spectacle, if only we could write, in Maximilian's own hand and for the guidance of any future monarchs who may lose their lives at the hands of their subjects, [. . .] an *Etiquette for the Shooting of an Emperor.* (645)

Combining serious intent with humor and satire, the conclusion to "The Last of the Mexicans" envisages a full-blown alternative account of Maximilian's death: a mortigraphy (to adopt a neologism coined by Julio Ortega in his brilliant 1992 study of *El general en su laberinto*), which replaces the conventional truths of recorded history with a spectacle of pomp and make-believe. What is more, the stuff of the author-narrator's fantasy materializes immediately in the third and final section of chapter

22, which conveys the novel's final assessment of Maximilian. The last words of *Noticias del Imperio* may be reserved literally for Carlota in her concluding monologue, but as far as the author-narrator is concerned, his involvement in the narrative ends with the witty and poignant "Etiquette for the Shooting of an Emperor."

As a means of narrative closure, the ten-page "Etiquette" is noteworthy for several reasons. It is formally appropriate because by this stage of narrative proceedings the author-narrator has unburdened himself of his hostility toward the institutions and ideologies of empire and can now express regret, exclusive of sentimentality, over the fate of Maximilian. Beyond that, it carves out a well-defined position for the author-narrator in the debate, begun by previous commentators including Juan A. Mateos (in *El Cerro de las Campanas*) and Rodolofo Usigli, concerning "the political and ethical responsibility of Maximilian and Carlota" (641). And, most interestingly in the context of this study, the alternative mortigraphy for Maximilian satisfies a moral imperative that Hayden White identifies with all narrative history. On the specific subject of narrative closure, White writes in *Content of the Form:* "The demand for closure in the historical story is a demand [. . .] for moral meaning, a demand that sequences of real events be assessed as to their significance as elements in a moral drama." He asks, "Has any historical narrative ever been written that was not informed not only by moral awareness but specifically by the moral authority of the narrator?" (21). *Noticias* bears out these authoritative observations. Not only is it a text informed by "a moralizing impulse." It also assumes the form of a "moral drama," exploring discursively the often disturbing implications of its subject, before offering a narrative resolution to the moral dilemma of a nation.

Hayden White's insights into the narrative representation of historical issues allow the formulation of a final verdict on *Noticias*. They provide confirmation, first, of the humanist ethics which, along with a postcolonial sensibility, inform del Paso's narrative treatment of the tragic episode of Maximilian and Carlota's imperial venture. Second, White's insights help to define a non-postmodernist stratum in the construction of the text, which is at odds with the dominant postmodernist design of *Noticias*. Ten years after the composition of *Palinuro de México*, *Noticias* again negotiates the competing demands of literary modernism and postmodernism, this time tipping the balance more toward the latter than the former. The internal tug-of-war between conflicting paradigms of thought and feeling constitutes the specificity of Fernando del Paso's third novel; from an extrinsic point of view, it also serves to distinguish *Noticias* from other Mexican and Spanish American novels routinely ascribed to the category of postmodern historiographic metafiction.

Contemporary Intertextual Relations

The overt dialogue conducted in the pages of *Noticias del Imperio* with a multitude of historical and literary antecedents is the most conspicuous sign of an ambitious and systematic intertextuality that scholars from Juan José Barrientos to Inés Sáenz have recognized as an important area of study. Detailed comparison with a handful of novels composed and published at more or less the same time as *Noticias* promises to shed more light on the relationship of del Paso's novel to a contemporary field of writing on historical subjects in Spanish America. The texts that offer the most substantial grounds for comparison are *Terra nostra* and *La campaña* by Carlos Fuentes, *El general en su laberinto* by Gabriel García Márquez, and *Madero, el otro* by Ignacio Solares.

In *Terra nostra* (1975) are to be found important prefigurations of the central thematic patterns of *Noticias*. The figure of El Señor is a composite entity representing the Habsburg dynasty whose pernicious influence is as dominant a concern in Fuentes's novel as it is in that of del Paso. *Terra nostra* may dwell, as *Noticias* does not, on the genetic burden of a "multitude of murderous, cruel, incestuous, mad ghosts, mortally infected by syphilis and likely to bleed to death from a simple scratch" (213) and hold King Philip II (as the principal referent of El Señor) responsible for the suppression of a tradition of cultural pluralism that had flourished in some regions of medieval Spain. But both novels expose the Habsburg obsession with centralized power and deplore the marginalization and exploitation of overseas territories under Habsburg control (whether these be Mexico or the Congo). Making allowances for differences of kind in the imaginative treatment of political themes in *Terra nostra* and *Noticias*, the two texts present a common attitude vis-à-vis the abuses that have been perpetrated by the imperial powers of "The Old World."

Another substantial coincidence centers on the presence, in both novels, of an elderly female character who embodies the discourse of unreason. In *Terra nostra*, La Viajera is an archetypal mad wife and mother modeled on Princess Juana la loca. The metonymic relationship of la Viajera to the Habsburg dynasty, her nomadism, and her final incarceration and lament for the loss of a prince clearly anticipate the portrayal of Carlota in *Noticias*:

I see myself, I dream myself, I touch myself. [. . .] I wander from one
castle, one century, and one crypt to another, mother of all kings,
wife of them all, surviving every one of them, until finally I am
locked away in a castle surrounded by rainfall and misty pastures,
crying for someone who has died in a sunny clime, another prince of
our degenerate line. (*Terra nostra* 80)

Beyond her attachment to a specific referent, la Viajera represents the
most celebrated mothers, wives, and widows of Spanish and Spanish
American history, whose suffering she perpetuates:

I shall be what I was, Blanca, Leonor and Urraca, I shall be what I
am, Joan, I shall be what I shall be, Isabel, Mariana and Carlota,
forever close to the burial tombs of kings, forever a widow and dis-
consolate. (613)

In her boundless grief and multiple identifications across time and space,
La Viajera looks ahead to the extravagant narrative style and pathetic
desolation of Carlota in *Noticias*, as well as back to Fuentes's less extensive treatment of the figure of the mad woman in the castle in "Tlactocatzine, del jardín de Flandes," first published in *Los días enmascarados*
(1954).

As the examples of El Señor and La Viajera show, *Terra nostra* draws on
an almost infinite array of historical data, which it then subjects to a
process of carnivalization. The creation of composite figures out of several
historical referents, and the translation from one ontological realm to
another of Cervantes, la Celestina, Don Juan, and others, exemplify an
aesthetic of carnivalization that permeates the narrative of *Terra nostra*
and is not reproduced in *Noticias*. Also missing from del Paso's novel are
writing in the fantastic mode, which Carlos Fuentes had cultivated in both
Terra nostra and "Tlactocatzine, del jardín de Flandes"; an apocalyptic
scenario, such as that of Polo Febo in Paris; a sustained narrative sequence
made up of material drawn from pre-Columbian mythology; and a variety
of other cultural materials ranging from religious heterodoxies and literary archetypes to Renaissance painting and aesthetics—all of which are
specific to the diegesis of *Terra nostra*.

In respect of narrative architecture, *Terra nostra* differs substantially
from *Noticias*, whose mode of construction bears a somewhat closer resemblance to Fuentes's later novel, *La campaña* (1990). Basically mono-
linear, the narrative of *La campaña* follows the political and personal

evolution of a fictional character, Baltasar Bustos, who from 1810 to 1821 plays an active role in the fight of the Spanish American republics for independence. The story of "Balta" is embedded in a field of historical data that is as tightly packed as that re-created in *Noticias;* tracing Balta's passage from youthful idealism to a more sober maturity, it conforms to the pattern of the *Bildungsroman,* which also subtends the narrative devoted to Maximilian in approximately half of the chapters of del Paso's novel.

Yet fundamental differences in the nature of the stories of Maximilian and Balta limit the extent of any likeness between the two. Quite apart from the lack of a historical referent for Balta, his story belongs for the most part to the category of Romance, shading ultimately into Satire through a mechanism that is explained by Hayden White in a discussion about the limited compatibility of certain modes of emplotment. Insisting that the "notion of a Romantic Satire represents a contradiction in terms," White contends, "I can legitimately imagine a Satirical Romance, but what I would mean by that term would be a form of representation intended to expose, from an Ironic standpoint, the fatuity of a Romantic conception of the world" (*Metahistory* 9–10). Such an exposure takes place in *La campaña*'s final chapters when, upon reaching Mexico, Balta unexpectedly comes face to face with Ofelia, whom he had idealized throughout as a latter-day Dulcinea but who is now unmasked as a mother and covert political agent. Through this twist in its tail, Balta's story slots into a generic classification that is at odds with the tragic structure of Maximilian's life as represented in *Noticias.* What is more, the ironic perspective that the narrative offers on Balta at the close of *La campaña* reinforces other features of Fuentes's novel, including an unrestrained intertextuality, several kinds of parody, and forms of literary play correctly ascribed by Seymour Menton to a postmodern aesthetic that is more consistent and uniform than anything found in *Noticias* (163–85). In a telling contrast, the consistency of the postmodern aesthetic of *La campaña* throws into further relief the conflict between competing paradigms that characterizes *Noticias.*

More substantial parallels with *Noticias* are found in *El general en su laberinto* by Gabriel García Márquez, beginning with a common foundation in tragedy. The mortigraphy of Bolívar in *El general* (1989) duplicates that of Maximilian in the earlier *Noticias* (1987) and follows a similar process of dissolution in the personal and political spheres of a historical individual's life. The dual interest in the declining health and fortunes of Bolívar and Maximilian, on the one hand, and the corruption of the political systems that each sought idealistically to promote, on the other, evokes a sense of inevitable failure and pathos that is common to the two novels, being particularly marked in the concluding sections of each.

Without underestimating the specificities and obvious differences between the lives, personalities, and political creeds of Bolívar and Maximilian, it is also legitimate to register the use, made toward the end of the 1980s, of each of their stories to articulate an anti-imperialist philosophy around considerations of ethics and geopolitics, and to effect a revisionist reading of two front-line figures in the history of nineteenth-century Spanish America. In *El general,* the figure of Bolívar provides García Márquez with an ideal vehicle for championing, yet again, the independence and integrity of Spanish America vis-à-vis external sources of authority and control. El Libertador's testy conversation with the opinionated French opportunist, Diocles Atlantique, near the center point of the novel (128–32) spells out an authorial creed publicized on countless occasions and already glossed above in the section devoted to postcolonial themes in García Márquez and del Paso's work.

With regard to the revision of history, *El general* seeks to demystify the subject of Bolívar and to fill a gap in the historiography of a period of Bolívar's life that, according to García Márquez, is least documented (271). One significant point of convergence with *Noticias del Imperio* is the denunciation of inaccuracies, and indeed falsehoods, in the pictorial representation of Bolívar (see p. 186 of the García Márquez text), which echoes an identical observation about the distortion of history in paintings representing the execution of Maximilian (see p. 587 of *Noticias*). Another is the frank admission of reliance on what García Márquez terms "a torrent of documentary evidence that is contradictory and often dubious" (272), in the pursuit of an elusive historical truth that might be compatible with the requirements of fiction. To a certain extent, this coincidence, which is, in any case, a trademark of every historical novel, marks a site of difference between *Noticias* and *El general.* For, while in the former, contradictory source material is cited continuously in the body of the text and assessed in terms of its contribution to an ongoing historiographical inquiry, in the latter it forms part of the paratextual apparatus of *El general,* with a consequent diminution of the metafictional dimension of the Márquez text compared with the intertextual and metafictional carnival of *Noticias.*[10] Yet, all things considered, this differential reading of *El general* probably diverges only in emphasis from that of Rafael E. Correa, for whom "García Márquez's narrative style draws attention to the self-referential dimension [of *El general*], consciously articulating the principle of the impossibility of one History, one View, one Truth" (336). Where Correa perceives in *El general* symptoms of full-blown historiographic metafiction and a postmodernist rejection of a single authoritative historical truth, I detect a more elaborate metafictional structure in *Noticias* and emphasize a range of commonality between two new historical novels of Spanish America in which a humanist sensibility coexists with a postmodernist skepticism vis-à-vis the representation of history, and a shared mode of emplotment generates two narratives that are very similar in shape and tone.[11]

Another example of a tragic narrative is *Madero, el otro* (1989) by Ignacio Solares, which offers the fullest and most wide-ranging parallel with *Noticias* of those traced here. Narrated from a position of transcendence and judgment that recalls the "tú" sections of *La muerte de Artemio Cruz,* the novel plots the rise to the Mexican presidency of Francisco I. Madero and his vertiginous descent into political calamity and death. A combination of good moral intentions and political naiveté proves as fatal to Madero as it had to the equally ill-starred Maximilian of the earlier novel, and results in a similar characterization of part tragic hero, part misguided fool. The terms of the conflict embodied in Madero—forever oscillating between pragmatism and other-worldliness—and the inevitability of a tragic outcome both at the personal level and in the public affairs of the nation, are spelled out at the beginning of *Madero* by a narrator who calls the dead president to book:

> Do you remember when you wrote (or was it something *they* [the spirits] dictated to you?): "This world is nothing but the hazy blueprint of another world to come"? You were so caught up in that other world that you forgot about this one with its fragile foundations, its constraints, its stratagems, and its chicanery. Perhaps it is true that your feelings, your religious nature, your dreams allied you with the makers of the antidotes, rather than with those who produce the poisons. But it is no less true that by the end, there was no going back: your sacrifice alone would counteract the poison that was now spreading through everything, and if Huerta didn't kill you then Zapata or Carranza would, or, if you held out long enough, then you would die at the hands of Obregón and, if that were to happen, what picture would you leave behind of your sorry revolution? (16)

Reminiscent of the criticisms of Maximilian voiced by Carlota in sections of *Noticias del Imperio,* this and other passages in Solares's novel make no allowances for Madero's reputation as a decent, even saintly man as they subject him to cross-examination and rebuke.

Depiction as a sacrificial Christ figure is a key element in Madero's characterization and one that compares closely with the portrayal of Maximilian in *Noticias*. A sense of being destined to fulfill a messianic role culminating in inevitable martyrdom inspires Solares's Madero and is reflected in the diegetic presentation of the president throughout the narrative. Perhaps less ironic and self-aware than del Paso's handling of the motif, the Christological symbolism of *Madero* illustrates a common interest in the popular imaging of victim figures (including those who style themselves as such) in the terms of a dominant cultural archetype.

An aspect of the Christ analogy that possesses particular significance is the motif of shouldering a burden of guilt like Christ on the road to Golgotha. Already present in the first narrative segment of *Madero* (8–9), this motif fills out Madero's psychological profile and, beyond that, acts as a pointer to the ethical impulse behind Solares's investigation of the role and legacy of Madero in twentieth-century Mexican history. For, as in del Paso's history of Maximilian, Solares's narrative combines detailed character study of a historical individual with an examination of the collective conscience of a society troubled by its involvement in a tragic sequence of events. The reproduction, in the penultimate segment of *Madero,* of a speech delivered by Francisco Villa at Madero's grave acknowledging "the negative assistance or the culpability of his friends, none of whom is completely innocent" (245), highlights the book's concern with themes of morality and underlines its potential function as a vehicle for easing the guilt-stricken conscience of a community.

One final overlap between *Madero, el otro* and *Noticias* resides in the two books' express adherence to the formula—attributed to Borges—of "the subordination of historical exactitude to what is symbolically true" (*Noticias* 641; *Madero* 248). Like del Paso before him, Solares seeks to solve problems arising from "contradictions contained in the historical documentation" (249) by conjuring up an air of authenticity around events and, where necessary, resorting to legerdemain: a touch of invention here, a doctored attribution there, and the resulting version of events may turn out to be more verisimilar than a factually accurate account. As the author explains in a "Note" that reads like an epilogue to *Madero,* "After all, it is the halo surrounding events, more than the events themselves, that really matters" (250). This doctrine of creative freedom marks the closeness of the relationship between Solares's novel and that of del Paso. Indeed, from a comparative perspective, *Noticias* reveals itself quite emphatically to be a precursor text of *Madero* and a paradigm for writing on historical subjects in Mexican fiction and elsewhere.[12] On a general level, the multiple connections of *Noticias* with a range of texts considered here bears witness both to the complex operations of intertextuality and to the singularity of del Paso's novel in the contexts of national and continental Spanish American fiction written during the final quarter of the twentieth century.

5

Linda 67

The Homeland Strikes Back

> Postmodernism ought never to be viewed as a homogeneous
> phenomenon, but rather as one in which political contestation
> is central.
> **Cornel West**

Linda 67 is a unique event in del Paso's narrative production. A crime
novel set, for the most part, in the United States, it breaks with the modernist paradigm of both *José Trigo* and *Palinuro de Mexico* and also with
the mixed aesthetic of *Noticias del Imperio*. The modal variety cultivated
with virtuoso flamboyance in the three preceding novels is replaced in
Linda 67 by a strict adherence to the conventions of a single genre. The
grand proportions and totalizing parameters of *José Trigo, Palinuro de
México,* and *Noticias del Imperio* are scaled down to fewer than four
hundred pages, two-thirds the average length of the earlier novels. The
high-minded humanist message of each of the three forerunners is also
watered down in *Linda 67,* where it acquires the flimsy consistency of a
murderer's trite realization of his own betrayal of the values of love,
friendship, and freedom. In addition, the privileged, all-embracing mind
frames of *madrecita Buenaventura,* Grandfather Francisco, and Carlota
are recast, for the duration of a single chapter, in the stream of consciousness, overflowing with insults, threats, and obscenities, of a vulgar social
pariah who intervenes in the plot as the protagonist's blackmailer and
nemesis.

These and other differences notwithstanding, there are a number of
continuities with the previous works, ranging from the satire of consumerism, the nostalgic re-creation of a relationship of maternal and filial
devotion, and some highly charged erotic writing, all of which are reprised
from *Palinuro de Mexico,* to the display of encyclopedic knowledge (most
notably, about the cities of San Francisco and Berne) and exhaustive lists

(of consumer goods and details of interior décor, among other things) which are typical of del Paso's prose style in general. In particular, the author draws heavily on his lifetime experiences in milieux such as the world of advertising, the diplomatic service, and numerous cities in Europe and the Americas—including Paris, where he underwent heart surgery in 1990—to fashion a novel that in certain respects is a *roman-à- clef*.

At the center of the thematic design of *Linda 67* are the themes of nationality and personal identity and a critique of North American social mores. Built in part around a contrast with the values and attitudes of Mexican society, that critique articulates a thesis reminiscent of *Los pasos perdidos* by Carpentier—an author much admired by Fernando del Paso.[1] The echoes of Carpentier in turn illustrate a wider strategy of textual recycling of material derived from multiple sources; quotations from popular as well as highbrow culture combine with an interest in the mechanics of playacting and performance to produce what is arguably the most conspicuously intertextual and postmodernist novel in del Paso's output.

"What's in a Name?" *Linda 67,* the Plot, the Characters, and the Subject of Nationality

Dave Sorensen works as an executive for an advertising agency in San Francisco, where he lives with his wife, Linda. She is the only daughter of Samuel Lagrange, a millionaire from Texas, who refuses to accept Sorensen as his son-in-law. Disillusioned with their marriage, Linda has filed for divorce. Dave has a Mexican lover, an air hostess by the name of Olivia. Full of hatred for Linda, by whom he feels belittled and cheated, Dave conceives a plan to murder her and collect a ransom of $15 million. He carries out the murder on the night of Friday, 14 April 1995. However, he is seen pushing his wife's blue Daimler, registration "Linda 67" in commemoration of the year of her birth, over a cliff, where it sinks beneath the water with Linda's unconscious body trapped inside. The witness, an aging hippie who fought in Vietnam, threatens to tell the police all he knows unless Dave secures the ransom and passes it on to him. Dave follows the blackmailer's instructions and, in the process of handing over the money, receives a beating that lands him in hospital.

Neither the detective in charge of the case nor Linda's father believes in Dave's innocence. While Inspector Galvez pursues his investigations, Samuel Lagrange masterminds a ruse involving an invitation to Dave to travel to Berne where he is offered a lucrative job promoting a new Swiss watch. The offer, of course, is phony and sets Dave up as the recipient of the sum of $15 million, which is transferred into an account that he has opened, in his own name, in San Francisco. When Linda's body and car are discovered, Galvez can proceed to pin the murder on Dave: he has a body, a motive, and a suspect in possession of a sum of money identical to the ransom. In addition, there is the original set of ignition keys to Linda's Daimler, which, by an oversight, Dave had returned to one of the pockets of the jacket he wore on the night of the murder. Incriminated by his possession of them, Dave is remanded to a prison cell, where he repeatedly counts his losses and contemplates the choice that he will shortly have to make, between going to the electric chair or being given a lethal injection.

On this summary, *Linda 67* conforms to the type of the crime novel in many essential respects. The plot of *Linda 67* is built around a murder that is planned and executed with meticulous care; the reader has access to the criminal's mind and is presented, furthermore, with the details of a gruesome murder. In Dave Sorensen, del Paso creates an interesting criminal who pits his wits against a skilled detective and is ultimately incriminated by one telling piece of evidence. Inspector Galvez is a methodical detective whose character combines certain foibles (including an addiction to sugar) with a veneer of worldliness and sophistication: his knowledge of fine arts puts him in the same class as Tom Ripley, the detective in the series created by Patricia Highsmith, and Inspector Morse, the culture-snob created by Colin Dexter. This spotlight on the detective is sharpened by a reference to Sherlock Holmes and Alfred Hitchcock that Galvez makes in the course of a conversation with Sargeant Kirby, whom he playfully styles as Watson to his own Bay Area Holmes (345). However, it cannot be denied that Galvez radiates none of the aura of archetype surrounding Holmes, Ripley, or Héctor Belascoarán Shayne, the protagonist of a series of novels by del Paso's contemporary on the Mexican literary scene, Paco Ignacio Taibo II. Galvez fulfils the narrative requirements of his role but lacks the trademark quirkiness of the more celebrated examples of his kind. Where he makes an important contribution to *Linda 67* is in connection with the themes of nationality and personal identity, which are underscored in his very first appearance in the narrative.

Galvez only appears in twelve of the twenty-seven chapters of *Linda 67*. When he arrives in the second chapter of the second part of the book, Dave Sorensen remarks, "I assume you speak Spanish." Galvez replies, "No, my family first arrived here more than a hundred years ago. I am a North American citizen through and through" (201). Galvez's retort challenges conventional assumptions linking names to nationality and citizenship. For Sorensen, the name Galvez automatically implies the categories of "Hispanic" and "Spanish-speaking," with further inferences of low socioeconomic status generally granted to Hispanics in the United States over the last 150 years. For Galvez, the connotations of his name are eclipsed, along with any feeling of loyalty to the Spanish language, by the benefits of U.S. citizenship and by his sense of belonging to the greater sociopolitical entity that is the United States of America.

While at one level Galvez's opening exchange with Sorensen serves merely to reiterate the standard ideological perception of the United States as a melting pot/patchwork quilt/site of assimilation of peoples of different linguistic and ethnic origins, at another level it points up a noteworthy feature of *Linda 67*, which is the surface inconsistency between the names and identities of its leading players. Besides Inspector Galvez, Linda Lagrange combines a French-sounding surname with a Christian name originating in the Spanish language, which, while matching its bearer's physical appearance, is at odds with her reluctance to engage fully with things Mexican, as is signaled by her failure ever to get close to, let alone cross, the United States–Mexican border, on her regular weekend drives with Dave "Down Mexico Way" (33, 66). It is a function of the novel's moral economy that Linda should represent the archetypal *gringa*—a term Dave, in fact, uses to describe her to her face (24); in that context, her surname reveals its minimally coded significance as a transposition of all but one of the letters of the phrase "la gringa" > "la grange."

The conversation in which Dave and Linda trade names is reported in chapter 2 of *Linda 67*, where it forms part of a more extended narrative inquiry into the history of the Sorensen family after 1800. That is the date of birth, in Denmark, of Dave's great-great-grandfather, Isaías, who would emigrate to Mexico in the 1840s and found a family business based on the cultivation of coffee, in Coatepec in the state of Veracruz. Thereafter, the family tree extended through another Isaías to his sons, David Isaías and Salomón, and on to David "Papá" Sorensen, Dave's father. Contrary to Linda's impertinent and openly racist comment about their names, none of Dave's forefathers had any connection with Judaism: "They observed a Protestant tradition; [Dave's] great-great-grandmother was a devoted reader of the Holy Bible and her favorite prophet was Isaiah. It goes without saying that the Sorensens of Mexico were Catholic, from the moment of great-great-grandfather Isaías's conversion." This line of argument allows Dave to contradict Linda, insisting "So, that makes me Mexican, just as you are a *gringa* [. . .] in spite of the fact that your surname is French" (24). However, she had already called into question his professions of Mexican identity ("You, Mexican? With that Danish surname, that blond hair and those green eyes: Come on . . ."), and the narrative now confirms that "Dave knew very well that the only Mexican thing about him was his second surname, Armendáriz, which had belonged to his mother" (24). Observing that the circumstances of his birth (in London) and successive periods of residence with his parents in Ottawa, Paris, and San Francisco entitled him to neither English, Canadian, French, nor American nationality, the narrative concludes, "To be Mexican was the only alternative available to him, but that was something that didn't quite fit, and was alien to him" (25). For all his fascination and affinity with Mexico—its food, landscape, history, architecture, and so on—Dave remains an outsider to the nation, stuck in the role of "a curious tourist, enchanted by what he saw, but with no feeling that any of it belonged to him" (26).

This characterization depicts Dave as a man without a "patria chica," in the terms of del Paso's Rómulo Gallegos Prize acceptance speech of 1982. Furthermore, it identifies him as a paradigm of modern American and western mankind: the inheritor of both Northern Protestant and Hispano-Catholic traditions in the Americas, and a transnational who is equally at home, both literally and figuratively, in San Francisco and Cuernavaca, and yet condemned to feel *déraciné* wherever he goes. Admittedly, his cosmopolitan background and sophisticated manners open up real professional and social opportunities for him in the United States and, briefly, Switzerland, but he remains, ultimately, an outsider in both of those countries and in the continents of which they form part.

Consumerism, the *Malvinas,* and the State of the American Nation

At the same time as they point up themes of nationality and cultural disaffiliation, Dave Sorensen's profile and life serve as vehicles for a sustained critique of consumerism, imperialism, and relations between Mexico and the United States. This dimension of *Linda 67* merits separate treatment, in a section devoted to these three, sometimes converging focuses of narrative concern.

Minutely detailed and artfully slanted toward satire, the depiction of the world of advertising in *Linda 67* owes much to del Paso's early adult experience of that profession (to which he had already held up a distorting mirror in *Palinuro de México*) and to an acute sense of the many ills caused by consumerism in modern-day western society. The decision to situate the characters of *Linda 67* within the milieu of advertising and associated

circles of affluence provides ample opportunity to portray the materialism, opportunism, and cynicism that motivate the consumer industry at its
worst. An early image of Dave Sorensen reviewing the contents of his
wardrobe sets the tone for much of what is to follow. Filling the fourth
paragraph of the novel, it conveys his enthrallment with the idea of possession (the narrative registers the fact that Dave owns no fewer than 140
neckties) and his susceptibility to extreme forms of narcissism comparable
to that portrayed quite brilliantly on the screen by Richard Gere, in his
role as a lavishly provided, obsessively self-regarding American gigolo in
Paul Schrader's film of 1979.

At the agency where he works with Bob Morrison and other employees,
Dave Sorensen is doubly immersed in consumerism, first, as a connoisseur
of goods and market operations that it is his job to research thoroughly,
and then, as the inventor of brand names and slogans used in the promotion of new products. In the narrative of *Linda 67*, Sorensen plays a key
role in the development of a new line of cosmetics aimed at Hispanic
women living in California and Texas, but also targeted at the American
female population in general. Named "Olivia" after Dave's Mexican girlfriend, the product, along with the steamy television commercial designed
to promote it, appeals to and reinforces an ideology of surface appear-
ances that holds beauty to be skin deep. Susceptible audiences are hooked
by the manipulative strategies of an industry which plays on their sexual
desires through the means of a slogan that promises personal renewal and
unprecedented erotic fulfilment: "Olivia, a different way of being . . . a
different way of loving" (253). The visual narrative of the commercial
simulates a sexual encounter, filmed in black and white, between a man
"whose skin is white," and "a woman with light brown skin" whose
crimson nail varnish, in the "Olivia" range, is the only splash of colour in
the thirty-second long advertisement. Issues of color and social integration
are hinted at in this scenario, which ignores black America but suggests
the possibility of advancement for Hispanic women who "sink their
claws" into the male representatives of white American society (252). A
spoof of countless commercials that are shown every day on television
stations throughout the industrialized world, this one expresses its
author's profound disquiet about consumerism, advertising, and the stul-
tification of audiences in an era of mass media visual communication.

Del Paso's anti-imperialist convictions are also aired in *Linda 67* in
terms that hark back both to the previous novel, *Noticias del Imperio,* and
to the text of "Mi patria chica, mi patria grande." Chapter 5 evokes
Dave's childhood friendship with Chuck O'Brien, the son of the Irish

ambassador in Paris, and registers the telling, if unsurprising, observation that Ambassador O'Brien "would never have thought of enrolling his son at the Colegio Británico," so great was his hatred of the English: "The mere idea that his son could be taken for a subject of Her Royal Highness or that he should acquire even a trace of the pretentious, arrogant accent of the inhabitants of Mayfair or the graduates of Eton College was absolutely intolerable to him" (56). Bearing in mind del Paso's admiration of James Joyce, it is not difficult to detect here an echo of Joyce's hostility to Anglo-Saxon imperial rule, as expressed in the pages of *Ulysses* and elsewhere, or to infer sympathy with Irish animosity toward English attitudes.

Del Paso's years of residence in London afforded him the dubious privilege of witnessing the British government's conduct, in the spring of 1982, of a latter-day act of imperialist aggression overseas: the war against Argentine forces contesting possession of the Falkland Islands/Malvinas in the south Atlantic. The Malvinas episode is mentioned three times in *Linda 67,* as a temporal marker of Dave's youth and as a memory that invades his stream of consciousness as he wanders through the streets of San Francisco a few hours after murdering Linda. In that setting, he remembers his father's and others' indignation at the English sinking of the Belgrano battleship and their "cries of jubilation when, the following day, the Argentinians sank the Sheffield" (194). Evoking two of the most dramatic episodes of the conflict, the narrative furnishes a Spanish American perspective of events that is intended to counter Anglocentric versions of the Falklands War. Significantly, the text is not interested in warmongering. Rather, it laments a collective descent into irrationality ("Everybody had lost their reason," p. 194) on both sides of the conflict, and depicts the war as a historical nightmare which is still capable of haunting Dave, in the course of a drunken periplus, more than a decade after the event.

The connections established in the imperialist mind-set between geopolitics, race, and civilized values are clearly alluded to in *Linda 67*. A confrontation between Dave Sorensen and playboy Jimmy Harris over the latter's affair with Linda gives rise to the archetypal claim of the superiority of Anglo attitudes over Latin immaturity and hot-headedness: "I never imagined you'd react this way," Harris tells Dave. "Of course, that's very Latin. What else could be expected from a Mexican? We Anglos are more civilized, you know. I'm not afraid of a scandal, Dave, and I think that's all there is to say" (161). Arrogant and racist, Harris's words require no elaboration: readers know exactly how to respond to the novel's revisiting of ideological territory last explored in *Noticias del Imperio* and, contemporaneously, in *Discurso desde la marginación y la barbarie*—the 1988 essay by Leopoldo Zea which, together with del Paso's work, gave a pointed reformulation to the *civilización/barbarie* topos at a key moment in Latin American intellectual history.

Racist attitudes and stereotypes circulate freely around Jimmy Harris and form part of a larger critique of social behavior in the United States. Taking northern California as its primary setting, *Linda 67* exploits a series of references and metonymies to present a picture of the nation as a whole. Expanding on the repertoire of unflattering characteristics already noted, the novel portrays the United States as, essentially, a contemporary dystopia. Violence, urban poverty, and social deprivation are just three of the nation's social ills, festering in a climate of perversions and distorted appetites that lead Dave's friend, Chuck, to conclude, "The USA was becoming a country of monsters. Of every race and age: anglos, mulatos, chicanos, men and women, adolescents, who weighed 120, 150, 200 kilos" (42). This symbolic depiction of a bloated body politic is reinforced by a reference to AIDS (94) and by the evocation of a pervasive nausea that reaches fever pitch when Dave vomits during his periplus through the streets of San Francisco.

Beyond the physical symptoms of distemper, the novel uncovers deep-seated flaws in the moral and psychological constitution of the nation. Repeatedly and with clinical intent, it recalls a number of horrible *causes célèbres* that have etched themselves into the popular consciousness of the American people. They include the Oklahoma bombings carried out by Timothy McVeigh in April 1995; the trial of O. J. Simpson for the murder of Nicole Brown, which is mentioned three times in the narrative; a multiple murder committed in Novato, California, by a man from Laos "who pumped more than forty bullets into the bodies of his ex-girlfriend, her father and son in the town of Novato" (136); and, perhaps most disturbing of all, the case of a mother from South Carolina "who had plunged her car with her two small kids inside into the depths of John D. Long lake" (100). Considered "a horrendous crime" by Dave (100), the actions of Susan Smith haunt the narrative of *Linda 67*, which returns to them on no fewer than four occasions. For the blackmailer who saw action in Vietnam, they exemplify a perversion of natural instinct (he calls Susan Smith "la desnaturalizada," p. 258); diegetically, her actions are figured as a descent into dark and unfathomable depths; overall, they and the other criminal incidents that are reprised from contemporary U.S. news are orchestrated to indicate profound tears in the moral and mental fabric of the nation.

A contrast with Mexico illuminates the severity of this dystopian vision of life in the United States. Against the hell of San Francisco (as perceived by Dave when he is drunk, in chapter 15), Cuernavaca is pictured as Paradise. An early section of the narrative tells of Papá Sorensen's acquisition of a plot of land on which to build his family a home, and describes the setting thus:

> The fertility of the soil in Cuernavaca made it possible for the newly planted garden quickly to become a paradise. The flamboyanes grew in their new setting and were soon covered in orange flowers the color of fire. The bougainvilleas spread all over the walls, and every day they carpeted the grass and the watery surface of the swimming pool with red, purple, and white petals. Other climbing plants produced flowers that were sky-blue, shaped like bells. (30)

In its variety and profusion, the plant life thus described is a colorful illustration of the tropical fecundity that Julio Ortega, after Sarduy, has theorized as a trope of American writing (Ortega, "Para una teoría del texto latinoamericano"). In context, the passage of description functions additionally to promote "natural" values over and against the proliferation of material wealth in North American society.

The one-sidedness of the contrast drawn in *Linda 67* is plain to see, despite Olivia's reminder that Mexico is a country where corruption is endemic (149), kidnappings occur routinely (121), and the Indians of Chiapas remain mobilized against the forces of the state (136). Objective standards hardly apply at all in the ideologized atmosphere of the novel, which displays the hallmarks of contrivance associated with a thesis-novel. One such feature is the black-and-white characterization of Linda and Olivia. In line with its somber vision of life in the United States, *Linda 67* projects the nation's negativity onto Linda Lagrange, while investing Olivia with a positive set of characteristics and associations.

Linda is presented from the start as the personification of American materialism, the heiress to a millionaire's fortune amassed from the sale of plastics. Over the course of her relationship with Dave, she develops an obsession with domestic cleanliness and personal hygiene that signifies her total alienation from nature. The cans of air freshener that she instructs her domestics to use around the house produce "crude imitations of natural aromas" (54); her obsession with "taking a bath, not only before but also after making love, and with covering her body in soap repeatedly each time she had a bath" (102) is registered with narrative disapproval. In another sphere, Linda personifies the culture of denial, which, among other things, prohibits smoking and the consumption of meat and is suspicious of any foodstuffs that might be high in cholesterol (76).

For her part, Olivia represents the strict antithesis of Linda's moral and instinctual sterility. As detailed in chapters 12 and 23, she displays sincerity, loyalty, scruples, and an attitude of trust in her relationship with Dave, who is privileged to have access to her sexual intimacy. The narrative records Olivia's coyness at undressing in the light, her delicate speech and gestures during lovemaking, and her perfect attunement to her own and Dave's erotic desires. Time after time, all of this is contrasted with the mechanical regime and vulgarity of sex with Linda, who insists on Dave's taking a shower, brushing his teeth, applying deodorant to his armpits, and putting on a condom before making love to her (154). A significant detail in the presentation of Olivia is the likening of her sex to Paradise in the lush humidity of the garden at Cuernavaca; rooted in an archetypal store of celebratory images, Olivia thereby functions as a metonym of Mexico and, beyond that, of tropical America as a whole.

Together, Linda and Olivia help to flesh out the depiction of the United States and Mexico that is found in *Linda 67*. Patently, they belong to the realm not of verisimilitude but of stereotype, as exemplified in the novels of, say, D. H. Lawrence and any number of classic Hollywood films that revolved around the pairing of a "good girl" with a "bad girl." In the Spanish American literary tradition, Linda and Olivia descend most directly from Mouche and Rosario in *Los pasos perdidos* by Alejo Carpentier, which bears an unmistakeable family resemblance to the narrative of *Linda 67*.

Intertextual Recycling, the Noir Aesthetic, and the Author as Parasite and Nemesis

Los pasos perdidos lies barely concealed beneath the surface of *Linda 67*, like one of the constituent layers of a palimpsest. The narrative of *Linda 67* effectively refashions Carpentier's exploration of authentic American identity and the disorientation of twentieth-century western man, through the vehicle of a male protagonist who lacks a specific national identity and is burdened by the trappings of "civilized" life. Seen through the prism of *Los pasos perdidos*, Dave Sorensen can be likened both to Soren Kierkegaard and to another Danish writer, Villy Sorensen, who was the author of modernist short stories and philosophical works influenced by German Existentialism; less obviously versed in philosophical themes than his

Carpenterian predecessor, Dave Sorensen nevertheless replicates some of his Sartrean concerns, and confronts a similar ethical dilemma that is embodied in two female characters: Linda/Mouche, representing artifice, theatricality, and perverted instinct, and Olivia/Rosario, representing an idealized prelapsarian state of nature grounded in the terra firma of America.

On top of these coincidences of narrative detail, *Linda 67* replicates the schematic design and rhetorical overload of *Los pasos perdidos*. The allegorical structure and elaborate system of references to landmarks of western culture that obtrude like scaffolding around the narrative of *Los pasos perdidos* have their equivalents, in *Linda 67*, in a conspicuous and highly self-conscious practice of intertextual reference and pastiche. *Los pasos perdidos* certainly occupies a privileged position in the textual world of *Linda 67*, but it shares that space with countless other precursors ranging from the familiar lyrics of popular music (for example, "Down Mexico Way" sung by Patsy Cline, which provides the title for chapter 3), to the titles of "serious" works of literature (chapter 2 takes the heading of "Bajo el Volcán" from the novel by Malcolm Lowry), and famous scenes and characters in film (for example, the Eddie Murphy character in *Coming to America*, mentioned on p. 271). In particular, *Linda 67* cites well-known authors and works of crime and detective fiction, including Conan Doyle, Rex Stout, Patricia Highsmith, Dashiell Hammett and the writing of *The Maltese Falcon,* and the composite model of Jorge Luis Borges and Adolfo Bioy Casares, which inspires Samuel Lagrange's intricate and "providential" plot to entrap Sorensen (364).

The frank and often ironic tone of many of the references to detective fiction indicates a clear wish to write a pastiche of that mode, which comprises a finite stock of narrative formulae reworked constantly in literature and film.[2] This helps to explain some of the clichés that pepper the prose of *Linda 67* and the staginess and predictability of much of the action. (The sequence which narrates Dave and Olivia's idyllic weekend in Cuernavaca is paradigmatic in this respect.) Along with the overt intertextuality of *Linda 67,* the unmistakeable familiarity of its narrative schema and character types aligns it quite clearly with the aesthetic of postmodernism, as described by Fredric Jameson ("Postmodernism") and Jean Franco ("Pastiche"), among others.

For the majority of its commentators, the art of postmodern pastiche has the potential for conveying criticism of the social and political status quo. That potential is evidenced in the use that *Linda 67* makes of a type of crime fiction that combines psychological analysis with features of noir fiction (and film) that are applicable to contemporary urban life generally. Notwithstanding the existence of a vibrant tradition of noir fiction in Mexico and other parts of Spanish America,[3] *Linda 67* turns to North American examples such as Dashiell Hammett and Patricia Highsmith, to elaborate a dystopian vision of the darker sides of life in the United States.

Of all the novels written by Highsmith, *Those Who Walk Away* (1967) offers the closest fit with the narrative of *Linda 67*. Set in Venice, it conjures up an asphyxiating world of guilt, suspicion, bitterness, and violence, at the center of which are Ray Garrett and his vengeful father-in-law, Ed Coleman. Coleman hates Garrett because he failed to prevent his young wife, Peggy, from committing suicide. As in *Linda 67*, therefore, an older man holds his son-in-law responsible for the death of his only child. The extent of Coleman's loss is expressed in the following pathos-laden paragraph:

> He might, of course, marry and have another child—a son or another daughter, it didn't matter. Coleman admitted that he was as paternal as any mother was ever maternal. But a daughter, for instance, would never be another Peggy. And there simply wasn't time any longer to watch her grow up. No, never, never would there be anything for him like Peggy. (101)

For his part, Garrett carries a burden of guilt that makes him exceptionally vulnerable to Coleman's repeated assaults; a very different character from Dave Sorensen except when Sorensen is drunk, he feels a strange and constant need to explain himself to Coleman, until Coleman makes a second attempt on his life. Throughout the narrative, Garrett is the quarry of Coleman, in much the same way that Dave is tracked, and then cunningly tricked by old man Lagrange in the second part of *Linda 67*. Two psychological crutches support Garrett through his ordeal: a chamber maid named Elisabetta who works near the *pension* where he goes into temporary hiding, and the memory of his father. Elisabetta provides consolation for the grief caused by Peggy's death, while the memory of his father and certain childhood recollections to do with the family home are important points of reference for the adult Ray Garrett. Both elements reappear in *Linda 67*, where they help to define the situation and psychology of Dave Sorensen.

A more precise debt to noir traditions is the figure of the Vietnam veteran who highjacks Dave's plan for extracting a ransom from Linda's millionaire father. A familiar type from countless North American films and literary narratives of the last thirty years, the Vietnam vet typically carries the scars of his country's ill-judged and poorly rewarded involvement in Southeast Asia on his body (which is the case of the Tom Cruise character, Ron Kovic, in *Born on the Fourth of July*, 1990) or in his psyche (see the characters of Travis Bickle and Megs Megessey played by Robert de Niro in *Taxi Driver*, 1976, and *Jacknife*, 1989). Like his eponymous French counterpart in Claude Chabrol's *Le Boucher* (1970), he embodies a capacity for murderous violence, unleashed by war, that he simply cannot control.

The Vietnam veteran of *Linda 67* is an example of the social sickness and maladjustment of his type. "Alcoholic and addicted to drugs" (256), he had found a job in a hospital from which he would eventually be fired "for lack of hygiene" (365), and he now lives as a social pariah and outlaw. (He mentions a history of difficulties with the police.) His claim that "I used to swim amongst the crocodiles in the rivers of the Vietcong" (259) conveys a cunning and predatory nature that manifests itself in the action of *Linda 67*. The menace and brutality that he inflicts on Dave Sorensen, and the string of obscenities that he mouths at both Dave and Samuel Lagrange, complete the profile of a familiar type used in *Linda 67* to give the lie to utopian views of the United States as a nation representing the acme of civilization.

As well as reinforcing the text's dystopian vision of U.S. society, the character of the Vietnam veteran reflects ironically on the role of the author in and of *Linda 67*. Quite outrageously, he compares himself with the writer, whom he claims to outstrip in the inventiveness of his imagination, proudly boasting, "I have an imagination that you'd love to have yourself" (255). A facility for telling lies recalls the association of Carlota with the (re)generative powers of fiction in *Noticias del Imperio*, and culminates in the bragging pretense of "I, who am a poet and a novelist" (265), which rebounds on the (implied and real) author in several ways. First, the foul-mouthed degenerate who claims artistic status personifies the ambience and focus of noir writing, which is concerned with plumbing the depths of criminal instinct and disturbed psychological states.[4] In respect of his dark imagination and skill in plotting, the Vietnam veteran is more than the equal of the author of *Linda 67*. Second, the veteran's opportunistic blackmailing of Dave Sorensen for his own effortless gain is a parasitical ploy that mirrors the modus operandi of the literary author who feeds off other writers' clever schemes and material. Imitation of heterogeneous styles and experimentation with a genre like the *novela negra* add up to a strategy of mimicry and pastiche in which the figure of the author is consigned to the rank of a technician of textual rearrangement and a (mere) agent of intertextuality.

The veteran's role as nemesis to Dave Sorensen adds a final ironic detail to the allegory of authorship that is outlined in *Linda 67*. At a structural level of analysis, the veteran fulfills the needs of the plot by satisfying the requirement that Dave Sorensen should not ultimately profit from his immoral actions. Through sustained verbal and physical abuse, the former soldier metes out a punishment that helps to placate the reader who is appalled by murder, deceit, and immorality. Yet this too involves the veteran's subordination to a narrative formula, ultimately confirming his and the novel's character as derivative, parodic, and lacking the moral depth that had made an earlier text such as *Palinuro de México* devastatingly effective as political satire and truly poignant as a lament for lost youth. Instead, the veteran of *Linda 67* makes sense, partly as an emblem of the sociopathology of the nation and, more comprehensively, as an allegory of the intertextual impulse that feeds Fernando del Paso's fictional writings from *José Trigo* through to *Linda 67*, where it attains an unprecedented level of prominence and reflexivity.

Conclusion

> Any text is an intertext; other texts are present in it, at varying
> levels, in more or less recognisable forms: the texts of the previ-
> ous and surrounding culture. Any text is a new tissue of past ci-
> tations. Bits of codes, formulae, rhythmic models, fragments of
> social languages, etc., pass into the text and are redistributed
> within it.
> **Roland Barthes, "Theory of the Text"**

The above quotation from a seminal essay by Barthes will inevitably reso-
nate with the reader of *Linda 67: Historia de un crimen,* offering a rationale for the presence in del Paso's text of a heterogeneous body of material
ranging from snippets of music, newspaper headlines, and titles of well-
known literary works, to standard narrative formulae and preexisting
generic templates adapted from works by Alejo Carpentier and Patricia
Highsmith, among others. If a promiscuous intertextuality is symptomatic
of postmodernism, then *Linda 67* can be assigned without further ado to
that aesthetic category, in line and along with the epigraph from "Theory
of the Text" that heads these concluding remarks.

In relation to del Paso's fictional output as a whole, *Linda 67* accommodates the same intertextual impulse that we have seen at work in *José
Trigo, Palinuro de México,* and *Noticias del Imperio.* What is noteworthy
about *Linda 67* is the intense redoubling of that energy, resulting in a text
that is arguably the most self-consciously intertextual of del Paso's novels
and the most exclusively postmodern. In retrospect, the four novels from
José Trigo to *Linda 67* trace a meandering line of development from a
modernist paradigm of narrative to a postmodern paradigm and outlook.
At the start of the process, *José Trigo* and *Palinuro de México* exemplify a
fundamentally modernist aesthetic organized around the concept of totalization and grounded in a vision of the world that is expansive and anthro-
pocentric. In *Noticias del Imperio,* that vision gives way to a postmodern
mind-set and the adoption of some of the essential categories and procedures of postmodern historiographic metafiction. However, as I was keen
to argue in earlier chapters of this study, the impulse toward the
postmodern in *Palinuro de México* and *Noticias del Imperio* is held in

check by a continuing allegiance to the moral and aesthetic tenets of modernism. Only in *Linda 67* does the postmodern paradigm emerge as dominant, to the exclusion of its modernist alternative.

The trajectory outlined here runs *pari passu* with an evolving cultural and ideological agenda in del Paso's narrative. The word *culture,* as used (rather imprecisely) by Barthes in the quotation above, implies a context, or store, of signifying practices that acquire considerable clarity of definition in a study of the intertextual relations of the novels of Fernando del Paso. National, regional, continental, and intercontinental traditions provide the stimuli for a set of four novels that represent so many instances of cultural interaction. In the case of *José Trigo,* a metropolitan religious code undergoes a process of transculturation through interaction with local paradigms, the issue of which is a culturally hybrid text comparable with others from the narrative traditions of Mexico, Guatemala, and Paraguay. In *Palinuro de México,* the anxiety of influence suffered by Marechal in the creation of *Adán Buenosayres* gives way to an assurance of equal worth vis-à-vis the western canon, and eventuates in the most accomplished American version of *Ulysses.* After *Palinuro de México,* *Noticias del Imperio* takes European historiography and historical narrative as its starting point and exposes their failings in a spirit of postcolonial contestation. Finally, *Linda 67* cannibalizes the noir aesthetic of North American film and fiction and turns the weapons of a revised ideology of civilization and barbarism back against their source.

In the final analysis, ideological and aesthetic motivations coincide at every stage of del Paso's narrative trajectory. Together, *José Trigo, Palinuro de México, Noticias del Imperio,* and *Linda 67* intervene individually and serially in the political and cultural contexts of Mexican and American writing, reinterpreting, redeploying, and ultimately reinventing forms of narrative that have constituted the main lines of the western literary tradition of the twentieth century.

Notes

1. Paradigms, Contexts, and Affiliations: Reading the Novels of Fernando del Paso Intertextually

1. See, for example, Alvarez, "Fernando del Paso, de *José Trigo* a *Palinuro de México*," 15.

2. One obstacle to the recognition of the hybridity of a text such as *José Trigo* was an attitude of hostility and prejudice against "imported models" felt, in some circles, to be detrimental to the new novel of Spanish America. The greatest skeptic in this regard was Manuel Pedro González, who railed against the influence of James Joyce on Latin American fiction of the time in *Coloquio sobre la novela hispanoamericana*, 63, and elsewhere.

2. *José Trigo*: A Novel of Hybridity and Regeneration

1. Crucial to the progress of del Paso's literary apprenticeship was the support he received at the Centro Mexicano de Escritores from Juan Rulfo and Juan José Arreola, as reported in Carvajal, "Revelaciones y anticipaciones de Fernando del Paso y Miguel Angel Asturias," iii.

2. A vivid evocation of the period is provided by Carlos Fuentes in the essays "Radiografía de una década, 1953–1963" and "La muerte de Rubén Jaramillo," in *Tiempo mexicano*, 56–92, 109–22.

3. On the phenomenon of the railway workers' strike, see Antonio Alonso, *El movimiento ferrocarrilero en México, 1958/1959*. A brief discussion of the role of Vallejo can be found in Donald Hodges and Daniel Ross Gandy, *Mexico, 1910– 1976: Reform or Revolution?* 107.

4. Bakhtinian readings of Fuentes's work abound. Examples include Wendy Faris, *Carlos Fuentes*, and the text of an interview conducted by Julio Ortega, "Carlos Fuentes: para recuperar la tradición de la Mancha."

5. Alvaro Enrique situates Fuentes's novel within the tradition of writing about Mexico City, in "Nueva visita a *La región más transparente*."

6. A classic instance of the structuralist analysis of narrative in Latin American literature is found in Carlos Fuentes, *La nueva novela hispanoamericana*.

7. On the link between dismemberment and saintly status, see Joseph Campbell, *The Hero with a Thousand Faces*, 16–17, 245–46.

8. Benjamin Keen discusses structural aspects of the pre-Columbian picture of the universe in *The Aztec Image in Western Thought*, 32.

9. *Enciclopedia universal ilustrada europeo-americana* 48:1045.

10. The incident of Quetzalcóatl and the mirror is referred to in some detail by Carlos Fuentes in "From Quetzalcóatl to Pepsicóatl," *Tiempo mexicano,* 17–42.

11. The story of Castor and Pollux is told in *New Larousse Encyclopedia of Mythology,* 190, and invoked by Carlos Fuentes throughout *Terra nostra.*

12. Compare Borges's insight on this point with Fredric Jameson's commonsense proposition that "Totality is not available for representation, any more than it is accessible in the form of some ultimate truth": Jameson, *The Political Unconscious: Narrative as a Socially Symbolic Act,* 55.

13. The notion that *José Trigo* represents a summa of Mexican writing is a critical commonplace articulated as early as 1967 by Ramón Xirau, "José Agustín, Navarrete, del Paso," 25, and subsequently restated in 1972 by Luis Leal in "La nueva narrativa mexicana," 92.

14. Quoted by Donald Shaw in *Nueva narrativa hispanoamericana,* 163.

15. In my reading of *Hombres de maíz* I have found much useful material in René Prieto, *Miguel Angel Asturias's Archaeology of Return* and in the detailed introduction to the edition of *Hombres* prepared by Gerald Martin and published by Fondo de Cultura Económica.

16. Homi Bhabha comments on Fanon's "deep hunger for humanism" in "Remembering Fanon: Self, Psyche, and the Colonial Condition," 120. Zea's inclination toward humanist principles is documented at length in chapter 1 of this book.

17. The term *palimpsestuous* was coined by Gérard Genette in his landmark book *Palimpsestes* as a notation for extreme practices of intertextual inbreeding. By way of examples from the Arreola canon, "Prosodia" in *Confabulario* rewrites the *Quijote* and Garcí Sánchez de Badajoz, while *La feria* recycles chronicles, legal submissions, and other material from the colonial heritage of Mexican history and literature. It comes as no surprise that del Paso, in a schematic account of his Mexican precursors, should characterize Arreola as rhetorical brilliance (la retórica), vis-à-vis Rulfo who, he said, "es la sabiduría" (Carvajal, "Revelaciones y anticipaciones de Fernando del Paso y Miguel Angel Asturias," iii).

18. In conversation with Luis Sánchez Bordón and Javier Goñi, Fernando del Paso confirmed his admiration and affection for Juan Rulfo, whom he credited with being the author of "the most important book that has been written in Mexico" (Sánchez Bordón and Goñi, "Fernando del Paso: 'Uno escribe cuando camina, cuando lee, cuando sueña,'" 49).

3. *Palinuro de México:* The Body, the Nation, and the Book of the World

1. The erotic dimension of the novel is explored extensively by Claude Fell in "Sexo y lenguaje en *Palinuro de México,* de Fernando del Paso."

2. Two informative surveys of literary reactions to Tlatelolco are Dolly J. Young, "Mexican Literary Reactions to Tlatelolco 1968," and José Luis Martínez and Christopher Domínguez Michael, "La saga literaria de 1968," in *La literatura mexicana del siglo XX,* 222–29. The thirtieth anniversary of the Tlatelolco massa-

cre saw the publication of numerous historical studies; Sergio Aguayo Quezada, 1968: *Los archivos de la violencia* is particularly worthy of note.

3. A quarter century after the publication of *La noche de Tlatelolco*, Martínez and Domínguez Michael evaluated Poniatowska's testimony quite rightly as "a morally irreproachable book," in *La literatura mexicana del siglo XX*, 223.

4. Avilés Fabila has provided a fascinating account of the process of production of *El gran solitario del palacio* in his autobiographical memoirs, *Recordanzas*, 126–29.

5. The epigraph that I have lifted from a poem by Silvina Ocampo is just one of many instances of the Palinurus myth found in Spanish American (largely Argentine) writing. Before del Paso, Virgil's tragic hero is refracted through Marechal as well as through the Ocampo poem, and through Cortázar and his commentators as well. Cortázar reviewed Ricardo Baeza's translation of Connolly's essay in the pages of *Sur* in February 1950, and he mentions *The Unquiet Grave* again in *La vuelta al día en ochenta mundos*, 1:13. In the secondary literature, Graciela de Sola attests to Cortázar's sympathy for the figure of Palinurus, in *Julio Cortázar y el hombre nuevo*, 146.

6. Cortázar's search for a new humanist ethic is glossed in the following statement of 1963: "Everything that I have written is driven by a particular aim, which is to define a new metaphysics and a new ethics" (cited by Laszlo Scholz, *El arte poética de Julio Cortázar*, 36).

7. For a range of comments on the total novel, see Carlos Fuentes, *La nueva novela hispanoamericana*, 30–48, Mario Vargas Llosa, *La orgía perpetua*, and Fernando del Paso, in Fiddian, "James Joyce y Fernando del Paso."

8. Ethel Krauze captures the novel's spirit of engagement with universal culture when she observes that through del Paso's narrative, "Mexico assumes its rightful place on the planet, and achieves universality," in "Garibay, del Paso, Ibargüengoitia," 61.

9. I take the happy phrase "Oedipus without a complex" from Enrico Mario Santí, who applies it to José Cemí in a reading of *Paradiso* by José Lezama Lima. See "Escándalos de Paradiso," in Santí's *Por una politeratura: Literatura hispanoamericana e imaginación política*, 196.

4. Noticias del Imperio and the New Historical Novel

1. Work in progress was documented most informatively in interviews with the author such as those conducted by Maruja Echegoyen, "Nuevas conversaciones con Fernando del Paso," and Juan José Barrientos, "La locura de Carlota: novela e historia." For a sample of critical opinion at the time of publication, see Fabienne Bradu, "*Noticias del Imperio* de Fernando del Paso," in *Vuelta*, as well as views published in the cultural supplements of *Excelsior* (29 January 1988), *Unomásuno* (6 February 1988), and *Novedades* (7 February 1988).

2. Readings that give prominence to considerations of history and ideology in

the novel include Juan Bruce-Novoa, "*Noticias del Imperio:* la historia apasionada," and Claude Fell, "Historia y ficción en *Noticias del Imperio* de Fernando del Paso."

3. I draw attention again to the role played by Leopoldo Zea in the absorption of Fanon's work into the Spanish American intellectual mainstream. As noted in an earlier chapter, Zea hailed Fanon as a fellow Latin American and cited him a number of times in *Dependencia y liberación en la cultura latinoamericana.*

4. The "Addresses to the German Nation" ("Reden an die deutsche Nation") that Johann Gottlieb Fichte delivered 1807–8 are undoubtedly foremost in the author's mind as he criticizes German imperialism through the mouthpiece of Juárez.

5. In truth, Juárez's reference to the Scriptures is a loose translation and paraphrase of Genesis 10:1–32.

6. Del Paso nevertheless claims Carlota for the Mexican people in an open letter, dated 27 September 1993, to the king of Belgium. Complaining about official Belgian interference with the text of an article that he had earlier submitted to the organizing committee of Europalia, del Paso told King Albert, "The fact is that Carlota is more closely related to the history of Mexico than she ever was or could be to the history of Belgium. Or let us just say that Princess Charlotte belongs to you and Carlota to us" ("Carta de Fernando del Paso al Rey de Bélgica," 49).

7. The boardgames of Wallis and others like him belong to the same political category as the "Great Game" of British imperial intelligence in India, referred to by Edward Said in *Culture and Imperialism,* 56.

8. In characterizing Maximilian and Carlota's Mexican venture as "tragic," del Paso also echoes the terminology of his sources, including Edward Crankshaw, who describes Maximilian's reign as "the ghastliest tragi-comedy" (*Fall of the House of Habsburg,* 247).

9. My view of *Noticias del Imperio* as a demystifying text differs from that of Fabienne Bradu, who maintains that "Fernando del Paso persigue en Maximiliano una doble creación mítica: la que la Historia [*sic*] le encargó representar [. . .] y la que Carlota pretende hacer sobrevivir en su incansable memoria" ("*Noticias del Imperio* de Fernando del Paso," 49).

10. Carlos J. Alonso argues a much closer affiliation of *El general en su laberinto* with postmodernism in "The Mourning After: García Márquez, Fuentes, and the Meaning of Postmodernism in Spanish America."

11. Certain aspects of the relation between *Noticias del Imperio* and *El general en su laberinto* are discussed by Gustavo Pellón, who accords del Paso's novel pride of place in the genre of the New Historical Novel of Latin America. See "The Spanish American Novel: Recent Developments, 1975–1990," 287–94.

12. Alfonso González relates *Noticias del Imperio* to other Mexican novels on historical subjects including *Madero, el otro* and *Los pasos de López* by Jorge Ibargüengoitia, in *Euphoria and Crisis: Essays on the Contemporary Mexican Novel.*

5. *Linda 67:* The Homeland Strikes Back

1. Del Paso acknowledges his interest in Carpentier in the course of an interview conducted by Javier Aranda Luna, "Poesía de la ciencia, narrativa de la historia," 28.

2. The formulaic basis of the detective story or crime novel is the subject of Tzvetan Todorov, "The Typology of Detective Fiction," and of countless other classic studies of the genre.

3. Amelia S. Simpson surveys the genre in the River Plate, Brazil, Mexico, and Cuba in *Detective Fiction from Latin America.* For an up-to-date analysis of the Mexican tradition, see Ilán Stavans, *Antihéroes: México y su novela policial.* On parodic transgression in the work of Paco Ignacio Taibo II and others, see Elzbieta Sklodowska, *La parodia en la nueva novela hispanoamericana,* esp. 127–33.

4. On the *novela negra* proper, see, in addition to Stavans, Ian Michael, "From Scarlet Study to Novela Negra." For an account of the noir aesthetic in film, see Ian Cameron, ed., *The Movie Book of Film Noir,* and Joan Copjec, ed., *Shades of Noir.*

Bibliography

Aguayo Quezada, Sergio. *1968: Los archivos de la violencia.* Mexico City: Grijalbo/Reforma, 1998.

Aguilar Mora, Jorge. *Si muero lejos de ti.* Mexico City: Joaquín Mortiz, 1979.

———. "Pequeña relación de la más reciente narrativa mexicana." *Camp de l'Arpa* 74 (April 1980): 39–44.

Alazraki, Jaime. "La postmodernidad de Julio Cortázar." *Hacia Cortázar: aproximaciones a su obra.* Barcelona: Anthropos, 1994: 353–65.

Alonso, Antonio. *El movimiento ferrocarrilero en México, 1958/1959: De la conciliación a la lucha de clases.* Mexico City: Ediciones Era, 1972.

Alonso, Carlos J. "The Mourning After: García Márquez, Fuentes, and the Meaning of Postmodernism in Spanish America." *Modern Language Notes* 109 (1994): 252–67.

———, ed. *Julio Cortázar: New Readings.* Cambridge: Cambridge University Press, 1998.

Alvarez, Ildefonso. "Fernando del Paso, de *José Trigo* a *Palinuro de México.*" *La Estafeta Literaria* 627 (1 January 1978): 14–15.

Anderson, Danny J. "Cultural Conversation and Constructions of Reality: Mexican Narrative and Literary Theories after 1968." *Siglo XX/20th Century* 8, nos. 1–2 (1990–91): 11–30.

Aranda Luna, Javier. "Poesía de la ciencia, narrativa de la historia: Fernando del Paso" (An interview with the author). *Vuelta* 233 (April 1996): 25–28.

Aratán, Sonia, and René Depestre. "Entrevista con Aimé Césaire." *Casa de las Américas* 49 (July–August 1968): 130–42.

Aronne Amestoy, Lida. *Cortázar: la novela mandala.* Buenos Aires: Fernando García Cambeiro, 1972.

Asturias, Miguel Angel. *Hombres de maíz.* Buenos Aires: Losada, 1949. Ed. Gerald Martin. Mexico City: Fondo de Cultura Económica, 1981.

———. *Mulata de tal.* Buenos Aires: Losada, 1963.

Avilés Fabila, René. *El gran solitario del palacio.* Mexico City: Premia, 1988.

———. *Recordanzas.* Mexico City: Editorial Aldus, 1996.

Bailey, David C. *Viva Cristo Rey! The Cristero Rebellion and the Church-State Conflict in Mexico.* Austin: University of Texas Press, 1974.

Bakhtin, Mikhail. "Zakljuchitel'nye zamechanija" (Concluding remarks) (1973). *Voprosy literatury i éstetiki.* Moscow: Khudozhestvennaia literatura, 1975. 391–407. Cited in Tzvetan Todorov, *Mikhail Bakhtin: The Dialogical Principle.* Trans. Wlad Godzich. Manchester: Manchester University Press, 1984. 84–85.

Barcía, Pedro Luis, ed. *Leopoldo Marechal: Adán Buenosayres*. Madrid: Cátedra, 1994.

Barrientos, Juan José. "La locura de Carlota: una entrevista con Fernando del Paso." *Vuelta* 113 (April 1986): 30–34.

——. "Del Paso y la historia como *readymade*." *Biblioteca de México* 32 (March–April 1996): 51–56.

Barthes, Roland. "Theory of the Text" (1973). Trans. Ian McLeod. *Untying the Text: A Poststructuralist Reader*. Ed. Robert Young. London: Routledge, 1981. 31–46.

Bary, David. "Poesía y narración en cuatro novelas mexicanas." *Revista iberoamericana* 148–149 (July–December 1989): 903–14.

Basave Benítez, Antonio. *México mestizo: Análisis del nacionalismo mexicano en torno a la mestizofilia de Andrés Molina Enríquez*. Mexico City: Fondo de Cultura Económica, 1992.

Battilana, Carlos. *Reflexiones sobre "Hijo de hombre" de Augusto Roa Bastos*. Frankfurt am Main: Peter Lang, 1979.

Bendayán, P. L. *Palinuro de México*. Caracas: Universidad Simón Bolívar, 1990.

Beverley, John, Michael Aronna, and José Oviedo. *The Postmodernism Debate in Latin America*. Durham: Duke University Press, 1995.

Bhabha, Homi. "Remembering Fanon: Self, Psyche, and the Colonial Condition." *Colonial Discourse and Post-colonial Theory*. Ed. Patrick Williams and Laura Chrisman. New York: Columbia University Press, 1994. 112–23.

Bioy Casares, Adolfo. See Jorge Luis Borges.

Bloom, Harold. *The Anxiety of Influence: A Theory of Poetry*. Oxford: Oxford University Press, 1973.

Boehmer, Elleke. *Colonial and Postcolonial Literature*. Oxford: Oxford University Press, 1995.

Boldy, Steven. "Carlos Fuentes' *Las buenas conciencias*." *Bulletin of Hispanic Studies* 71 (1994): 359–80.

Borges, Jorge Luis. "El escritor argentino y la tradición." *Discusión*. Buenos Aires: M. Gleizer, 1932. Also in *Obras completas*. Vol. 1. Barcelona: Emecé, 1989. 267–74. 3 vols.

——. "El Aleph." *Sur* 131 (September 1945): 52–66. Also in *Obras completas*. Vol. 1. Barcelona: Emecé, 1989. 617–28. 3 vols.

——. With Adolfo Bioy Casares. *Seis problemas para don Isidro Parodi*. Buenos Aires: Ediciones Sur, 1942.

——. With Adolfo Bioy Casares and Silvina Ocampo. *Antología de la literatura fantástica*. Buenos Aires: Sudamericana, 1967.

Bradbury, Malcolm and James McFarlane. "The Name and Nature of Modernism." *Modernism*. Harmondsworth, Middlesex: Penguin, 1976. 19–55.

Bradu, Fabienne. "*Palinuro de México:* la picaresca de la desilusión." *Revista de la Universidad de México* 33, no. 12 (August 1979): 43–44.

——. "*Noticias del Imperio* de Fernando del Paso." *Vuelta* 138 (May 1988): 48–50.

————. "*Linda 67. Historia de un crimen.*" *Vuelta* 231 (February 1996): 39–41.

Brooker, Peter, ed. *Modernism/Postmodernism*. London: Longman, 1992. 1–33.

Bruce-Novoa, Juan. "*Noticias del Imperio:* la historia apasionada." *Literatura mexicana* 1 (1990): 421–38.

Cameron, Ian, ed. *The Movie Book of Film Noir*. London: Studio Vista, 1992.

Campbell, Federico. *Pretexta*. Mexico City: Fondo de Cultura Económica, 1979.

Campbell, Joseph. *The Hero with a Thousand Faces*. 2nd ed. Princeton: Princeton University Press, 1968.

Campos, Jorge. "*Palinuro de México* de Fernando del Paso." *Insula* 378 (May 1978): 11.

Campos, Marco Antonio. *Que la carne es hierba*. Mexico City: Joaquín Mortiz, 1982.

Carter, Angela. *The Sadeian Woman: An Exercise in Cultural History*. London: Virago, 1979.

Carvajal, Juan. "Revelaciones y anticipaciones de Fernando del Paso y Miguel Angel Asturias." *La Cultura en México* 225 (8 June 1966): i–vi.

Castellanos, Rosario. "Memorial de Tlatelolco." *Poesía no eres tú*. México City: Fondo de Cultura Económica, 1972. 287–88.

Castañón, Adolfo. "*Noticias del Imperio* de Fernando del Paso." *Vuelta* 142 (September 1988): 32–33.

Cawelti, John G. *Adventure, Mystery, and Romance*. Chicago: Chicago University Press, 1976.

Chavarri, Raúl. "El personaje en la moderna novela mexicana: A propósito de *José Trigo* de Fernando del Paso." *Cuadernos hispanoamericanos* 215 (November 1967): 395–400.

Clark, Stella, and Alfonso González. "*Noticias del Imperio:* la 'verdad histórica' y la novela finisecular en México." *Hispania* 77 (1994): 731–37.

Connolly, Cyril. *The Unquiet Grave: A Word Cycle by Palinurus*. London: Horizon, 1944.

Conte, Rafael. "Un largo viaje entre el exceso y la totalidad (*Palinuro de México*)." *EL PAIS* (Madrid), Arte y pensamiento, 1, no. 11 (24 December 1977): iii.

Copjec, Joan, ed. *Shades of Noir*. London: Verso, 1993.

Corral Peña, Elizabeth. "Del Paso; entre historia y ficción." *Literatura mexicana* 4 (1993): 125–47.

————. *Noticias del Imperio y los nuevos caminos de la novela histórica*. Xalapa, Veracruz: Universidad Veracruzana, 1997.

Correa, Rafael E. "Por el Magdalena de García Márquez o la excentricidad de la escritura." *Asociación Internacional de Hispanistas. Actas Irvine-92*. Ed. Juan Villegas. Vol 4. California: Asociación Internacional de Hispanistas, 1994. 331–37. 5 vols.

Cortázar, Julio. Review of Cyril Connolly, *La tumba sin sosiego*. Trans. Ricardo Baeza. *Sur* 184 (February 1950): 61–63.

————. "Situación de la novela." *Cuadernos americanos* 9, no. 4 (July–August 1950): 223–43.

————. *La vuelta al día en ochenta mundos.* Madrid: Siglo XXI, 1972.

————. *Rayuela.* Buenos Aires: Editorial Sudamericana, 1963. Barcelona: Edhasa, 1977.

Corti, Count Egon Caesar. *Maximiliano y Carlota.* 1924. Trans. Vicente Caridad. Mexico City: Fondo de Cultura Económica, 1944.

Crankshaw, Edward. *The Fall of the House of Habsburg.* London: Longman, 1963.

Davies, Tony. *Humanism: The New Critical Idiom.* London: Routledge, 1997.

de Sola, Graciela. *Julio Cortázar y el hombre nuevo.* Buenos Aires: Editorial Sudamericana, 1968.

de Toro, Alfonso, ed. *Postmodernidad y postcolonialidad: Breves reflexiones sobre Latinoamérica.* Frankfurt am Main: Vervuert/Madrid: Iberoamericana, 1997.

del Paso, Fernando. *José Trigo.* 2nd ed. Mexico City: Siglo XXI, 1969.

————. "La imaginación al poder. El intelectual y sus medios." *Revista de la Universidad de México* 34, no. 2 (October 1979): 15–16.

————. *Palinuro de México.* Madrid: Alfaguara, 1977; Mexico City: Joaquín Mortiz, 1980.

————. "Las Nuevas Hébridas. El paraíso perdido . . . o casi." *Triunfo* (Madrid) 33, no. 910 (5 July 1980): 35–36.

————. "Latinoamérica para los latinoamericanos." *Proceso* 284 (12 April 1982): 38–39.

————. "Malvinas: Inglaterra y Argentina en un posible punto sin retorno." *Proceso* 287 (3 May 1982): 40–44.

————. "Malvinas: falló la diplomacia y ya se combate por los derechos humanos ¿de quiénes?" *Proceso* 290 (24 May 1982): 43–45.

————. "Mi patria chica, mi patria grande." *Proceso* 301 (9 August 1982): 48–52. Reprinted in *Casa de las Américas* 136 (January–February 1983): 154–60.

————. *Noticias del Imperio.* Mexico City: Diana, 1987.

————. "La novela que no olvidé." *Revista de Bellas Artes* 3 (July 1982): 46–49. Reprinted in *Los novelistas como críticos.* Comp. Norma Klahn and Wilfrido Corral. Mexico City: Fondo de Cultura Económica, 1991. 318–22.

————. Excerpts of the address delivered in Paris at the Sorbonne on 11 March 1991, reproduced in Anne Mergier, "Como 'Hizo trizas' Fernando del Paso un texto de Octavio Paz en la reunión de escritores en París." *Proceso* 750 (19 March 1991): 46–47.

————. "Carta de Fernando del Paso al Rey de Bélgica." *Proceso* 882 (27 September 1993): 48–49.

————. *Linda 67: Historia de un crimen.* Mexico City: Plaza y Janés, 1995.

Dessau, Adalbert. "*José Trigo:* Notas acerca de un acontecimiento literario en la novela mexicana." *Bulletin Hispanique* 70 (1968): 510–19.

Díaz Infante, Fernando. *Quetzalcóatl (Ensayo psicoanalítico del mito nahua).* With a prologue by Angel Ma. Garibay. Xalapa, Veracruz: Universidad Veracruzana, 1963.

Dominguez, Mignon, coord. *Historia, ficción y metaficción en la novela latinoamericana*. Buenos Aires: Corregidor, 1969.

Domínguez Michael, Christopher. "Fernando del Paso o el banquete de la historia." *Proceso* 588 (8 February 1988): 58–59.

———. "Notas sobre mitos nacionales y novela mexicana (1955–1985)." *Revista iberoamericana* 148/149 (July–December 1989): 915–24.

Donoso, José. *Historia personal del "boom."* Barcelona: Anagrama, 1972.

Dottori, Nora. "*José Trigo*: el terror a la historia." *Nueva novela latinoamericana*. Ed. J. Lafforgue. Vol. 2. Buenos Aires: Paidós, 1969. 262–99. 2 vols.

Eagleton, Terry. *The Illusions of Postmodernism*. Oxford: Blackwell, 1996.

Echegoyen, Maruja. "Entrevista binaria con Fernando del Paso." *Cuadernos de Marcha* 17/18 (January/April 1982): 23–28.

———. "Nuevas conversaciones con Fernando del Paso." *Cuadernos de Marcha* 23 (September 1983): 24–33.

Enciclopedia universal ilustrada europeo-americana. Madrid: Espasa Calpe, 1922.

Enrique, Alvaro. "Nueva visita a *La región más transparente*." *Insula* 611 (November 1997): 22–24.

Espinosa-Jácome. "Palinuro: escultura del artista adolescente." *Bulletin Hispanique* 99 (1997): 457–70.

Fanon, Frantz. *Black Skin, White Masks*. 1952. Trans. Charles Lan Markmann. London: Grove Press, 1967. London: Pluto Press, 1986.

———. *The Wretched of the Earth*. 1961. Trans. Constance Farrington. Harmondsworth, Middlesex: Penguin, 1967.

Faris, Wendy. *Carlos Fuentes*. New York: Fredrick Ungar, 1983.

Fell, Claude. "Sexo y lenguaje en *Palinuro de México*, de Fernando del Paso." *Coloquio internacional: Escritura y sexualidad en la literatura hispanoamericana*. Poitiers: Centre de Recherches Latino-Americaines/Madrid: Fundamentos, 1990. 181–94.

———. "Histoire et fiction dans *Noticias del Imperio* de Fernando del Paso." *Cahiers du C.R.I.A.R.* 11 (1991): 25–32. Also printed as "Historia y ficción en *Noticias del Imperio* de Fernando del Paso." *Cuadernos americanos* (New series) 4, no. 28 (July–August 1991): 77–89.

Fiddian, Robin. "*Palinuro de México*, a World of Words." *Bulletin of Hispanic Studies* 58 (1981): 121–33.

———. "Beyond the Unquiet Grave and the Cemetery of Words: Myth and Archetype in *Palinuro de México*." *Iberoamerikanisches Archiv*, n.s., 8, no. 3 (1982): 243–55.

———. "A Case of Literary Infection: *Palinuro de México* and *Ulysses*." *Comparative Literature Studies* 19 (1982): 220–35.

———. "James Joyce y Fernando del Paso." *Insula* 455 (October 1984): 10.

———. "Religious Symbolism and the Ideological Critique in 'El perseguidor' by Julio Cortázar." *Revista canadiense de estudios hispánicos* 9 (1985): 149–63.

———. "James Joyce and Spanish-American Fiction: A Study of the Origins and Transmission of Literary Influence." *Bulletin of Hispanic Studies* 66 (1989): 23–39.

———. "The Pursuit of Knowledge and Pleasure." *Times Literary Supplement,* 15–21 December 1989: 1386.

———. "Fernando del Paso y el arte de la renovación." *Revista iberoamericana* 150 (January–May 1990): 143–58.

———. "*Palinuro de México:* entre la protesta y el mito." *Literatura mexicana hoy. Del 68 al ocaso de la revolución.* Ed. Karl Kohut. Frankfurt am Main: Vervuert Verlag, 1991. 214–22.

Flores Sevilla, Jesús. "*José Trigo:* un mito sobre Nonoalco-Tlatelolco." *Hojas de crítica,* Suplemento de *Revista de la Universidad de México* 24, nos. 5–6 (January–February 1970): 4–7.

Forster, Edward Morgan. *Aspects of the Novel.* London: Edward Arnold, 1927.

Foster, David William. *Augusto Roa Bastos.* Boston: G. K. Hall, 1978.

Foster, Hal. "Postmodernism: A Preface." *The Anti-Aesthetic: Essays on Postmodern Culture.* Ed. Hal Foster. Port Townsend, Wash.: Bay Press, 1984.

Foster, Merlin H., ed. *Tradition and Renewal: Essays on Twentieth-Century Latin American Literature and Culture.* Urbana: University of Illinois Press, 1975.

Franco, Jean. *Lectura sociocrítica de la obra novelística de Agustín Yáñez.* Guadalajara, Mexico: Unidad Editorial, 1988.

———. "Pastiche in Contemporary Latin American Literature." *Studies in Twentieth-Century Literature* 14 (1989–90): 95–107.

Frazer, James George. *The Golden Bough: A Study in Magic and Religion.* New York: Macmillan, 1935.

Frenk, Susan. "Rewriting History: Carlos Fuentes' *Aura.*" *Forum for Modern Language Studies* 30 (1994): 256–76.

Freud, Sigmund. *On Sexuality: Three Essays on the Theory of Sexuality and Other Works* (1905–31). Pelican Freud Library, ed. Angela Richards. Trans. from the original German under the general editorship of James Strachey. Vol. 7. Harmondsworth, Middlesex: Penguin, 1977.

Fuentes, Carlos. *La región más transparente.* Mexico City: Fondo de Cultura Económica, 1958.

———. *La nueva novela hispanoamericana.* Mexico City: Joaquín Mortiz, 1969.

———. *Casa de guardar.* Mexico City: Joaquín Mortiz, 1970.

———. *Tiempo mexicano.* 4th ed. Mexico City: Joaquín Mortiz, 1972.

———. *Terra nostra.* Mexico City: Joaquín Mortiz, 1975.

———. *Cervantes o la crítica de la lectura.* Mexico City: Joaquín Mortiz, 1976.

———. *Los días enmascarados.* Mexico City: Los Presentes, 1954. Mexico City: Ediciones Era, 1982.

———. *Valiente mundo nuevo.* Madrid: Mondadori España, 1990.

———. *La campaña.* Mexico City: Fondo de Cultura Económica, 1990.

Gambetta Cruk, Aida Nadi. "Las coordenadas míticas en *José Trigo.*" *Revista de literatura hispanoamericana* 7 (1974): 153–85.

García Gutiérrez, Georgina. *Los disfraces: la obra mestiza de Carlos Fuentes*. Mexico City: Colegio de México, 1981.

——, ed. Carlos Fuentes, *La región más transparente*. Madrid: Cátedra, 1982.

García Márquez, Gabriel. *Cien años de soledad*. Buenos Aires: Sudamericana, 1967.

——. *La hojarasca*. Bogotá: Sipa, 1955; Barcelona: Bruguera, 1970.

——. "¿Problemas de la novela?" (1950). *Obra periodística*. Ed. Jacques Gilard. Vol. 1. Barcelona: Bruguera, 1981–83. 267–69. 6 vols.

——. *La soledad de América latina: Brindis por la poesía*. Cali: Corporación de Editorial Universitaria de Colombia, 1983.

——. *El general en su laberinto*. Madrid: Mondadori España, 1989.

Garibay K., Angel María. *La literatura de los aztecas*. Mexico City: Joaquín Mortiz, 1970.

Genette, Gérard. *Palimpsestes: La littérature au second degré*. Paris: Editions du Seuil, 1982.

Giardinelli, Mempo. "Panorama de la narrativa mexicana en los 80's." *Insula* 512–513 (August–September 1989): 22–25.

Glantz, Margot. *Repeticiones: Ensayos sobre literatura mexicana*. Xalapa, Veracruz: Universidad Veracruzana, 1979.

González, Alfonso. *Euphoria and Crisis: Essays on the Contemporary Mexican Novel*. National Library of Canada, York Press, 1990.

——. "Neobarroco y carnaval medieval en *Palinuro de México*." *Hispania* 74 (March 1991): 45–49.

——. "*Noticias del Imperio* y la historiografía postmodernista." *Asociación Internacional de Hispanistas. Actas Irvine-92*. Ed. Juan Villegas. Vol. 4. California: Asociación Internacional de Hispanistas, 1994. 251–58. 5 vols.

González, Manuel Pedro. "La novela hispanoamericana en el contexto de la internacional." In Manuel Pedro González, Ivan Schulman et al., *Coloquio sobre la novela hispano-americana*. Mexico City: Fondo de Cultura Económica, 1967. 35–109.

González Bermejo, E. "Juan Rulfo: la literatura es una mentira que dice la verdad." *Revista de la Universidad de México* 43, no. 1 (September 1979): 8.

González del Alba, Luis. "1968: La fiesta y la tragedia." *Nexos* 189 (September 1993): 23–31.

González Echevarría, Roberto. *Myth and Archive: A Theory of Latin American Narrative*. Cambridge: Cambridge University Press, 1990.

Gordon, Ambrose. "Dublin and Buenos Aires, Joyce and Marechal." *Comparative Literature Studies* 19 (1982): 208–19.

Gramsci, Antonio. *Selections from the Prison Notebooks*. Ed. Quinton Hoare and Geoffrey Nowell-Smith. London: Lawrence and Wishart, 1971.

Guevara Niebla, Gilberto. "Volver al '68." *Nexos* 190 (October 1993): 31–41.

Gutiérrez Mouat, Ricardo. "Postmodernity and Postmodernism in Latin America: Fuentes's *Christopher Unborn*." *Critical Theory, Cultural Politics, and Latin*

American Narrative. Ed. Steven M. Bell, Albert H. LeMay, and Leonard Orr. Notre Dame: University of Notre Dame Press, 1993. 153–79.

Hancock, Joel. "New Directions in Historical Fiction: *Noticias del Imperio,* Fernando del Paso, and the Self-Conscious Novel." *Hispanic Journal* 12 (1991): 109–21.

Hassan, Ihab. *The Postmodern Turn: Essays in Postmodern Theory and Culture.* Columbus: Ohio State University Press, 1987.

Highsmith, Patricia. *Those Who Walk Away.* London: Heinemann, 1967; New York: First Atlantic Monthly Press, 1988.

Hirschkop, Ken, and David Shepherd. *Bakhtin and Cultural Theory.* Manchester: Manchester University Press, 1989.

Hodges, Donald Clark, and Daniel Ross Gandy. *Mexico, 1910–1976: Reform or Revolution?* London: Zed Press, 1979.

Hunt, Eva. *The Transformation of the Humming Bird: Cultural Roots of a Zinacantecan Mythical Poem.* Ithaca: Cornell University Press, 1977.

Hutcheon, Linda. *A Poetics of Postmodernism: History, Theory, Fiction.* London: Routledge, 1988.

———. *The Politics of Postmodernism.* London: Routledge, 1989.

Jakobson, Roman. "Linguistics and Poetics." *Style and Language.* Ed. Thomas E. Sebeok. Cambridge: Massachusetts Institute of Technology Press, 1960. 350–77.

Jameson, Fredric. *The Political Unconscious: Narrative as a Socially Symbolic Act.* Ithaca: Cornell University Press, 1981.

———. "Postmodernism, or the Cultural Logic of Late Capitalism." *New Left Review* 146 (1984): 53–92. Reproduced in *Postmodernism or the Cultural Logic of Late Capitalism.* London: Verso, 1991.

Joyce, James. *Finnegans Wake.* 1939. London: Faber and Faber, 1975.

———. *Ulysses.* 1922. Ed. Hans Walter Gabler et al. Harmondsworth, Middlesex: Penguin, 1986.

Keen, Benjamin. *The Aztec Image in Western Thought.* New Brunswick: Rutgers University Press, 1971.

Kerr, Lucille. *Reclaiming the Author: Figures and Fictions from Spanish America.* Durham: Duke University Press, 1992.

Klor de Alva, Jorge J. "The Postcolonization of the (Latin) American Experience: A Reconsideration of 'Colonialism,' 'Postcolonialism,' and 'Mestizaje'." *After Colonialism: Imperial Histories and Postcolonial Displacements.* Ed. Gyan Prakash. Princeton: Princeton University Press, 1995. 241–75.

Kohut, Karl, ed. *Literatura mexicana hoy: Del 68 al ocaso de la revolución.* Frankfurt am Main: Vervuert Verlag, 1991.

Krauze, Ethel. "Garibay, del Paso, Ibargüengoitia. Tres imaginerías mexicanas." *Revista de Bellas Artes* 3, no. 2 (May 1982): 60–61.

Kristeva, Julia. "Word, Dialogue, and Novel." Trans. Alice Jardine, Thomas Gora, and Leon S. Roudiez. *Desire in Language: A Semiotic Approach to Literature and Art.* Ed. Leon S. Roudiez. Oxford: Blackwell, 1980. 64–91.

Kuhn, Annette. *The Power of the Image: Essays in Representation and Sexuality.* London: Routledge and Kegan Paul, 1985.

Lafaye, Jacques. *Quetzalcóatl and Guadalupe: The Formation of the National Mexican Consciousness, 1531–1813.* Trans. Benjamin Keen. Chicago: Chicago University Press, 1976.

Langford, Walter. *The Mexican Novel Comes of Age.* Notre Dame: University of Notre Dame Press, 1971.

Larsen, Neil. "Cortázar and Postmodernity: New Interpretive Liabilities." *Julio Cortázar: New Readings.* Ed. Carlos J. Alonso. Cambridge: Cambridge University Press, 1998. 57–75.

Leal, Luis. "La nueva narrativa mexicana." *Nueva narrativa hispanoamericana* 2 (1972): 89–97.

Lenherdt, U. "Ensayo de interpretación de *Hijo de hombre* a través de su simbolismo cristiano y social." *Homenaje a Augusto Roa Bastos.* Ed. Helmy F. Giacoman. New York: Las Américas, 1973. 169–85.

León-Portilla, Miguel. *Pre-Columbian Literatures of Mexico.* Trans. Grace Lobanov and Miguel León-Portilla. Norman: Oklahoma University Press, 1969.

Levitt, Morton P. "Joyce and Fuentes: Not Influence but Aura." *Comparative Literature Studies* 19 (1982): 254–71.

López González, Aralia. "Una obra clave en la narrativa mexicana: *José Trigo.*" *Revista iberoamericana* 150 (January–March 1990): 117–41.

Manjarrez, Héctor. *Lapsus.* Mexico City: Joaquín Mortiz, 1971.

Mansour, Monica. *Los mundos de Palinuro.* Xalapa, Veracruz: Universidad Veracruzana, 1986.

Marechal, Leopoldo. *Las claves de adán buenosayres y tres artículos de Julio Cortázar, Adolfo Prieto y Graciela de Sola.* Mendoza, Argentina: Azor, 1966.

———. *Adán Buenosayres.* Buenos Aires: Sudamericana, 1948. Ed. Pedro Luis Barcía. Madrid: Castalia, 1994.

Marra, Nelson. "México, una literatura en movimiento." *Temas* (Montevideo) 14 (October–December 1967): 28–32.

Martin, Gerald. "Boom, Yes, 'New Novel,' No: Further Reflections on the Optical Illusions of the 1960s in Latin America." *Bulletin of Latin American Research* 3 (1984): 53–63.

———. *Journeys through the Labyrinth.* London: Verso, 1989.

Martínez, José Luis. "Nuevas letras, nueva sensibilidad" *Revista de la Universidad de México* 22, no. 8 (April 1968): 1–10. Reproduced in *La crítica de la novela mexicana contemporánea.* Ed. Aurora M. Ocampo. Mexico City: Universidad Nacional Autónoma de México, 1981. 191–213.

Martínez, José Luis, and Christopher Domínguez Michael. *La literatura mexicana del siglo XX.* Mexico City: Consejo Nacional para la Cultura y las Artes, 1995.

Mata, Oscar. *Acercamiento a la obra narrativa de Fernando del Paso.* Mexico City: Universidad Autónoma Metropolitana, 1981.

———. *Un océano de narraciones: Fernando del Paso.* Mexico City: Universidad Autónoma de Tlaxcala-UAP, 1991.

Mateos, Juan A. *El cerro de las campanas: memorias de un guerrillero: novela histórica.* Mexico City: Cumplido, 1868. Mexico City: Editora Nacional, 1956.

McGuirk, Bernard J. *Latin American Literature: Symptoms, Risks, and Strategies of Post-structuralist Criticism.* London: Routledge, 1997.

McHale, Brian. *Constructing Postmodernism.* London: Routledge, 1992.

Menton, Seymour. *Latin America's New Historical Novel.* Austin: University of Texas Press, 1993.

Merino Juti, Blanca. *Two Sides of a Mirror: The Dialectical Relation of History and Literature in the Novels of Fernando del Paso.* Ph.D. diss., University of Cambridge, 1994.

Meyer, Jean A. *The Cristero Rebellion: The Mexican People between Church and State, 1926–1929.* Trans. Richard Southern. Cambridge: Cambridge University Press, 1976.

Michael, Ian (David Serafín). "From Scarlet Study to Novela Negra: The Detective Story in Spanish." *Thrillers in Transition: Novela Negra and Political Change in Spain.* Ed. Rob Rix. Leeds: Trinity and All Saints College, 1992. 17–47.

Mignolo, Walter. "Occidentalización, imperialismo, globalización: herencias coloniales y teorías postcoloniales." *Revista iberoamericana* 170–171 (January–June 1995): 27–40.

Miller, Karl. *Doubles: Studies in Literary History.* New York: Oxford University Press, 1985.

Monsiváis, Carlos. *Días de guardar.* Mexico City: Ediciones Era, 1970.

Montes de Oca, Marco Antonio. "*Palinuro de México* de Fernando del Paso." *Vuelta* 40 (March 1980): 42–44.

Moran, Dominic. *Questions of the Liminal in the Fiction of Julio Cortázar.* Ph.D. diss., University of Cambridge, 1997.

Moreno Durán, Rafael Humberto. "PALINURO: las varas de Esculapio y el médico como actor." *Camp de l'Arpa* 67–68 (1979): 60–66.

New Larousse Encyclopedia of Mythology. Trans. Richard Aldington and Delano Ames, with an introduction by Robert Graves. London: Hamlyn, 1968.

Ngugi wa Thiong'o. *Decolonising the Mind: The Politics of Language in African Literature.* London: Currey, 1986.

Novo, Salvador. *Nueva grandeza mexicana: Ensayo sobre la ciudad de México y sus alrededores en 1946.* Mexico City: Hermes, 1947.

Ocampo, Silvina. "Palinuro insomne." *Enumeración de la patria y otros poemas.* Buenos Aires: Ediciones Sur, 1942. 81–82.

Olivier, Florence. "Mythe et histoire dans *El luto humano,* de José Revueltas." *América: Cahiers du CRICCAL* 3 (1988): 21–35.

Orrantia, Dagoberto. "The Function of Myth in Fernando del Paso's *José Trigo.*" *Tradition and Renewal: Essays in Twentieth- Century Latin American Literature and Culture.* Ed. Merlin H. Foster. Urbana: University of Illinois Press, 1975. 129–38.

Ortega, José. *La estética neobarroca en la narrativa hispanoamericana.* Madrid: José Porrúa Turanzas, 1984.

Ortega, Julio. *La contemplación y la fiesta: Notas sobre la novela latinoamericana actual.* Caracas: Monte Avila, 1969.

———. "Para una teoría del texto latinoamericano: Colón, Garcilaso, y el discurso de la abundancia." *Revista de crítica literaria latinoamericana* 14, no. 28 (1988): 101–15.

———. "Postmodernism in Latin America." In *Postmodern Fiction in Europe and the Americas.* Ed. Theo D'haen and Hans Bertens. Amsterdam: Rodopi, 1988. 193–208.

———. "Carlos Fuentes: para recuperar la tradición de la Mancha." *Revista iberoamericana* 148–149 (1989): 637–54.

———. "El lector en su laberinto." *Hispanic Review* 60 (1992): 165–79.

Parkinson Zamora, Lois. "European Intertextuality in Vargas Llosa and Cortázar." *Comparative Literature Studies* 19 (1982): 21–38.

———. *The Usable Past: The Imagination of History in Recent Fiction of the Americas.* Cambridge: Cambridge University Press, 1997.

Parra, Ernesto. "Trópico de Palinuro: Entrevista con Fernando del Paso." *El topo viejo* (Madrid) 24 (1978): 68–71.

Paz, Octavio. *Posdata.* Mexico City: Siglo XXI, 1970.

———. *El laberinto de la soledad.* Ed. Enrico Mario Santí. Madrid: Cátedra, 1993.

Pechey, Graham. "On the Borders of Bakhtin: Dialogisation, Decolonisation." *Bakhtin and Cultural Theory.* Ed. Keith Hirschkop and D. Shepherd. Manchester: Manchester University Press, 1989. 39–67.

Pellón, Gustavo. "The Spanish American Novel: Recent Developments, 1975–1990." *The Cambridge History of Latin American Literature.* Ed. Roberto González Echevarría and Enrique Pupo Walker. Vol. 2. Cambridge: Cambridge University Press, 1996. 279–302. 3 vols.

Peñuel, Arnold. *Intertextuality in García Márquez.* York, S.C.: Spanish Literature Publications, 1994.

Pérez Firmat, Gustavo. *The Cuban Condition: Translation and Identity in Modern Cuban Literature.* Cambridge: Cambridge University Press, 1989.

Pláa, Monique. "Histoire et mythe dans *José Trigo*." *América: Cahiers du CRICCAL* 3 (1988): 63–80.

———. "De l'instabilité des frontières à l'organisation du récit." *América: Cahiers du CRICCAL* 8 (1991): 209–22.

Planells, Antonio. "El género detectivesco en Hispanoamérica." *Revista interamericana de bibliografía* 36 (1986): 460–72.

Poe, Edgar Allan. "The Power of Words." *The Works of Edgar Allan Poe.* Ed. John H. Ingram. Vol. 2. London: A. and C. Black, 1899. 189–93. 4 vols.

Poniatowska, Elena. *La noche de Tlatelolco: Testimonios de historia oral.* Mexico City: Era, 1971.

Pons, María Cristina. "*Noticias del Imperio:* entre la imaginación delirante y los desvaríos de la historia." *Hispamérica* 69 (1994): 97–108.

Portal, Marta. *Proceso narrativo de la revolución mexicana.* Madrid: Espasa Calpe, 1980.

Prieto, Adolfo. "Los dos mundos de Adán Buenosayres." In Leopoldo Marechal, *Las claves de adán buenosayres y tres artículos de Julio Cortázar, Adolfo Prieto y Graciela de Sola.* Mendoza, Argentina: Azor, 1966. 31–50.

Prieto, René. *Miguel Angel Asturias's Archaeology of Return.* Cambridge: Cambridge University Press, 1993.

Quirarte, Vicente. "*Noticias del Imperio* de Fernando del Paso: la visión omnipotente de la historia." *Perfiles: ensayos sobre literatura mexicana reciente.* Ed. Federico Patán. Boulder, Colorado: Society of Spanish and Spanish-American Studies, 1992. 141–46.

Rama, Angel. "La tecnificación narrativa." *Hispamérica* 30 (December 1981): 29–82.

———. *Transculturación narrativa en América Latina.* Mexico City: Siglo XXI, 1982.

———. *La novela en América Latina: Panoramas 1920–1980.* Xalapa: Universidad Veracruzana, 1986.

Revueltas, Eugenia. "La novela policíaca en México y en Cuba." *Cuadernos Americanos,* n.s., 1 (January–February 1987): 102–20.

Revueltas, José. *El luto humano.* Mexico City: Editorial Mexico, 1943. Mexico City: Editorial Novaro, 1970.

———. *Mexico '68: Juventud y revolución.* Mexico City: Ediciones Era, 1978.

Reyes, Alfonso. "Notas sobre la inteligencia americana." *Sur* 24 (September 1936): 7–15.

———. "Visión de Anáhuac [1519]." In *Obras completas de Alfonso Reyes.* Vol. 2. Mexico City: Fondo de Cultura Económica, 1956. 9–34. 25 vols.

———. "Sobre la novela policial." In *Obras completas de Alfonso Reyes.* Vol. 9. Mexico City: Fondo de Cultura Económica, 1959. 457–61. 25 vols.

Reyes, Juan José. "Coartadas sanfranciscanas. Fernando del Paso. *Linda 67: Historia de un crimen.*" *Nexos* 218 (February 1996): 85–86.

Richards, Nelly. "Cultural Peripheries: Latin America and Postmodernist Decentering." In *The Postmodernism Debate in Latin America.* Ed. John Beverley, Michael Aronna, and José Oviedo. Durham: Duke University Press, 1995. 217–22.

Roa Bastos, Augusto. *Hijo de hombre.* Buenos Aires: Losada, 1960.

Rodríguez Lozano, Miguel G. *José Trigo: el nacimiento discursivo de Fernando del Paso.* Mexico City: Universidad Nacional Autónoma de México, 1997.

Rodríguez Monegal, Emir. *El BOOM de la novela latinoamericana.* Caracas: Editorial Tiempo Nuevo, 1972.

Ross, Andrew, ed. *Universal Abandon? The Politics of Postmodernism.* Edinburgh: Edinburgh University Press, 1989.

Rossner, Michael. "Fernando del Paso: realismo loco o lo real maravilloso europeo." *Literatura mexicana hoy: Del 68 al ocaso de la revolución*. Ed. Karl Kohut. Frankfurt am Main: Vervuert Verlag, 1991. 223–29.

Ruffinelli, J. "Entrevista con Fernando del Paso." *Vuelta* 37 (December 1979): 45–49.

———. "Fernando del Paso: la novela como exorcismo." *El lugar de Rulfo*. Xalapa: Universidad Veracruzana, 1980. 191–200.

———. "New Voices/Fernando del Paso: Notes on *Palinuro de México*." Trans. Jo Anne Engelbert. *Review: Latin American Literature and Arts* 28 (January–April 1981): 31–33.

———. "Notas sobre la novela en México (1975–1980)." *Cuadernos de Marcha* 14 (July–August 1981): 47–59.

Rulfo, Juan. *El llano en llamas*. Mexico City: Fondo de Cultura Económica, 1953.

———. *Pedro Páramo*. Mexico City: Fondo de Cultura Económica, 1955.

Sáenz, Inés. *Hacia la novela total*. Madrid: Pliegos, 1994.

Said, Edward. *Orientalism*. London: Routledge and Kegan Paul, 1978.

———. *Culture and Imperialism*. New York: Vintage Books, 1994.

Sainz, Gustavo. "Novela y cuento." *La cultura en México: Suplemento de "Siempre"* 255 (28 December 1966): ii–iv.

———. "Carlos Fuentes: A Permanent Bedazzlement." Trans. Tom J. Lewis. *World Literature Today* 57, no. 4 (autumn 1983): 568–72.

Saldivar, Dasso. "La totalidad equívoca de *Palinuro de México*." *Estafeta Literaria* 636 (15 May 1978): 3201–2.

Sánchez Bardón, Luis, and Javier Goñi. "Fernando del Paso: 'Uno escribe cuando camina, cuando lee, cuando sueña'." *Triunfo* (Madrid) 788 (4 March 1978): 48–49.

Santí, Enrico Mario. *Por una politeratura: Literatura hispanoamericana e imaginación política*. Mexico City: Ediciones del Equilibrista, 1997.

Sarduy, Severo. "El barroco y el neobarroco." *América Latina en su literatura*. Ed. César Fernández Moreno. Mexico City: Siglo XXI, 1974. 167–84.

Schama, Simon. *Dead Certainties (Unwarranted Speculations)*. London: Granta Books, in association with Penguin Books, 1991.

Scholz, Laszlo. *El arte poética de Julio Cortázar*. San Antonio de Padua, Buenos Aires: Castañeda, 1977.

Sejourné, Laurette. *Pensamiento y religión en el México antiguo*. Mexico City: Fondo de Cultura Económica, 1984.

Seligson, Esther. "*José Trigo*: una memoria que se inventa." *Texto crítico* 7, no. 5 (September–December 1976): 162–69.

Shaw, Donald Leslie. *Nueva narrativa hispanoamericana*. Madrid: Cátedra, 1981.

———. "Inverted Christian Imagery and Symbolism in Modern Spanish American Fiction." *Romance Studies* 10 (Summer 1987): 71–82.

———. *The Post-Boom in Spanish American Fiction*. Albany: State University of New York Press, 1998.

Sheldon, Helia A. *Mito y desmitificación en dos novelas de José Revueltas*. Mexico City: Editorial Oasis, 1985.

Simpson, Amelia. *Detective Fiction from Latin America*. Cranbury, N.J.: Associated Universities Press, 1990.

Sklodowska, Elzbieta. *La parodia en la nueva novela hispanoamericana*. Purdue University Monographs. Amsterdam: Benjamins, 1991.

Solares, Ignacio. *Madero, el otro*. Mexico City: Joaquín Mortiz, 1989.

Sontag, Susan. "The Pornographic Imagination." *Styles of Radical Will*. London: Secker and Warburg, 1969.

Soto, Lilvia. "Tres aproximaciones a *José Trigo*." *Revista chilena de literatura* 30 (November 1987): 125–54.

Soustelle, Jacques. *The Daily Life of the Aztecs on the Eve of the Spanish Conquest* (1954). Trans. Patrick O'Brien. London: Weidenfield and Nicolson, 1961.

Spitta, Silvia. *Between Two Waters: Narratives of Transculturation in Latin America*. Houston: Rice University Press, 1995.

Stavans, Ilan. *Antihéroes: México y su novela policial*. Mexico City: Joaquín Mortiz, 1993.

———. "A Conversation with Fernando del Paso." *Review of Contemporary Fiction* 16 (1996): 122–32.

Steele, Cynthia. *Politics, Gender, and the Mexican Novel, 1968–1988: Beyond the Pyramid*. Austin: University of Texas Press, 1992.

Stephanson, Anders. "An Interview with Cornel West." *Universal Abandon? The Politics of Postmodernism*. Ed. Andrew Ross. Edinburgh: Edinburgh University Press, 1989. 269–86.

Swanson, Philip. "Romancing the Stone with Carlos Fuentes: Reading and Writing *La cabeza de la hidra*." *La Chispa '93: Selected Proceedings*. Ed. Gilbert Paolini. New Orleans: Tulane University, 1993. 240–47.

Symons, Julian. *Bloody Murder: From the Detective Story to the Crime Novel*. London: Faber and Faber, 1972.

Taylor, Kathy. *The New Narrative of Mexico: Subversions of History in Mexican Fiction*. Cranbury, N.J.: Associated University Presses, 1994.

Tejera, María Luisa. "Fernando del Paso: *José Trigo*." *Imagen*, suplemento no. 5 (15–30 July 1967): 12–13.

Thomas, P. N. "Historiographic Metafiction and the Neo-Baroque in del Paso's *Noticias del Imperio*." *Indiana Journal of Hispanic Literature* 6–7 (1995): 169–84.

Todorov, Tzvetan. "The Typology of Detective Fiction." In *The Poetics of Prose*. Trans. Richard Howard. Oxford: Basil Blackwell, 1977. 42–52.

———. *Mikhail Bakhtin: The Dialogical Principle*. Trans. Wlad Godzich. Manchester: Manchester University Press, 1984.

Toledo, Alejandro, ed. *El imperio de las voces: Fernando del Paso ante la crítica*. Mexico City: Ediciones Era, 1997.

Trejo Fuentes, Ignacio. "El que despalinurice a palinuro será un buen despalin-urizador: entrevista con Fernando del Paso." *La Semana de Bellas Artes* 138 (23 July 1980): 6–11.

Usigli, Rodolfo. *Corona de sombra* (1943). Collected in *Teatro completo de Rodolfo Usigli*. Vol. 2. Mexico City: Fondo de Cultura Económica, 1966. 147–222. 3 vols.

Vaillant, Georges. *The Aztecs of Mexico*. Harmondsworth, Middlesex: Penguin, 1950.

Van Delden, Maarten. *Carlos Fuentes, Mexico, and Modernity*. Nashville: Vanderbilt University Press, 1998.

Vargas Llosa, Mario. *La orgía perpetua: Flaubert y "Madame Bovary."* Barcelona: Seix Barral, 1975.

Vasconcelos, José. *La raza cósmica*. Paris: Agencia Mundial de Librería, 1925.

West, Cornel. See Anders Stephanson, "An Interview with Cornel West." *Universal Abandon? The Politics of Postmodernism*. Ed. Andrew Ross. Edinburgh: Edinburgh University Press, 1989. 269–86.

White, Hayden. *Metahistory: The Historical Imagination in Nineteenth-Century Europe*. Baltimore: Johns Hopkins University Press, 1973.

———. *The Content of the Form: Narrative Discourse and Historical Representation*. Baltimore: Johns Hopkins University Press, 1987.

Williams, Raymond. "Modern and Postmodern *Terra nostra*." *The Writings of Carlos Fuentes*. Austin: University of Texas Press, 1996. 95–104.

Worton, Michael, and Judith Still, eds. *Intertextuality: Theories and Practices*. Manchester: Manchester University Press, 1990.

Xirau, Ramón. "José Agustín, Navarrete, del Paso." *Diálogos* 3, no. 1 (January–February 1967): 24–26.

Yáñez, Agustín. *Al filo del agua*. México: Porrúa, 1947.

———. *Las tierras flacas*. Mexico City: Joaquín Mortiz, 1962.

Yates, Donald. "The Mexican Detective Story." *Kentucky Foreign Language Quarterly* 8 (1961): 42–47.

Young, Dolly. "Mexican Literary Reactions to Tlatlelolco 1968." *Latin American Research Review* 20 (1985): 71–85.

Young, Richard A., ed. *Latin American Postmodernisms*. Amsterdam: Rodopi, 1997.

Young, Robert. *Untying the Text: A Poststructuralist Reader*. London: Routledge and Kegan Paul, 1981.

———. *White Mythologies: Writing History and the West*. London: Routledge, 1990.

Zea, Leopoldo. *La filosofía como compromiso y otros ensayos*. Mexico City: Tezontle, 1952.

———. "Gabino Barreda and Positivism." *The Latin American Mind*. Trans. James H. Abbott and Lowell Dunham. Norman: University of Oklahoma Press, 1963. 276–79.

————. *América latina en el mundo*. Buenos Aires: Eudeba, 1965.

————. *Dependencia y liberación en la cultura latinoamericana*. Mexico City: Joaquín Mortiz, 1974.

————. *Discurso desde la marginación y la barbarie*. Barcelona: Anthropos, 1988.

————. *Filosofar a la altura del hombre*. Mexico City: Universidad Nacional Autónoma de Mexico, 1993.

Index

Adán Buenosayres (Marechal), 4, 9, 96–
101, 156; and *Palinuro de México,* 95–
96, 99–101

Aguilar Mora, Jorge, 4, 98; *Si muero lejos
de ti,* 5, 86

Agustín, José: *De perfil,* 3

Alazraki, Jaime, 102

Al filo del agua (Yáñez), 2, 31, 56, 99

Arguedas, José María, 25, 26

Aronne Amestoy, Lida, 96, 102

Arreola, 56, 60, 158n.17; *Confabulario,* 3,
70; *La feria,* 3, 70

Asturias, Miguel Angel, 20, 26, 60;
Hombres de maiz, 64–65; *Mulata de tal,*
64–65

Avilés Fabila, René, 159n.4; *El gran
solitario del palacio,* 87–89

Azuela, Arturo: *Manifestación de silencios,*
5, 86

Azuela, Mariano, 56; *La luciérnaga,* 34

Bakhtin, Mikhail, 9, 121

Barreda, Gabino: *Oración cívica,* 115–16

Barrientos, Juan José, 134, 159n.1

Barthes, Roland, 120, 155, 156

Battilana, Carlos, 62

Bergson, Henri, 22

Black Skin, White Masks (Fanon), 14

Bloom, Harold, 9, 94

Boehmer, Elleke, 104

Bolívar, Simón, 20, 136–37

Borges, Jorge Luis, 8, 20, 73, 101, 139; acknowledged by del Paso as an influence,
35; author of decentered model of global
cultural relations, 69; and Bioy Casares,
151; *El escritor argentino y la tradición,*
10; and the *figura,* 82, 97: identified with

the cosmopolitan pole of the field of
Latin American culture, 26; *Los teólogos,*
83; and theories of intertextuality, 9; and
totalization, 158n.12; valorization of the
periphery, 11

Born on the Fourth of July (Stone), 153

Boullosa, Carmen, 6

Campos, Marco Antonio, 88–89; *Que la
carne es hierba,* 86, 88

Cantú, Cesar, 122

Carpentier, Alejo: acknowledged by del Paso
as an influence, 19, 142, 161n.1; the
America/Europe dichotomy in, 114; *Los
pasos perdidos,* 7, 142, 150; model for
Linda 67, 7, 26, 150, 155

Carroll, Lewis, 73

Carter, Angela, 80

Caso, Antonio, 11, 12

Castellanos, Rosario, 89

Castor and Pollux, 45–46, 67, 81, 92, 95,
158n.11

Césaire, Aimé, 13, 14–15

Chabrol, Claude: *Le Boucher,* 153

Cien años de soledad (García Márquez), 77,
113

colonialism, 15, 16, 109

Coming to America (Landis), 151

Confabulario (Arreola), 3, 70

Connolly, Cyril, 73; *The Unquiet Grave,* 92,
131, 159n.5

Corona de sombra (Usigli), 105, 130

Cortázar, Julio, 9, 94; acknowledged by del
Paso as an influence, 19; identified with
the cosmopolitan pole of the field of
Latin American culture, 26; and the rejection of the Christian dialectic, 40;

Cortázar, Julio—*continued*
relation to postmodernism, 102–3;
reviewer of Spanish translation of *The
Unquiet Grave,* 159n.5; and the theory
of the *figura,* 82
—works: "El perseguidor," 62; *Libro de
Manuel,* 103; *Rayuela,* 4, 33, 40, 79,
101–3; 62 *modelo para armar,* 10
Corti, Egon Caesar, 123–24

decolonization, 13, 16; of the mind, 14, 116
del Paso, Fernando, 1–8, 16–24; and
Arreola, 3, 157n.1, 158n.17; commitment to the Third World, 18; and crime
fiction, 6; and Fuentes, 31; and Joyce, 66;
and Latin America, 17–24; opposition to
imperialism, 18; polemic with Paz, 22;
and transculturation, 21–22, 25, 27. *See
also José Trigo; Linda 67: Historia de un
crimen;* "Mi patria chica, mi patria
grande"; *Noticias del Imperio; Palinuro
de México*
de Sola, Graciela, 94, 102
Días de guardar (Monsiváis), 4, 86
Díaz Ordaz, Gustavo, 84, 87–88
Dos Passos, John, 2, 27, 31
Dottori, Nora, 41
Dussel, Enrique, 13

"El Aleph" (Borges), 53
El general en su laberinto (García Márquez),
5, 106, 132; and *Noticias del imperio,*
134, 136–38
El gran solitario del palacio (Avilés Fabila),
87–89
Elizondo, Salvador, 3, 94; *Farabeuf,* 4, 84
El laberinto de la soledad (Paz), 100
El luto humano (Revueltas), 2, 31; and *José
Trigo,* 57–60
"Escritura," 4

Fanon, Frantz, 13, 69, 109, 158n.16; *Black
Skin, White Masks,* 14; cited by Zea, 14,
15, 160n.3
Farabeuf (Elizondo), 4, 84
Faulkner, William, 2, 8, 22, 27, 31, 66
Fichte, Johann Gottlieb, 111, 160n.4

Finnegans Wake (Joyce), 4, 117; and *José
Trigo,* 27, 66–70
Flores Sevilla, Jesús, 7, 36
Foster, David William, 62
Foster, Hal, 102
Foucault, Michel, 121
Franco, Jean, 151
Frazer, James George, 17; *The Golden
Bough,* 55
Freud, Sigmund, 76
Fuentes, Carlos, 2, 3, 7, 104; and Cortázar,
10, 97; identified with the cosmopolitan
pole of the field of Latin American cul-
ture, 26–27; and James Joyce, 34, 94;
modernist experiments of, 56
—works: *Cambio de piel,* 75; *Cervantes o la
crítica de la lectura,* 34; "Chac Mool,"
26; *Cumpleaños,* 75, 77; *La campaña,* 5;
La muerte de Artemio Cruz, 33, 38, 74;
La región más transparente, 2–3, 26, 31–
34, 47; "Los días enmascarados," 29;
Terra nostra, 4, 26, 81, 103, 117, 134–
35; "Tlactocatzine, jardín de Flandes,"
135; *Valiente mundo nuevo,* 105; *Zona
sagrada,* 77

García Márquez, Gabriel, 7, 13, 104;
identified with the transculturating pole
of the field of Latin American culture,
26; Nobel Prize acceptance speech,
113–14
—works: *Cien años de soledad,* 77, 113; *El
general en su laberinto,* 5, 106, 113, 132,
134, 136–38; *La hojarasca,* 92; *La
soledad de América latina,* 114;
"¿Problemas de la novela?," 100
García Saldaña, Parménides: *Pasto verde,* 3
Garibay, Angel María, 37, 44
Gazapo (Sainz), 3, 81
González, Manuel Pedro, 33, 95, 157n.2
González del Alba, Luis, 4–5
González Echevarría, Roberto, 117
Gramsci, Antonio: *Prison Notebooks,* 113
Guadalupe de Anda, José, 2, 56

Hammett, Dashiell, 151, 152
Hegel, Friedrich, 111

Highsmith, Patricia, 28, 143, 151, 155; *Those that Walk Away,* 152
Hombres de maiz (Asturias), 64–65; and *José Trigo,* 65
humanism, 16, 62, 69, 103, 106, 111
Hunt, Eva, 43
Hutcheon, Linda, 102, 103, 120–21, 122–23
Huxley, Aldous, 8

Ibargüengoitia, Jorge, 5, 160n.12
imperialism, 111, 119; denounced by del Paso, 18–19, 106; personified by Carlota in *Noticias del Imperio,* 108, 118

Jacknife (Jones), 153
Jakobson, Roman, 51, 54
Jameson, Fredric, 50, 70, 120, 151, 158n.12
Jitrik, Noé, 94
José Trigo, 1, 29–71; divergent from *Palinuro de México,* 4, 90; and *El luto humano,* 57–60; and *Finnegans Wake,* 66–70; first authorial pronouncements about, 16–17; and *Hijo de hombre,* 60–64; and *Hombres de maiz,* 64–65; imprint of Manicheanism in, 41–43; influence of Arreola on, 3; and *La región más transparente,* 31–35, 47, 51, 52; and *Las tierras flacas,* 56–60; networking of characters in, 81; and the paradigm of the modernist novel, 8, 27, 30, 50, 141; as precursor of *Noticias del Imperio,* 105–6; as a summa of Mexican fiction, 3, 35; totalizing strategies in, 50–53; transculturation in, 25, 27, 156; and *Ulysses,* 27, 35, 52, 66
Joyce, James, 10, 20, 35, 79, 101; architect of the "total novel," 97; debt of Fuentes to, 34; dialogue of *Noticias del Imperio* with, 105; identified with international currents of modernism, 8, 27, 30–31; influence of, denied by Marechal, 94; moral outlook of, 99; narrative style of, 2. *See also Finnegans Wake;* Joycean paradigm; *Ulysses*
Joycean paradigm, 92–93, 95–99
Juárez, Benito, 26, 119, 124, 126, 128; characterization of, 111–17; life and political career of, 107–8; as object of denigration, 125

Kafka, Franz, 27
Kierkegaard, Soren, 150
Kristeva, Julia, 9,
Kuhn, Annette, 79–80

La campaña (Fuentes), 134, 135–36
La feria (Arreola), 3, 70
La noche de Tlatelolco (Poniatowska), 4, 86
Lapsus (Manjarrez), 75, 81, 85
La región más transparente (Fuentes), 26, 40, 47, 99; influence on *José Trigo,* 31–35; as landmark text, 2–3, 33
Larsen, Neil, 102, 103
Las claves de "Adán Buenosayres" (Marechal), 93–94
Las tierras flacas (Yáñez), 3; compared with *José Trigo,* 56–60
La tierra pródiga (Yáñez), 3
Le Boucher (Chabrol), 153
Lezama Lima, José, 19
Libro de Manuel (Cortázar), 79
Linda 67: Historia de un crimen, 1, 141–54; allegory of authorship in, 153–54; critique of consumerism in, 145–46; critique of imperialism in, 145–48; and *José Trigo,* 141, 154, 155–56; and *Los pasos perdidos,* 7, 142, 150–51; narrative summary of, 6–7; and *noir* traditions, 152–53; and *Noticias del Imperio,* 141, 147, 153, 155–56; and the *novela negra,* 6–7, 28, 143, 151–52; and *Palinuro de México,* 141–42, 154, 155–56; portrayal of the United States in, 7, 26, 148–50, 153; and postmodernism, 155; themes of nationality and personal identity in, 142–45; and *Those Who Walk Away,* 152
López González, Aralia, 60
Los adioses (Onetti), 77
Los pasos perdidos, 7, 142, 150–51

Madero, el otro (Solares), 5, 134, 138–39
Mal de amores (Mastretta), 5
Manjarrez, Héctor, 4, 6, 85; *Lapsus,* 75, 81

Marcuse, Herbert, 77
Marechal, Leopoldo, 4, 20, 92, 93–96, 156; acknowledgment of debt to Dante and Quevedo, 94; *Adán Buenosayres,* 4, 9, 96–101; and the anxiety of influence, 94–95; and *Palinuro de México,* 95–96, 99–101
Martí, José, 114
Martínez, José Luis, 74, 158n.2, 159n.3
Mastretta, Angeles: *Mal de amores,* 5
Mauthner, Fritz, 83
Maximilian I (Emperor), 110–11
Maximilian III (Emperor), 26, 108, 110–12, 126–27, 129–30
McHale, Brian, 101–2
Merino Juti, Blanca, 70
mestizaje, 21, 25, 32–33, 60
Miller, Henry, 73
"Mi patria chica, mi patria grande," 19–21, 23–24, 72, 113–14, 145, 146
modernism, 8, 20, 65, 71, 101–3, 133
modernist paradigm of narrative, 8, 70–71, 102, 155
Monsiváis, Carlos, 86; *Días de guardar,* 4
Moran, Dominic, 102, 103

Napoleon III (Emperor), 108, 111, 116, 119, 124; contrasted with Benito Juárez, 114; political failings of, 115; as wager of colonial wars, 109
Neruda, Pablo, 13, 19, 20
"new historical novel," 5
Ngugi wa Thiong'o, 23
Noticias del Imperio, 5, 7, 88, 105–40; Christian imagery in, 126–28, 139; critique of imperialism in, 108–19; and *El general en su laberinto,* 134, 136–38; and *José Trigo,* 105–6, 118, 127; and *La campaña,* 135–36; and *Madero, el otro,* 134, 138–40; and *Palinuro de México,* 105–6, 118, 127, 131; and the paradigm of the historical novel, 27–28; the postcolonial orientation of, 104, 125, 133; relation to postmodern historiography, 106, 120–23; residue of humanist and modernist elements in, 128–34; and *Terra nostra,* 117, 134–35; and

"Tlactocatzine, del jardín de Flandes," 135; and "Universal History," 122; and Usigli, 130–31, 133
"novela negra," 6, 153, 161n.4
Novo, Salvador, 34, 52

Ocampo, Silvina, 72, 159n.5
"Onda," la, 3–4
Onetti, Juan Carlos: *Los adioses,* 77
Orozco, José Clemente: *The Man of Fire,* 90
Ortega, Julio, 10–11, 70, 102, 132, 149
Ortiz, Fernando, 25

Palinuro de México, 4, 5, 7, 18, 25–26, 72–104; and *Adán Buenosayres,* 92, 95–96; and the *Aeneid,* 90–92; caricature of pornography in, 78–81; and the *Commedia dell' Arte,* 85–87; family relations in, 75–77; and humanism, 88–89; incest in, 77, 81; and modernism, 103, 141, 155–56; and the myth of Palinurus, 90–92, 100–101, 104; the postcolonial connection, 104; postmodernist elements of, 103; and *Que la carne es hierba,* 88; and *Rayuela,* 73, 82, 92, 97, 98; relation to "Escritura," 3; relation to "la Onda," 3; and *Ulysses,* 27, 73, 75, 92–93, 97–98, 99, 101, 103; view of the human condition, 73, 82–83
Parkinson Zamora, Lois, 8, 9, 10
Paz, Octavio, 20, 73, 79, 101, 104; polemic with del Paso, 21–22
—works: *Conjunciones y disjunciones,* 81; *El laberinto de la soledad,* 100; *Posdata,* 10
Pechey, Graham, 9, 10
Pedro Páramo (Rulfo), 2, 77
Peñuel, Arnold, 9, 10,
Pérez Firmat, Gustavo, 8, 9, 11, 35,
Poe, Edgar Allan, 17, 20, 35, 54–55
Poniatowska, Elena, 4, 6, 86, 88, 89; *La noche de Tlatelolco,* 4, 86
Posse, Abel: *Los perros del paraíso,* 5
postcolonialism, 15; relation of Del Paso to, 112, 137
postcolonial societies, 24; empathy of Leopoldo Zea with, 14

postmodern historiographic metafiction, 106, 128, 134, 138, 155
postmodernism, 71, 101–4, 120–23, 127–28, 133, 141, 151, 155
Prieto, Adolfo, 94, 95
Prison Notebooks (Gramsci), 113
Puga, María Luisa, 6

Que la carne es hierba (Campos), 86, 88
Quetzalcóatl, 37–39, 42–46, 59, 65, 67, 81, 91, 158n.10
Quevedo, Francisco de, 73, 84, 94

Rabelais, François, 73, 84
Rama, Angel, 8, 10, 26–27, 65
Rayuela (Cortázar), 4, 33, 40, 79; and modernism, 103; and *Palinuro de México*, 73, 82, 92; as postmodernist text, 102–3; and *Ulysses*, 92, 96–97
resurrection, myth of, 44–47, 64, 67, 68–69, 73
Revueltas, José, 7, 60, 61, 65; *El luto humano*, 2, 57–58; *Los errores*, 3
Reyes, Alfonso, 11, 34, 43, 52, 55–56; "Notas sobre la inteligencia americana," 10, 23, 89; "Visión de Anáhuac," 56
Richards, Nelly, 101, 104
Riffaterre, Michael, 9
Rivera, Diego: *The Legend of Quetzalcóatl*, 37
Roa Bastos, Augusto, 19, 26, 104; *Hijo de hombre*, 60–64
Rodó, José Enrique, 12
Rodríguez Lozano, Miguel G., 36
Rulfo, Juan, 3, 20, 56, 60; *El llano en llamas*, 2, 70; identified with the transculturating pole of the field of Latin American culture, 26; *Pedro Páramo*, 2, 77; relations with del Paso, 157n.1, 158nn.17, 18; subject of a pastiche in *José Trigo*, 70

Sáenz, Inés, 117, 134
Said, Edward, 16, 160n.7
Sainz, Gustavo, 6, 31
—works: *Compadre Lobo*, 5; *Gazapo*, 3, 81; *Obsesivos días circulares*, 98

Salazar Bondy, Augusto, 13, 14,
Sarduy, Severo, 53, 149
Schama, Simon, 120
Schrader, Paul, 146
Scott, Walter, 122
Sédar Senghor, Leopold, 13, 14–15
Shaw, Donald Leslie, 62
Si muero lejos de ti (Aguilar Mora), 5, 86, 98
Solares, Ignacio, 6, 7; *Madero, el otro*, 5, 134, 138–39
Sontag, Susan, 79
Sophocles, 92
Soustelle, Jacques, 37, 38, 40, 44–45, 48, 49
Spitta, Silvia, 24–26, 35
Sterne, Lawrence, 66
surrealism, 20, 77
Swift, Jonathan, 73
Symbolism, 20, 54–55, 56
syncretism, 43, 54, 60, 64

Taibo II, Paco Ignacio, 6, 143, 161n.3
Taxi Driver (Scorsese), 153
Terra nostra (Fuentes), 4, 26, 81; and modernist paradigm of narrative, 103; and *Noticias del Imperio*, 117, 134–35
Tezcatlipoca, 33, 38–39, 58, 67
The Golden Bough (Frazer), 55
The Unquiet Grave (Connolly), 92, 131, 159n.5
Those Who Walk Away (Highsmith), 152
"Tlactocatzine, del jardín de Flandes" (Fuentes), 135
"Tlatelolco literature," 85–89
totalizing consciousness, 50, 105, 106, 118
"total novel," 4, 50, 97
transculturation, 8, 21, 24–27, 43, 156

Ulysses, 4, 42, 79, 147; and *Adán Buenosayres*, 93–95; and *José Trigo*, 66, 70; major properties of, 92–93; Mexicanization of, 27, 99; and *Palinuro de México*, 72, 92, 98–99, 156; and postmodernism, 102; as quintessential example of the modernist paradigm of narrative, 3, 27, 34, 101; and *Rayuela*, 92, 96–97, 102. *See also* Joycean paradigm

Usigli, Rodolfo: *Corona de sombra,* 105, 130–31
Uslar Pietri, Arturo, 19

Vaillant, George C., 38, 39
Valiente mundo nuevo (Fuentes), 105
Vargas Llosa, Mario, 9, 10
Vasconcelos, José, 11, 43
Villoro, Juan, 6
Virgil, 26, 73, 90, 92, 100–101

West, Cornel, 141
White, Hayden, 120, 122, 125–26, 128, 133, 136
White Mythologies (Young), 120

Yáñez, Agustín: *Al filo del agua,* 2; *Las tierras flacas,* 3, 56–60; *La tierra pródiga,* 3, 56
Young, Robert, 120

Zea, Leopoldo, 8, 11–16, 69, 114; and Césaire, 14–15; and humanism, 23; postcolonial awareness of, 13–14; promoter of Fanon, 14, 158n.16, 160n.3; and Sédar Senghor, 15
—works: "Colonization and Decolonization of Latin American Culture," 13, 23, 116; *Dependence and Liberation in Latin American Culture,* 13, 14, 24; *Discourse from the Site of Marginalization and Barbarism,* 13, 15–16, 115–16, 147–48; "From the History of Ideas to the Philosophy of Latin American History," 13; "Latin American Philosophy as Philosophy of Liberation," 13, 14; "Negritude and Indigenism," 14–15; "North America in the Spanish American Consciousness," 11–12, 15, 116; *Philosophizing at the Level of Mankind,* 15; "Philosophy as Commitment," 11, 12

Robin Fiddian is University Reader in Spanish and Fellow of Wadham College, Oxford. He is the author of three books and numerous articles on topics in Spanish literature and film. In the field of Latin American literature, he has published *Gabriel García Márquez* (1995) and more than a dozen articles on authors such as Julio Cortázar, Gabriel García Márquez, Carlos Fuentes, and Fernando del Paso. A forthcoming volume entitled *Postcolonial Perspectives on the Cultures of Latin America and Lusophone Africa* includes a substantial essay on the Mexican thinker and author Leopoldo Zea.